By Donald J. Trump

The Art of the Deal

Surviving at the Top

The Art of the Comeback

The America We Deserve

How to Get Rich

Think Like a Billionaire

TRUMP
THE ART OF THE DEAL

MORE . . .

TRUMP
THE ART OF THE DEAL

DONALD J. TRUMP
with TONY SCHWARTZ

BALLANTINE BOOKS • NEW YORK

The Art of the Deal is a commonsense guide to personal finance. In practical-advice books, as in life, there are no guarantees, and readers are cautioned to rely on their own judgment about their individual circumstances and to act accordingly.

A Ballantine Book
Published by The Random House Publishing Group

Published in the United States by Ballantine Books, an imprint of The Random House Publishing Group, a division of Random House, Inc., New York, and simultaneously in Canada by Random House of Canada Limited, Toronto.

Ballantine and colophon are registered trademarks of Random House, Inc.

www.ballantinebooks.com

ISBN 0-345-47917-3

Manufactured in the United States of America

First Edition: 1987
First Mass Market Edition: January 2005

OPM   19 18 17 16 15 14 13 12

To my parents—Fred and Mary Trump

Acknowledgments

I owe special thanks to several people who made it possible for me to complete this book in the face of my other responsibilities. Ivana Trump, my wonderful wife, and my three children were understanding about the many weekends that I spent working on the book. Si Newhouse first came to me and convinced me to do a book despite my initial reluctance. Howard Kaminsky, Peter Osnos, and many others at Random House have been enthusiastic, energetic supporters of the book.

Tony Schwartz wishes to thank the many people who gave generously of their time, in particular, Robert Trump, Der Scutt, Nick Ribis, Blanche

Sprague, Norman Levine, Harvey Freeman, Tony Gliedman, Al Glasgow, John Barry, and Dan Cooper. For typing, photocopying, copyediting, research, and fact checking, thanks to Ruth Mullen, Gail Olsen, Adina Weinstein, Deborah Immergut, and Nancy Palmer. Without Norma Foerderer, sweet Norma, running interference for me, I never could have gotten the time and access I needed. My agent, Kathy Robbins, is the best at what she does, but also much more: editor, cheerleader, confidante. Ed Kosner, the extraordinary editor of *New York*, has long been a source of ideas, inspiration and sage counsel. My children, Kate and Emily, are a joy, a challenge, and an inspiration. My wife, Deborah, is the most supportive person I've ever known, my first editor, my best friend, and—after ten years still the love of my life.

Contents

1

DEALING

A Week in
the Life

IDON'T do it for the money. I've got enough, much
more than I'll ever need. I do it to do it. Deals are
my art form. Other people paint beautifully on
canvas or write wonderful poetry. I like making deals,
preferably big deals. That's how I get my kicks.

Most people are surprised by the way I work. I play
it very loose. I don't carry a briefcase. I try not to
schedule too many meetings. I leave my door open.
You can't be imaginative or entrepreneurial if you've
got too much structure. I prefer to come to work each
day and just see what develops.

There is no typical week in my life. I wake up most

mornings very early, around six, and spend the first hour or so of each day reading the morning newspapers. I usually arrive at my office by nine, and I get on the phone. There's rarely a day with fewer than fifty calls, and often it runs to over a hundred. In between, I have at least a dozen meetings. The majority occur on the spur of the moment, and few of them last longer than fifteen minutes. I rarely stop for lunch. I leave my office by six-thirty, but I frequently make calls from home until midnight, and all weekend long.

It never stops, and I wouldn't have it any other way. I try to learn from the past, but I plan for the future by focusing exclusively on the present. That's where the fun is. And if it can't be fun, what's the point?

MONDAY

9:00 A.M. My first call is to Alan ("Ace") Greenberg, on the trading floor of Bear Stearns, a major Wall Street investment banking firm. Alan is the CEO of Bear Stearns, he's been my investment banker for the past five years, and he's the best there is. Two weeks ago, we began buying stock in Holiday Inns. It was selling in the 50s. As of this morning, Alan tells me, I own just over one million shares, or slightly more than 4 percent of the company. The stock closed Friday at $65 a share, mostly, Alan says, because word is out on the street that I've been a big buyer, and there's speculation I am planning a run at the company.

The truth is I'm keeping my options open. I may ultimately go for control of Holiday, which I think is somewhat undervalued. At the current stock price, I could get control for less than $2 billion. Holiday's three casino-hotels could be worth nearly that much—and the company owns another 300,000 hotel rooms besides.

A second option, if the stock price goes high enough, is to sell my stake and take a very nice profit. If I did that today, I'd already be up about $7 million. The third possibility is that Holiday may eventually offer to buy back my shares, at a premium, simply to get rid of me. If the premium is big enough, I'll sell.

In any case, I enjoy seeing the lengths to which bad managements go to preserve what they call their independence—which really just means their jobs.

9:30 A.M. Abraham Hirschfeld calls me, looking for advice. Abe is a successful real estate developer but he wants to be a politician. Unfortunately for Abe, he's a far better developer than politician.

This fall, Abe tried to run for lieutenant governor against Governor Cuomo's hand-picked candidate, Stan Lundine. Cuomo led a court fight to get Hirschfeld off the ballot on technical grounds, and sure enough, halfway into the campaign, the court ruled Hirschfeld out. Abe knows I'm friendly with the governor, and he wants my advice now on whether he should endorse Cuomo or switch parties and endorse Cuomo's opponent. I tell him it's a no-contest question—stick with a winner and a good guy at that.

We set a meeting for Thursday.

10:00 A.M. I call Don Imus to thank him. Imus has one of the most successful radio shows in the United States on WNBC, and he's been helping to raise money for the Annabel Hill fund.

I'm amazed at how this has snowballed into such a media event. It began last week when I saw a national news report by Tom Brokaw about this adorable little lady from Georgia, Mrs. Hill, who was trying to save her farm from being foreclosed. Her sixty-seven-year-old husband had committed suicide a few weeks earlier, hoping his life insurance would save the farm, which had been in the family for generations. But the insurance proceeds weren't nearly enough. It was a very sad situation, and I was moved. Here were people who'd worked very hard and honestly all their lives, only to see it all crumble before them. To me, it just seemed wrong.

Through NBC I was put in touch with a wonderful guy from Georgia named Frank Argenbright, who'd become very involved in trying to help Mrs. Hill. Frank directed me to the bank that held Mrs. Hill's mortgage. The next morning, I called and got some vice president on the line. I explained that I was a businessman from New York, and that I was interested in helping Mrs. Hill. He told me he was sorry, but that it was too late. They were going to auction off the farm, he said, and "nothing or no one is going to stop it."

That really got me going. I said to the guy: "You

listen to me. If you do foreclose, I'll personally bring a lawsuit for murder against you and your bank, on the grounds that you harassed Mrs. Hill's husband to his death.'' All of a sudden the bank officer sounded very nervous and said he'd get right back to me.

Sometimes it pays to be a little wild. An hour later I got a call back from the banker, and he said, "Don't worry, we're going to work it out, Mr. Trump.'' Mrs. Hill and Frank Argenbright told the media, and the next thing I knew, it was the lead story on the network news.

By the end of the week, we'd raised $40,000. Imus alone raised almost $20,000 by appealing to his listeners. As a Christmas present to Mrs. Hill and her family, we've scheduled a mortgage-burning ceremony for Christmas Eve in the atrium of Trump Tower. By then, I'm confident, we'll have raised all the money. I've promised Mrs. Hill that if we haven't, I'll make up any difference.

I tell Imus he's the greatest, and I invite him to be my guest one day next week at the tennis matches at the U.S. Open. I have a courtside box and I used to go myself almost every day. Now I'm so busy I mostly just send my friends.

11:15 A.M. Harry Usher, the commissioner of the United States Football League, calls. Last month, the jury in the antitrust suit we brought against the National Football League ruled that the NFL was a monopoly, but awarded us only token damages of one dollar. I've already let the better players on my team, the

New Jersey Generals, sign with the NFL. But the ruling was ridiculous.

We argue about the approach we should take. I want to be more aggressive. "What worries me," I say to Harry, "is that no one is pushing hard enough on an appeal."

12:00 noon Gerry Schoenfeld, head of the Shubert Organization, the biggest Broadway theater owners, calls to recommend a woman for a job as an office administrator. He tells me the woman specifically wants to work for Donald Trump, and I say she's crazy but I'll be happy to see her.

We talk a little about the theater business, and I tell Gerry I'm about to take my kids to see *Cats*, one of his shows, for a second time. He asks if I'm getting my tickets through his office. I tell him that I don't like to do that sort of thing. "Don't be silly," he says. "We have a woman here whose job it is to handle tickets for our friends. Here's her number. Don't hesitate to call."

It's a nice gesture from a very nice guy.

1:15 P.M. Anthony Gliedman stops by to discuss the Wollman Rink project. Gliedman was housing commissioner under Ed Koch. At the time we fought a lot, and even though I ended up beating him in court, I always thought he was bright. I don't hold it against people that they have opposed me. I'm just looking to hire the best talent, wherever I can find it.

Tony has been helping to coordinate the rebuilding of the Wollman Skating Rink in Central Park, a project the city failed at so miserably for seven years. In June I offered to do the job myself. Now we're ahead of schedule, and Tony tells me that he's set up a press conference for Thursday to celebrate the last important step in construction: pouring the concrete.

It doesn't sound like much of a news event to me, and I ask him if anyone is likely to show up. He says at least a dozen news organizations have RSVPd yes. So much for my news judgment.

2:00 P.M. I get deposed in a lawsuit we've brought against a contractor on Trump Tower. Halfway into the job we had to fire the company for total incompetence, and we're suing for damages. I hate lawsuits and depositions, but the fact is that if you're right, you've got to take a stand, or people will walk all over you. In any case, there's no way I could avoid depositions, even if I never brought a lawsuit myself. Nowadays, if your name is Donald Trump, everyone in the world seems to want to sue you.

3:00 P.M. I ask Norma Foerderer, my executive assistant and the person who keeps my life organized, to bring me lunch: a can of tomato juice. I rarely go out, because mostly, it's a waste of time.

3:15 P.M. I put in a call to Sir Charles Goldstein; he's out, and I leave a message. He's a successful real estate attorney, but not one of my favorites.

I'm pretty sure Charlie Goldstein is from the Bronx, but he's a very pompous guy and has a tendency to act like royalty, so I call him Sir Charles. Over the weekend, I heard that Lee Iacocca had hired Sir Charles to represent him on a deal in Palm Beach where Lee and I intend to be partners. Lee had no way of knowing about my past experience with Sir Charles. A while back, I was in the middle of making a deal with a guy who needed an attorney, and I recommended Sir Charles. The next thing I knew, Sir Charles was recommending to his client that he not make the deal with me. I couldn't believe it!

This deal is to buy two condominium towers in the Palm Beach area. I own a house in Palm Beach—a spectacular place called Mar-a-Lago—and one day last winter, when I was down for the weekend, I went out to have lunch with some friends. On the way, a pair of beautiful gleaming white towers caught my eye. I made a couple of calls. It turned out they'd been built for about $120 million and a major New York bank had just foreclosed on the developers. The next thing I knew I was making a deal to buy the project for $40 million.

A mutual friend, William Fugazy, first mentioned that Lee and I should do a real estate deal together. I think Lee is an extraordinary businessman who has done wonders in turning Chrysler around, and I also like him a great deal personally. So one thing led to another and we began talking about the towers. It's a substantial investment, and I'm not certain Lee is absolutely sure yet that he wants to go forward. If that's the case, it occurs to me, he's done the perfect thing by hiring an attorney I don't like. And that's precisely what I intend to tell Sir Charles when he calls me back.

3:30 P.M. I call my sister, Maryanne Barry, to discuss a recent decision in a lawsuit we are contesting in Atlantic City. Maryanne is a federal court judge in New Jersey, and her husband, John, is a talented attorney I have used on many occasions.

"Can you believe they ruled against us?" I ask her. Maryanne is very smart, she obviously knows a lot more about the law than I do, and she's as surprised as I am. I tell her that I've arranged to have all the materials from the case sent to John immediately, because I want him to handle the appeal.

4:00 P.M. I go to our conference room to look at slides of potential Christmas decorations for the atrium in Trump Tower. The spectacular six-story marble atrium has become one of the leading tourist attractions in New York City. More than 100,000 people a week come from all over the world to see it and shop in it, and it's now a symbol of the Trump Organization. That's why I still get involved in details like what Christmas decorations we should use.

I don't like most of what I'm shown. Finally, I see a huge and magnificent gold wreath for the entrance to the building, and decide we should use just that. Sometimes—not often, but sometimes—less is more.

* * *

4:30 P.M. Nicholas Ribis, a New Jersey attorney who handled the licensing of both my Atlantic City casinos, calls to say he's about to leave for Sydney, Australia, to pursue a deal I'm considering. He tells me it's a twenty-four-hour flight, and I tell him I'm very glad he's going instead of me.

The deal, however, may be worth the trip. The government of New South Wales is in the midst of choosing a company to build and operate what they envision as the world's largest casino. We're a front-runner for the job, and Nick is going over to meet with the key government people. He tells me he'll call from Australia as soon as he has any news.

5:15 P.M. I call Henry Kanegsberg, the NBC executive in charge of choosing a new site for the network's headquarters. We've been courting NBC for more than a year, trying to get them to move to our West Side yards site—seventy-eight acres along the Hudson River that I bought a year ago and on which I've announced plans to build the world's tallest building.

I know Henry has just been shown our latest plans for the site, and I'm following up. I mention that Bloomingdale's is dying to become the anchor store in our shopping center, which will give it real prestige. I also tell him the city seems very excited about our latest plans. Then I say we expect to get our preliminary approvals in the next several months.

Kanegsberg seems enthusiastic. Before I get off, I also put in a plug for NBC's locating its offices in the world's tallest building. "Think about it," I say. "It's the ultimate symbol."

5:45 P.M.   My nine-year-old son, Donny, calls to ask when I'll be home. I always take calls from my kids, no matter what I'm doing. I have two others—Ivanka, six, and Eric, three—and as they get older, being a father gets easier. I adore them all, but I've never been great at playing with toy trucks and dolls. Now, though, Donny is beginning to get interested in buildings and real estate and sports, and that's great.

I tell Donny I'll be home as soon as I can, but he insists on a time. Perhaps he's got my genes: the kid won't take no for an answer.

6:30 P.M.   After several more calls, I leave the office and take the elevator upstairs to my apartment in the residential part of Trump Tower. Of course, I have a tendency to make a few more calls when I get home.

TUESDAY

9:00 A.M.   I call Ivan Boesky. Boesky is an arbitrageur, but he and his wife are also the majority owners of the Beverly Hills Hotel and I've just read that he's decided to sell it. I have no idea when I call that just two weeks from now Boesky will plead guilty to insider trading, and that the real reason he's eager to sell the hotel is that he needs to raise cash fast.

My idea is to hire Steve Rubell and Ian Schrager, the creators of Studio 54 and the Palladium, to run the Beverly Hills Hotel for me. Steve's an incredible promoter, and he'd make the hotel hot as hell again. I get Boesky and tell him I'm very interested. He tells me Morgan Stanley and Company is handling the deal, and I will get a call from their people shortly.

I like Los Angeles. I spent a lot of weekends there during the 1970s, and I always stayed at the Beverly Hills. But I won't let my personal preferences affect my business judgment. Much as I like the hotel, I'm interested in it only if I can get it for a much better price than they're now asking.

9:30 A.M. Alan Greenberg calls. We've bought another 100,000 shares of Holiday, and the stock is up another point and a half. Trading is very active. I tell Alan I've heard that the top guys at Holiday are in a panic and that they're holding emergency meetings to discuss how to react to me. Alan says that he thinks Holiday will enact some kind of "poison pill" as a way of fending off any attempts I make at a hostile takeover.

Our call lasts less than two minutes. That's one thing I love about Alan: he never wastes time.

10:00 A.M. I meet with the contractors in charge of building my 2,700-space parking garage and transportation center across the street from Trump Plaza on the Boardwalk in Atlantic City. It's a $30 million job, and they're here to give me a progress report. They tell me we're on schedule and under budget.

The garage will be ready in time for Memorial Day, 1987—the biggest weekend of the year in Atlantic City—and it's going to increase our business enormously. Right now we are doing well with virtually no parking. The new lot is located at the end of the main road leading to the Boardwalk, and it's connected by a walkway to our casino. Anyone who parks in the garage funnels directly into our facility.

11:00 A.M. I meet with a top New York banker at my office. He's come to try to solicit business, and we have a general talk about deals I'm considering. It's funny what's happened: bankers now come to me, to ask if I might be interested in borrowing their money. They know a safe bet.

12:15 P.M. Norma comes in and tells me that we have to switch the Wollman Rink press conference from Thursday to Wednesday. Henry Stern, the New York City parks commissioner, has a conflict: on Thursday he is also scheduled to dedicate a new Central Park playground on the Upper West Side, underwritten by Diana Ross, the singer.

The problem is that there's no way we can move our concrete-pouring, which was why we called the press conference in the first place. But what the hell? I'll wing it and things will work out. I'm reluctant to give Henry a hard time. Last week, my security force refused to let him into Wollman without my written permission. This was taking good security a step too far. As you can imagine, Henry wasn't thrilled.

12:45 P.M. Jack Mitnik, my accountant, calls to discuss the tax implications of a deal we're doing. I ask him how bad he thinks the new federal tax law is going to be for real estate, since it eliminates a lot of current real estate write-offs.

To my surprise, Mitnik tells me he thinks the law is an overall plus for me, since much of my cash flow comes from casinos and condominiums and the top tax rate on earned income is being dropped from 50 to 32 percent. However, I still believe the law will be a disaster for the country, since it eliminates the incentives to invest and build—particularly in secondary locations, where no building will occur unless there are incentives.

1:30 P.M. I tell Norma to call John Danforth, the Republican senator from Missouri. I don't know Danforth personally, but he's one of the few senators who fought hard against the new tax bill. It's probably too late, but I just want to congratulate him on having the courage of his convictions, even though it might cost him politically.

Danforth isn't in, but his secretary says he'll call back.

1:45 P.M. Norma sees an opening between calls, and she comes in to ask me about several invitations. Dave Winfield, the New York Yankee outfielder, has asked me to be the chairman of a dinner to benefit his foundation, which fights drug abuse. I'm already chairing two dinners this month, one for United Cerebral Palsy and the other for the Police Athletic League.

I don't kid myself about why I'm asked to speak at or chair so many events. It's not because I'm such a great guy. The reason is that the people who run charities know that I've got wealthy friends and can get them to buy tables. I understand the game, and while I don't like to play it, there is no graceful way out. However, I've already hit up my friends twice this month—and there's only so many times you can ask people to donate $10,000 for a table. I tell Norma to turn Winfield down, with regrets.

The other invitation is from the Young President's Organization, asking me to speak at a dinner they're having. YPO admits businessmen under the age of forty who are chief executives of their companies. I turned forty two months ago, so in their eyes, I guess I now qualify as an elder statesman.

Norma also asks me about a half dozen party invitations. I say yes to two. One is being given by Alice Mason, the real estate broker who has managed to turn herself into a major socialite by getting the hottest people to come to her parties. The other is a reception for two wonderful people, Barbara Walters of ABC and Merv Adelson, the head of Lorimar-Telepictures, who were married a few months ago in California.

Frankly, I'm not too big on parties, because I can't stand small talk. Unfortunately, they're part of doing business, so I find myself going to more than I'd like—and then trying hard to leave early. A few, fortunately, I enjoy. But more often I will accept an invitation many months in advance, thinking the date is so far off that it will never arrive. When it does, I get mad at myself for having accepted in the first place. By then it's usually too late to pull out.

2:00 P.M. I get an idea and call Alan Greenberg again. My idea is based on the fact that if I make a takeover move against Holiday, I have to get licensed as a casino operator in Nevada, where Holiday owns two casinos. "What do you think," I ask him, "about just selling out Holiday shares right now, taking a profit, and then rethinking a takeover bid after I get licensed?"

Alan argues for holding tight with what we've got. I say okay, for now. I like to keep as many options open as I can.

2:15 P.M. John Danforth calls back. We have a nice talk, and I tell him to keep up the good work.

2:30 P.M. I return a call from one of the owners of the Dunes Hotel in Las Vegas. They also own perhaps the best undeveloped site on the Vegas strip. For the right price, I'd consider buying it.

I like the casino business. I like the scale, which is huge, I like the glamour, and most of all, I like the cash flow. If you know what you are doing and you run your operation reasonably well, you can make a very nice profit. If you run it very well, you can make a ton of money.

2:45 P.M. My brother, Robert, and Harvey Freeman, both executive vice presidents in my company, stop by to report on a meeting they've had that day with Con Edison and executives from NBC about the West Side yards project. Con Ed has a large smokestack on the southern end of the site, and the meeting was to discuss whether the fumes from the stack would dissipate as effectively if a large building goes up adjacent to it.

Robert, who is two years younger than I am, is soft-spoken and easygoing, but he's very talented and effective. I think it must be hard to have me for a brother, but he's never said anything about it and we're very close. He is definitely the only guy in my life whom I ever call "honey."

Robert gets along with almost everyone, which is great for me, since I sometimes have to be the bad guy. Harvey is a different type: no-nonsense, not too big on laughs, but he's got an absolutely brilliant analytic mind.

The Con Ed people, I'm happy to hear, told the NBC executives that there is no reason to believe the presence of the NBC building will affect the smokestack. Unfortunately, Con Ed won't be the last word. Before we can get our approvals, we'll have to get an independent environmental-impact statement.

3:15 P.M. I call Herbert Sturz of the City Planning Commission, which will be the first city agency to approve or disapprove our latest plan for the West Side yards. Sturz and his people are scheduled to have a preliminary look on Friday.

He isn't in, so I leave a message with his secretary. I just say I'm looking forward to seeing him Friday morning.

3:20 P.M. Gerald Schrager calls. Jerry's a top attorney at Dreyer & Traub, one of the best real estate firms in the country, and he's handled nearly every one of my major deals since I bought the Commodore Hotel back in 1974. Jerry is more than an attorney. He's an absolute business machine, and he can see through to the essence of a deal as fast as anyone I know.

We talk about the Holiday Inns situation and several other deals that are in various stages. Like Alan Greenberg, Schrager isn't big on wasting time. We cover a half dozen subjects in less than ten minutes.

3:30 P.M. My wife, Ivana, stops in to say good-bye. She's on her way to Atlantic City, by helicopter. I like to kid her that she works harder than I do. Last year, when I bought my second casino from the Hilton Corporation and renamed it Trump's Castle, I decided to put Ivana in charge. She's incredibly good at anything she's ever done, a natural manager.

Ivana grew up in Czechoslovakia, an only child. Her father was an electrical engineer and a very good athlete, and he started Ivana skiing very early. By the age of six she was winning medals, and in 1972 she was an alternate on the Czechoslovakian ski team at the Sapporo Winter Olympics. A year later, after graduating from Charles University in Prague, she moved to Montreal and very quickly became one of the top models in Canada.

We met at the Montreal Summer Olympic Games in August 1976. I'd dated a lot of different women by then, but I'd never gotten seriously involved with any of them. Ivana wasn't someone you dated casually. Ten months later, in April 1977, we were married. Almost immediately, I gave her responsibility for the interior decorating on the projects I had under way. She did a great job.

Ivana may be the most organized person I know. In addition to raising three children, she runs our three homes—the apartment in Trump Tower, Mar-a-Lago, and our home in Greenwich, Connecticut—and now she also manages Trump's Castle, which has approximately 4,000 employees.

The Castle is doing great, but I still give Ivana a hard time about the fact that it's not yet number one. I tell her she's got the biggest facility in town, so by all rights it should be the most profitable. Ivana is almost as competitive as I am and she insists she's at a disadvantage with the Castle. She says she needs more suites. She isn't concerned that building the suites will cost $40 million. All she knows is that not having them is hurting her business and making it tougher for her to be number one. I'll say this much: I wouldn't bet against her.

* * *

3:45 P.M. The executive vice president for marketing at the Cadillac Division of General Motors is on the phone. He's calling at the suggestion of his boss, John Gretenberger, the president of the Cadillac Motors Division whom I know from Palm Beach. Cadillac, it turns out, is interested in cooperating in the production of a new superstretch limousine that would be named the Trump Golden Series. I like the idea. We set a date to sit down and talk in two weeks.

4:00 P.M. Daniel Lee, a casino analyst for Drexel Burnham Lambert, stops by with several of his colleagues to discuss being my investment bankers on a deal to purchase a hotel company.

Michael Milken, the guy who invented junk-bond financing at Drexel, has called me regularly for the last several years to try to get me to bring my business to Drexel. I have no idea that Drexel is about to get enmeshed in the insider-trading scandal that will soon rock Wall Street. In any case, I happen to think Mike's a brilliant guy. However, Alan Greenberg is exceptional himself, and I'm loyal to people who've done good work for me.

I hear Lee and his guys out on their deal, but in truth, it doesn't excite me much. We leave it that I'll get back to them.

5:00 P.M. Larry Csonka, former running back for the Miami Dolphins, calls. He has an idea for keeping the USFL alive. He wants to merge it with the Canadian Football League. Larry's both a bright and a nice guy, and he's very enthusiastic, but he doesn't convince me. If the USFL couldn't get off the ground with players like Herschel Walker and Jim Kelly, how is Canadian football, with a lot of players nobody has heard of, going to help? We've got to win in the courts first, to break up the NFL monopoly.

5:30 P.M. I call Calvin Klein, the designer, to congratulate him. Back when Trump Tower first opened, Klein took a full floor of offices for his new perfume line, Obsession. It did so well that within a year, he expanded to a second floor. Now he's doing better than ever, and so he's taking over a third floor.

I have a lot of admiration for Calvin, and I tell him so. He's a very talented designer, but he's also a very good salesman and businessman—and it's the combination of those qualities that makes him so successful.

6:00 P.M. I draft a letter to Paul Goldberger, architecture critic of the *New York Times*. A week ago, in a Sunday column, Goldberger gave a great review to the design of Battery Park City, the new development in lower Manhattan. He also called it "a stunning contrast" to what he claimed we're doing with the Television City project at the West Side yards. In other words, he killed us.

There's just one catch: we're in the middle of designing our project with new architects and concepts, and nobody—including Goldberger—has seen our new plan. He was knocking a design he hadn't even looked at yet.

"Dear Paul," I write. "Your recent article is an obvious 'setup' in preparation for the negative review you intend to do on Television City—no matter how great it is. Just think, if you are negative enough (which I am sure you will be) you might even help convince NBC to move to New Jersey."

My people keep telling me I shouldn't write letters like this to critics. The way I see it, critics get to say what they want to about my work, so why shouldn't I be able to say what I want to about theirs?

WEDNESDAY

9:00 A.M. I go with Ivana to look at a private school for my daughter. If you had told me five years ago that I'd be spending mornings looking at kindergarten classrooms, I would have laughed.

11:00 A.M. I have a press conference for the Wollman Rink. When I get there, I'm amazed. There are at least twenty reporters and photographers milling around.

Henry Stern, the parks commissioner, goes to the microphone first and he is very complimentary to me. He says that if the city had tried to undertake the current renovation by itself, "we would now be awaiting Board of Estimate approval for what Donald Trump has already done."

When it's my turn, I explain that we've laid twenty-two miles of pipes, that they've all been thoroughly tested and there are no leaks, that the project is ahead of schedule by at least a month, and under budget by about $400,000. I also announce that we've set a grand opening for November 13—and that we have a show planned for that day which will include most of the world's great skaters.

After I finish, the reporters ask a million questions. Finally Henry and I step down into the rink. If we can't have a real concrete-pouring, at least we'll have a ceremonial one. A couple of workmen pull over a wheelbarrow full of wet concrete and point it down toward us. Henry and I shovel some concrete onto the pipes while the photographers click away.

As many times as I've done these things, I have to say I still find them a little ridiculous. Think of it: a couple of guys in pinstripe suits shoveling wet concrete. But I like to be accommodating. As long as they want to shoot, I'll shovel.

12:45 P.M. The minute I get back to my office, I start returning calls. I want to get as much done as I can now, because I have to leave early for Trenton, to attend a retirement dinner for a member of the New Jersey Casino Control Commission.

The first person I call back is Arthur Barron, the president of Gulf & Western's entertainment group, which includes Paramount Pictures. Martin Davis, the chairman of G&W, has been my friend for a long time, and Barron apparently called in response to a letter I wrote to Marty two weeks ago. In the letter I explained to Marty that I'd recently purchased a fantastic site and was in the midst of designing a building with eight motion picture theaters at its base, and I wondered if he might be interested in making a deal for them.

"As you are aware," I wrote, "there is no one I would rather do business with than Marty Davis."

That happened to be true, for Martin Davis is a truly talented man, but there are also a dozen other companies who would kill to have eight theaters in a top location. In other words, if I can't make a deal I like with Marty, I've got a lot of other options.

As I anticipated, when I get Art Barron on the phone, he wants to set up a meeting to discuss the theaters. We make a date for the following week.

1:30 P.M. I return a call from Arthur Sonnenblick, one of the city's leading brokers. Three weeks ago, Arthur called to say he had some foreign clients who were interested in buying the West Side yards. He wouldn't tell me their names, but he said they were serious people, and they were prepared to make me a very substantial offer for the site—far more than the $100 million I paid a year ago.

I didn't get too excited. On the contrary, I say to Arthur, "The bid sounds low. If you can get them higher, I might be interested." Now Arthur's calling to give me a status report.

The truth is, I really don't want to sell the yards at any price. To me, those one hundred acres overlooking the Hudson River are the best undeveloped real estate site in the world. On the other hand, I don't want to rule out anything. Arthur tells me his clients are still very interested, that they may come up a little, but he doubts they'll go much higher. "Keep pushing," I tell him.

2:00 P.M. The contractor who's building my pool at Mar-a-Lago is on the phone. I'm busy, but I take the call anyway. We're going to great lengths to build a pool in keeping with the original design of the house, and I want to make sure every detail is right.

Buying Mar-a-Lago was a great deal even though I bought it to live in, not as a real estate investment. Mar-a-Lago was built in the early 1920s by Marjorie Merriweather Post, the heiress to the Post cereal fortune and, at the time, Mrs. Edward F. Hutton. Set on twenty acres that face both the Atlantic Ocean and Lake Worth, the house took four years to build and has 118 rooms. Three boatloads of Dorian stone were brought from Italy for the exterior walls, and 36,000 Spanish tiles dating back to the fifteenth century were used on the exterior and the interior.

When Mrs. Post died she gave the house to the federal government for use as a presidential retreat. The government eventually gave the house back to the Post Foundation, and the foundation put it up for sale at an asking price of $25 million. I first looked at Mar-a-Lago while vacationing in Palm Beach in 1982. Almost immediately I put in a bid of $15 million, and it was promptly rejected. Over the next few years, the foundation signed contracts with several other buyers at higher prices than I'd offered, only to have them fall through before closing. Each time that happened, I put in another bid, but always at a lower sum than before.

Finally, in late 1985, I put in a cash offer of $5 million, plus another $3 million for the furnishings in the house. Apparently, the foundation was tired of broken deals. They accepted my offer, and we closed one month later. The day the deal was announced, the Palm Beach *Daily News* ran a huge front-page story with the headline MAR-A-LAGO'S BARGAIN PRICE ROCKS COMMUNITY.

Soon, several far more modest estates on property a fraction of Mar-a-Lago's size sold for prices in excess of $18 million. I've been told that the furnishings in Mar-a-Lago alone are worth more than I paid for the house. It just goes to show that it pays to move quickly and decisively when the time is right. Upkeep of Mar-a-Lago, of course, isn't cheap. For what it costs each year, you could buy a beautiful home almost anywhere else in America.

All of which is a long way of explaining why I take this call from the pool contractor. He has a small question about the matching of the Dorian stone we're using for the decking and I care about every detail when it comes to Mar-a-Lago. The call takes two minutes, but it will probably save two days of work— and ensure that the job doesn't have to be ripped out and done over later.

2:30 P.M. A prominent businessman who does a lot of business with the Soviet Union calls to keep me posted on a construction project I'm interested in undertaking in Moscow. The idea got off the ground after I sat next to the Soviet ambassador, Yuri Dubinin, at a luncheon held by Leonard Lauder, a great businessman who is the son of Estée Lauder. Dubinin's daughter, it turned out, had read about Trump Tower and knew all about it. One thing led to another, and now I'm talking about building a large luxury hotel, across the street from the Kremlin, in partnership with the Soviet government. They have asked me to go to Moscow in July.

3:00 P.M. Robert stops in, and we talk about several issues relating to NBC and the West Side yards.

3:30 P.M. A friend from Texas calls, to tell me about a deal he's got working. He happens to be a very charming guy—wonderful looking, wonderfully dressed, with one of those great Texas drawls that make you feel very comfortable. He calls me Donny, a name that I hate, but which he says in a way that somehow makes it okay.

Two years ago, this same friend called me about another deal. He was trying to put together a group of wealthy people to take over a small oil company. "Donny," he said, "I want you to invest fifty million. This is a no-lose proposition. You'll double or triple your money in a matter of months." He gave me all the details, and it sounded very good. I was all set to go forward. The papers were being drawn up, and then one morning I woke up and it just didn't feel right.

I called my friend back and I said, "Listen, there's something about this that bothers me. Maybe it's that oil is underground, and I can't see it, or maybe it's that there's nothing creative about it. In any case, I just don't want to go in." And he said, "Okay, Donny, it's up to you, but you're missing a great opportunity." The rest is history, of course. Oil went completely to hell several months later, the company his group bought went bankrupt, and his investors lost every dime they put up.

That experience taught me a few things. One is to listen to your gut, no matter how good something sounds on paper. The second is that you're generally better off sticking with what you know. And the third is that sometimes your best investments are the ones you don't make.

Because I held back, I saved $50 million and the two of us have remained friends. As a result, I don't want to reject him outright on his new deal. Instead, I tell him to send up the papers. In reality, I'm not too likely to get involved.

4:00 P.M. I call back Judith Krantz. You've got to give it to her: how many authors have written three number-one best-selling books in a row? She also happens to be a very nice woman. Trump Tower is the setting for her latest novel, *I'll Take Manhattan*, and I'm a character in the book. At Judy's request, I agreed to play the role of myself in a scene from the miniseries based on her book, and filmed at Trump Tower.

Now Judy is calling to say that the scene, with Valerie Bertinelli, came off well. I'm happy to hear it, although I'm not about to quit my day job. Still, I figure it's not a bad way to promote Trump Tower—on national television, in a miniseries that runs during sweeps week and is virtually guaranteed to get huge national ratings.

4:30 P.M. My last call is to Paul Hallingby, a partner at Bear Stearns who handled the $550 million in bond issues we did successfully for our two casinos in Atlantic City during 1985.

Now we're talking about setting up something called the Trump Fund, through which we'd buy distressed and foreclosed real estate, particularly in the Southwest, at bargain-basement prices.

Hallingby tells me that he's putting together a prospectus, and that he's confident we'll easily be able to raise $500 million in a public offering. What I like about the deal is that I'd retain a large equity position in any purchase we made, but I wouldn't be at any personal risk, in the event that any of the deals went bad. What I don't like is the idea of competing with myself. What happens, for example, if I see a piece of distressed property that I want to buy on my own but that might also be good for the fund?

In any case, I'll look at the prospectus.

* * *

5:00 P.M. I'm driven to the 60th Street heliport, in time to catch a helicopter and be in Trenton for cocktails at 5:30 P.M.

THURSDAY

9:00 A.M. I sit down with Abe Hirschfeld. Basically, Abe feels hurt that Governor Cuomo personally led a fight to push him off the ballot. I tell Abe I understand how he feels, but that the governor is a good guy, and that in any event it would look ridiculous for Abe, who is a Democrat, to suddenly turn around now and endorse a Republican. I also point out that as a practical matter, Cuomo is going to win re-election by a landslide, and that it's a lot better to side with a winner than a loser.

Abe is a pretty stubborn guy, but finally he says, "Look, why don't you get the governor to call me?" I tell him I'll do my best. Abe has always been considered difficult. But I like him and his family a lot.

10:15 A.M. Alan Greenberg calls. The market is down 25 points less than an hour after opening. Alan tells me everyone's a seller, that nearly all stocks are down, but that Holiday is holding firm. I can't decide whether I should be happy or sad. Part of me wants Holiday to drop off, so I can buy more at a better price. The other part of me wants it to go up, because at this point, every time the stock rises a point, I make a lot of easy money.

* * *

10:30 A.M. Harvey Myerson, the attorney who handled our USFL antitrust case, comes in for a meeting. Harvey is an incredible trial lawyer. He took a case in which no one gave us a prayer going in, and he managed to win on antitrust grounds, even though we were awarded only token damages.

Even so, I've wondered, since the trial, whether perhaps Harvey was just a little too sharp for some of the jurors. Every day he'd show up in one of his beautiful pinstripe suits, with a little handkerchief in his pocket, and I'm just not sure how well that went over.

Overall, I think he did as good a job as anyone could, and I still believe he's our best hope on the appeal. One thing I like about Harvey is his enthusiasm. He's still absolutely convinced he's going to win the appeal.

11:30 A.M. Stephen Hyde calls. After I bought out Holiday Inns' interest in the Trump Plaza Hotel and Casino in Atlantic City and took over the management in June, I hired Steve to run the facility. Steve had been working as a vice president for Stephen A. Wynn at the Golden Nugget. Wynn is one of the best gaming guys around, and my philosophy is always to hire the best from the best. After a long-running negotiation, I offered Hyde a bigger job and more money, and he said yes. I think he also liked the idea of working for me, and he didn't mind leaving Steve Wynn.

Wynn is very slick and smooth, but he's also a very

strange guy. A couple of weeks ago, he called and said, "Donald, I just wanted to let you know that my wife and I are getting divorced." So I said, "Oh, I'm sorry to hear that, Steve." He said, "Oh, don't be sorry, it's great, we're still in love, it's just that we don't want to be married anymore. In fact, she's right here with me. Do you want to say hello?" I politely declined.

Hyde is calling to report on the August figures for the Plaza, which just came in. He tells me that gross operating profit was just over $9,038,000 compared with $3,438,000 for the same period a year ago, when I was still partners with Holiday Inns, and they were managing the facility.

"Not too bad," I say to Steve, "considering we still don't have any parking." Still, I can't resist razzing him a little: "Now all you've got to do is get the hotel in mint condition." I'm a stickler for cleanliness, and last time I visited the hotel, I wasn't totally happy.

"We're working on it, Donald," Steve says good-naturedly. "It's already improving."

12:00 noon I walk over to the Wollman Rink, to watch the pouring of the concrete. This morning all of the papers had stories about our press conference.

When I get to the rink, it's surrounded by a convoy of cement trucks lined up as if they're in a military operation. HRH, the construction company in charge of the project, has done a fantastic job moving things along, but this has to be the most incredible sight yet:

thousands of pounds of wet concrete being poured from truck after truck into this huge rink. It's like watching the world's biggest cake get iced.

Even though the press conference was yesterday, I notice photographers and camera crews all over the place. This is the event everyone was waiting for.

1:30 P.M. I sit down with a reporter from *Fortune* who is doing a story about real estate and the new tax laws—with me on the cover. Contrary to what a lot of people think, I don't enjoy doing press. I've been asked the same questions a million times now, and I don't particularly like talking about my personal life. Nonetheless, I understand that getting press can be very helpful in making deals, and I don't mind talking about them. I just try to be very selective. Norma must turn down twenty requests a week from all over the world. Also, when I do give an interview, I always keep it short. This reporter is in and out in less than twenty minutes. If I didn't limit myself, I could spend my life talking to the press.

2:45 P.M. A friend of mine, a highly successful and very well known painter, calls to say hello and to invite me to an opening. I get a great kick out of this guy because, unlike some artists I've met, he's totally unpretentious.

A few months back he invited me to come to his studio. We were standing around talking, when all of a sudden he said to me, "Do you want to see me earn twenty-five thousand dollars before lunch?" "Sure,"

I said, having no idea what he meant. He picked up a large open bucket of paint and splashed some on a piece of canvas stretched on the floor. Then he picked up another bucket, containing a different color, and splashed some of that on the canvas. He did this four times, and it took him perhaps two minutes. When he was done, he turned to me and said, "Well, that's it. I've just earned twenty-five thousand dollars. Let's go to lunch."

He was smiling, but he was also absolutely serious. His point was that plenty of collectors wouldn't know the difference between his two-minute art and the paintings he really cares about. They were just interested in buying his name.

I've always felt that a lot of modern art is a con, and that the most successful painters are often better salesmen and promoters than they are artists. I sometimes wonder what would happen if collectors knew what I knew about my friend's work that afternoon. The art world is so ridiculous that the revelation might even make his paintings *more* valuable! Not that my friend is about to risk finding out.

4:00 P.M. A group of us meet in our conference room to go over the latest plans for the West Side yards project, which we're scheduled to show to the city tomorrow morning. It turns out that Herb Sturz of the planning commission won't be able to attend, but his key people will be there.

There are perhaps fifteen people at this meeting, including Robert and Harvey Freeman, and Alexander

Cooper and his team. Alex is the architect-city planner I hired two months ago to take over the design of the project, after it became clear that my original architect, Helmut Jahn, just wasn't making it with the city. I don't know if the reason was his Germanic style, or the fact that he is based in Chicago rather than New York, or just that he's a little too slick. I do know that he wasn't getting anywhere with the City Planning Commission.

Alex, by contrast, was formerly a city planner himself and he's almost a legend in that office. He's also the guy who designed Battery Park City, which has gotten great press. Politically, he's a much better choice than Helmut Jahn, and I'm a very practical guy.

We've been meeting like this every week for the past couple of months to hash out a broad plan, including where to locate the residential buildings, the streets, the parks, and the shopping mall. Today Alex has brought preliminary drawings of the layout we've agreed on. At the southern end are the prospective NBC studios, adjacent to the world's tallest building. Then, heading north, there are the residential buildings, facing east over a boulevard, and west over a huge eight-block-long shopping mall and out at the river. Every apartment has a great view, which I believe is critical.

I am very happy with the new layout, and Alex seems happy too. I happen to think that tall buildings are what will make this project special, but I'm not naïve about zoning. Eventually, I know, we're going to have to make some concessions. On the other hand, if the city won't approve something I think makes sense economically, I'll just wait for the next administration and try again. This site is only going to get more valuable.

6:00 P.M. I excuse myself, because I am due at an early dinner, and it's not the kind to be late for. Ivana and I have been invited, by John Cardinal O'Connor, to have dinner at St. Patrick's Cathedral.

7:00 P.M. No matter whom you've met over the years, there is something incredible about sitting down to dinner with the cardinal and a half dozen of his top bishops and priests in a private dining room at St. Patrick's Cathedral. It's hard not to be a little awed.

We talk about politics, the city, real estate, and a half dozen other subjects, and it's a fascinating evening. As we leave, I tell Ivana how impressed I am with the cardinal. He's not only a man of great warmth, he's also a businessman with great political instincts.

FRIDAY

6:30 A.M. I'm leafing through the *New York Times* when I come to a huge picture of the concrete being poured onto Wollman Rink. It's on the front page of the second section. This story just won't quit.

* * *

9:15 A.M. We meet with the city on the West Side yards project. Almost everyone from yesterday's meeting is there, and we are joined by four city planners, including Rebecca Robinson and Con Howe, who are directly in charge of evaluating our project.

Alex does the presentation, and he's very good. Mostly he emphasizes the things we know the city is going to like—the public parks, the easy access to the waterfront, the ways we've devised to move traffic in and out. The only time the density issue comes up—how tall the buildings will be—Alex just says we're still working it out.

When it's over, we all agree it went very well.

10:30 A.M. I go back to my office for a meeting to discuss progress on construction at Trump Parc, the condominium I'm building out of the steel shell of the Barbizon-Plaza Hotel on Central Park South. It's an incredible location, and the building we're redoing will be a great success.

The meeting includes Frank Williams, my architect on the project, Andrew Weiss, the project manager, and Blanche Sprague, an executive vice president, who is in charge of sales. Frank, who is very soft-spoken, is a fine architect. Blanchette—my nickname for her—is a classic. She's got a mouth that won't quit, which is probably why she's so good at sales. I like to tell her that she must be a very tough woman to live with. The truth is I get a great kick out of her.

We start by talking about what color to use on the frames of the windows. Details like these make all the difference in the look and ambience of a building. After almost a half hour, we finally agree on a light beige that will blend right into the color of the stone. I happen to like earth tones. They are richer and more elegant than primary colors.

11:00 A.M. Frank Williams leaves, and we turn to a discussion of the demolition work at Trump Parc. Andy tells me it's not finished, and that the contractor has just given us a $175,000 bill for "extras." Extras are the costs a contractor adds to his original bid every time you request any change in the plan you initially agreed on. You have to be very rough and very tough with most contractors or they'll take the shirt right off your back.

I pick up the phone and dial the guy in charge of demolition at Trump Parc. "Steve," I say when I get him, "this is Donald Trump. Listen, you've got to get your ass moving and get finished. You're behind. I want you to get personally involved in this." He starts to give me explanations but I cut him off. "I don't want to know. I just want you to get the job done and get out. And listen, Steve, you're killing me on these extras. I don't want you to deal with Andy anymore on the extras. I want you to deal with me personally. If you try screwing me on this job, you won't be getting a second chance. I'll never hire you again."

My second concern is the laying of floors. I ask Andy for the number of our concrete guy. "Okay," I say, only half joking, "I'm going to take my life in my hands now." Concrete guys can be extremely rough. J get the number-two guy on the line. "Look," I say to him, "your boss wanted this contract very badly. I was set to give it to someone else, but he told me he'd do a great job. I walked the site yesterday, and the patches you're making aren't level with the existing concrete. In some places, they're as much as a quarter-inch off."

The guy doesn't have any response, so I keep talking. "Nobody has the potential to give you more work in the future than Trump. I'm going to be building when everyone else has gone bust. So do me a favor. Get this thing done right."

This time the guy has a response. "Every guy on the job is a pro," he says. "We've given you our best men, Mr. Trump."

"Good," I say. "Call me later and let me know how you're doing."

12:00 noon Alan Greenberg calls to tell me that Holiday has gone ahead and enacted some "poison pill" provisions that will weigh the company down with debt and make it much less attractive as a take-over target. I'm not worried. No poison pill is going to keep me from going after Holiday Inn, if that's what I decide I want to do.

The market is still taking a drubbing. It was off 80 points yesterday, and it's down another 25 today. But Holiday is off only a point. Alan tells me that we've now bought almost 5 percent of the company.

* * *

12:15 P.M. Blanche stays on after Andy leaves to get me to choose a print advertisement for Trump Parc. She shows me a half dozen choices, and I don't like any of them. She is furious.

Blanche wants to use a line drawing that shows the building and its panoramic views of Central Park. "I like the idea of a line drawing," I tell her. "But I don't like these. Also, I want a drawing that shows more of the building. Central Park is great, but in the end I'm not selling a park, I'm selling a building and apartments."

12:30 P.M. Norma comes in, carrying a huge pile of forms I have to sign as part of my application for a Nevada gaming license. While I'm signing, Norma asks who I want to use as character references. I think for a minute, and tell her to put down General Pete Dawkins, a great Army football hero, a terrific guy, and a good friend who's now an investment banker at Shearson; Benjamin Hollaway, chairman and CEO of Equitable Real Estate Group; and Conrad Stephenson of Chase Manhattan Bank.

"Also," I tell Norma, "put down John Cardinal O'Connor."

12:45 P.M. Ivana rings. She's in the office and wants me to go with her to see another school we're considering sending our daughter to next fall. "Come on, Donald," she says. "You haven't got anything else to do." Sometimes I think she really believes it.

"Actually, honey, I'm a little busy right now," I tell

her. It doesn't work. Three minutes later she's in my office, tugging at my sleeve. I finish signing the forms, and we go.

2:30 P.M. Bill Fugazy calls. I like to call him Willie the Fug, but he doesn't seem to appreciate it. Fugazy's business is limousines, but he really should have been a broker. The guy knows everyone. He's one of Lee Iacocca's best friends, and he's the person who recommended to the cardinal that he meet with me to discuss real estate and get to know each other better.

Fugazy asks me how dinner went last night at St. Pat's and I tell him it was great. Before we hang up, we set a golf date for the weekend.

2:45 P.M. John D'Alessio, the construction manager on my triplex in Trump Tower, comes by to discuss the progress. He is carrying drawings. Except for the third floor, where the kids are, and the roof, where someday I'm going to build a park sixty-eight stories up, I've gutted the whole apartment. In truth, I've gone a little overboard. First of all, I practically doubled the size of what I have by taking over the adjacent apartment. What I'm doing is about as close as you're going to get, in the twentieth century, to the quality of Versailles. Everything is made to order. For example, we had the finest craftsmen in Italy hand-carve twenty-seven solid marble columns for the living room. They arrived yesterday, and they're beautiful. I can afford the finest workmanship, and when it comes to my own apartment, I figure, why spare any expense? I want the best, whatever it takes.

I look over the drawings with John and mark up a few changes. Then I ask him how the job is going. "Not bad," he said. "We're getting there."

"Well, push, John," I say. "Push hard."

3:30 P.M. A Greek shipping magnate is on the line. "How's the shipping business?" I ask. He tells me he has a deal he'd like to discuss. He doesn't say what it is, but with certain people you don't ask. If it wasn't big, I assume he wouldn't waste my time. We set a date.

4:00 P.M. I get a call from a guy who sells and leases corporate airplanes. I've been considering buying a G-4, the jet that most corporations use. I tell the guy on the phone that I'm still interested in a plane, but that he should keep his eye out for a 727, which is what I really want.

4:30 P.M. Nick Ribis calls from Australia. He tells me things are going very well on our negotiations to be designated builder and operator of the world's largest casino. Nick fills me in on the details and says that we should know more by the following Monday. "Sounds great," I tell him. "Call me before you fly back."

4:45 P.M. Norma tells me that David Letterman, the talk-show host, is downstairs in the atrium of Trump

Tower, filming a day in the life of two out-of-town tourists. He'd like to know if they could stop up and say hello.

I almost never stay up late enough to watch Letterman, but I know he's hot. I say sure. Five minutes later, Letterman walks in, along with a cameraman, a couple of assistants, and a very nice-looking married couple from Louisville. We kid around a little, and I say what a great town I think Louisville is—maybe we should all go in together on a deal there. Letterman asks me how much an apartment goes for in Trump Tower. I tell him that he might be able to pick up a one-bedroom for $1 million.

"Tell me the truth," Letterman says after a few minutes of bantering. "It's Friday afternoon, you get a call from us out of the blue, you tell us we can come up. Now you're standing here talking to us. You must not have much to do."

"Truthfully, David," I say, "you're right. Absolutely nothing to do."

2

TRUMP CARDS

The Elements
of the Deal

MY STYLE of deal-making is quite simple and straightforward. I aim very high, and then I just keep pushing and pushing and pushing to get what I'm after. Sometimes I settle for less than I sought, but in most cases I still end up with what I want.

More than anything else, I think deal-making is an ability you're born with. It's in the genes. I don't say that egotistically. It's not about being brilliant. It does take a certain intelligence, but mostly it's about instincts. You can take the smartest kid at Wharton, the one who gets straight A's and has a 170 IQ, and if he doesn't have the instincts, he'll never be a successful entrepreneur.

Moreover, most people who do have the instincts will never recognize that they do, because they don't have the courage or the good fortune to discover their potential. Somewhere out there are a few men with more innate talent at golf than Jack Nicklaus, or women with greater ability at tennis than Chris Evert or Martina Navratilova, but they will never lift a club or swing a racket and therefore will never find out how great they could have been. Instead, they'll be content to sit and watch stars perform on television.

When I look back at the deals I've made—and the ones I've lost or let pass—I see certain common elements. But unlike the real estate evangelists you see all over television these days, I can't promise you that by following the precepts I'm about to offer you'll become a millionaire overnight. Unfortunately, life rarely works that way, and most people who try to get rich quick end up going broke instead. As for those among you who do have the genes, who do have the instincts, and who could be highly successful, well, I still hope you won't follow my advice. Because that would just make it a much tougher world for me.

Think Big

I like thinking big. I always have. To me it's very simple: if you're going to be thinking anyway, you might as well think big. Most people think small, because most people are afraid of success, afraid of making decisions, afraid of winning. And that gives people like me a great advantage.

My father built low-income and middle-income buildings in Brooklyn and Queens, but even then, I gravitated to the best location. When I was working in Queens, I always wanted Forest Hills. And as I grew older, and perhaps wiser, I realized that Forest Hills was great, but Forest Hills isn't Fifth Avenue. And so I began to look toward Manhattan, because at a very early age, I had a true sense of what I wanted to do.

I wasn't satisfied just to earn a good living. I was looking to make a statement. I was out to build something monumental—something worth a big effort. Plenty of other people could buy and sell little brownstones, or build cookie-cutter red-brick buildings. What attracted me was the challenge of building a spectacular development on almost one hundred acres by the river on the West Side of Manhattan, or creating a huge new hotel next to Grand Central Station at Park Avenue and 42nd Street.

The same sort of challenge is what attracted me to Atlantic City. It's nice to build a successful hotel. It's a lot better to build a hotel attached to a huge casino that can earn fifty times what you'd ever earn renting hotel rooms. You're talking a whole different order of magnitude.

One of the keys to thinking big is total focus. I think of it almost as a controlled neurosis, which is a quality I've noticed in many highly successful entrepreneurs. They're obsessive, they're driven, they're single-minded and sometimes they're almost maniacal, but it's all channeled into their work. Where other people are paralyzed by neurosis, the people I'm talking about are actually helped by it.

I don't say this trait leads to a happier life, or a better life, but it's great when it comes to getting what you want. This is particularly true in New York real estate, where you are dealing with some of the sharpest, toughest, and most vicious people in the world. I happen to love to go up against these guys, and I love to beat them.

Protect the Downside and the Upside Will Take Care of Itself

People think I'm a gambler. I've never gambled in my life. To me, a gambler is someone who plays slot machines. I prefer to own slot machines. It's a very good business being the house.

It's been said that I believe in the power of positive thinking. In fact, I believe in the power of negative thinking. I happen to be very conservative in business. I always go into the deal anticipating the worst. If you plan for the worst—if you can live with the worst—the good will always take care of itself. The only time in my life I didn't follow that rule was with the USFL. I bought a losing team in a losing league on a long shot. It almost worked, through our antitrust suit, but when it didn't, I had no fallback. The point is that you can't be too greedy. If you go for a home run on every pitch, you're also going to strike out a lot. I try never to leave myself too exposed, even if it means sometimes settling for a triple, a double, or even, on rare occasions, a single.

One of the best examples I can give is my experience in Atlantic City. Several years ago, I managed to piece together an incredible site on the Boardwalk. The individual deals I made for parcels were contingent on my being able to put together the whole site. Until I achieved that, I didn't have to put up very much money at all.

Once I assembled the site, I didn't rush to start construction. That meant I had to pay the carrying charges for a longer period, but before I spent hundreds of millions of dollars and several years on construction, I wanted to make sure I got my gaming license. I lost time, but I also kept my exposure much lower.

When I got my licensing on the Boardwalk site, Holiday Inns came along and offered to be my partner. Some people said, "You don't need them. Why give up fifty percent of your profits?" But Holiday Inns also offered to pay back the money I already had in the deal, to finance all the construction, and to guarantee me against losses for five years. My choice was whether to keep all the risk myself, and own 100 percent of the casino, or settle for a 50 percent stake without putting up a dime. It was an easy decision.

Barron Hilton, by contrast, took a bolder approach when he built his casino in Atlantic City. In order to get opened as quickly as possible, he filed for a license and began construction on a $400 million facility at the same time. But then, two months before the hotel was scheduled to open, Hilton was denied a license. He ended up selling to me at the last minute, under a lot of pressure, and without a lot of other options. I renamed the facility Trump's Castle and it is now one of the most successful hotel-casinos anywhere in the world.

Maximize Your Options

I also protect myself by being flexible. I never get too attached to one deal or one approach. For starters, I keep a lot of balls in the air, because most deals fall out, no matter how promising they seem at first. In addition, once I've made a deal, I always come up with at least a half dozen approaches to making it work, because anything can happen, even to the best-laid plans.

For example, if I hadn't gotten the approvals I wanted for Trump Tower, I could always have built an office tower and done just fine. If I'd been turned down for licensing in Atlantic City, I could have sold the site I'd assembled to another casino operator, at a good profit.

Perhaps the best example I can give is the first deal I made in Manhattan. I got an option to purchase the Penn Central railyards at West 34th Street. My original proposal was to build middle-income housing on the site, with government financing. Unfortunately, the city began to have financial problems, and money for public housing suddenly dried up. I didn't spend a lot of time feeling sorry for myself. Instead, I switched to my second option and began promoting the site as ideal for a convention center. It took two years of pushing and promoting, but ultimately the city did designate my site for the convention center—and that's where it was built.

Of course, if they hadn't chosen my site, I would have come up with a third approach.

Know Your Market

Some people have a sense of the market and some people don't. Steven Spielberg has it. Lee Iacocca of Chrysler has it, and so does Judith Krantz in her way. Woody Allen has it, for the audience he cares about reaching, and so does Sylvester Stallone, at the other end of the spectrum. Some people criticize Stallone, but you've got to give him credit. I mean, here's a man who is just forty-one years old, and he's already created two of the all-time-great characters, Rocky and Rambo. To me he's a diamond-in-the-rough type, a genius purely by instinct. He knows what the public wants and he delivers it.

I like to think I have that instinct. That's why I don't hire a lot of number-crunchers, and I don't trust fancy marketing surveys. I do my own surveys and draw my own conclusions. I'm a great believer in asking everyone for an opinion before I make a decision. It's a natural reflex. If I'm thinking of buying a piece of property, I'll ask the people who live nearby about the area—what they think of the schools and the crime and the shops. When I'm in another city and I take a cab, I'll always make it a point to ask the cabdriver questions. I ask and I ask and I ask, until I begin to get a gut feeling about something. And that's when I make a decision.

I have learned much more from conducting my own random surveys than I could ever have learned from the greatest of consulting firms. They send a crew of people down from Boston, rent a room in New York, and charge you $100,000 for a lengthy study. In the end, it has no conclusion and takes so long to complete that if the deal you were considering was a good one, it will be long gone.

The other people I don't take too seriously are the critics—except when they stand in the way of my projects. In my opinion, they mostly write to impress each other, and they're just as swayed by fashions as anyone else. One week it's spare glass towers they are praising to the skies. The next week, they've rediscovered old, and they're celebrating detail and ornamentation. What very few of them have is any feeling for what the public wants. Which is why, if these critics ever tried to become developers, they'd be terrible failures.

Trump Tower is a building the critics were skeptical about before it was built, but which the public obviously liked. I'm not talking about the sort of person who inherited money 175 years ago and lives on 84th Street and Park Avenue. I'm talking about the wealthy

Italian with the beautiful wife and the red Ferrari. Those people—the audience I was after—came to Trump Tower in droves.

The funny thing about Trump Tower is that we ended up getting great architectural reviews. The critics didn't want to review it well because it stood for a lot of things they didn't like at the time. But in the end, it was such a gorgeous building that they had no choice but to say so. I always follow my own instincts, but I'm not going to kid you: it's also nice to get good reviews.

Use Your Leverage

The worst thing you can possibly do in a deal is seem desperate to make it. That makes the other guy smell blood, and then you're dead. The best thing you can do is deal from strength, and leverage is the biggest strength you can have. Leverage is having something the other guy wants. Or better yet, needs. Or best of all, simply can't do without.

Unfortunately, that isn't always the case, which is why leverage often requires imagination, and salesmanship. In other words, you have to convince the other guy it's in his interest to make the deal.

Back in 1974, in an effort to get the city to approve my deal to buy the Commodore Hotel on East 42nd Street, I convinced its owners to go public with the fact that they were planning to close down the hotel. After they made the announcement, I wasn't shy about pointing out to everyone in the city what a disaster a boarded-up hotel would be for the Grand Central area, and for the entire city.

When the board of Holiday Inns was considering whether to enter into a partnership with me in Atlantic City, they were attracted to my site because they believed my construction was farther along than that of any other potential partner. In reality, I wasn't that far along, but I did everything I could, short of going to work at the site myself, to assure them that my casino was practically finished. My leverage came from confirming an impression they were already predisposed to believe.

When I bought the West Side railyards, I didn't name the project Television City by accident, and I didn't choose the name because I think it's pretty. I did it to make a point. Keeping the television networks in New York—and NBC in particular—is something the city very much wants to do. Losing a network to New Jersey would be a psychological and economic disaster.

Leverage: don't make deals without it.

Enhance Your Location

Perhaps the most misunderstood concept in all of real estate is that the key to success is location, location, location. Usually, that's said by people who don't know what they're talking about. First of all, you don't necessarily need the best location. What you need is the best deal. Just as you can create leverage, you can enhance a location, through promotion and through psychology.

When you have 57th Street and Fifth Avenue as your location, as I did with Trump Tower, you need less promotion. But even there, I took it a step further, by promoting Trump Tower as something almost larger than life. By contrast, Museum Tower, two blocks away and built above the Museum of Modern Art, wasn't marketed well, never achieved an "aura," and didn't command nearly the prices we did at Trump Tower.

Location also has a lot to do with fashion. You can take a mediocre location and turn it into something considerably better just by attracting the right people. After Trump Tower I built Trump Plaza, on a site at Third Avenue and 61st Street that I was able to purchase very inexpensively. The truth is that Third Avenue simply didn't compare with Fifth Avenue as a location. But Trump Tower had given a value to the Trump name, and I built a very striking building on Third Avenue. Suddenly we were able to command premium prices from very wealthy and successful people who might have chosen Trump Tower if the best apartments hadn't been sold out. Today Third Avenue is a very prestigious place to live, and Trump Plaza is a great success.

My point is that the real money isn't made in real estate by spending the top dollar to buy the best location. You can get killed doing that, just as you can get killed buying a bad location, even for a low price.

What you should never do is pay too much, even if that means walking away from a very good site. Which is all a more sophisticated way of looking at location.

Get the Word Out

You can have the most wonderful product in the world, but if people don't know about it, it's not going to be worth much. There are singers in the world with voices as good as Frank Sinatra's, but they're singing in their garages because no one has ever heard of them. You need to generate interest, and you need to create excitement. One way is to hire public relations people and pay them a lot of money to sell whatever you've got. But to me, that's like hiring outside consultants to study a market. It's never as good as doing it yourself.

One thing I've learned about the press is that they're always hungry for a good story, and the more sensational the better. It's in the nature of the job, and I understand that. The point is that if you are a little different, or a little outrageous, or if you do things that are bold or controversial, the press is going to write about you. I've always done things a little differently, I don't mind controversy, and my deals tend to be somewhat ambitious. Also, I achieved a lot when I was very young, and I chose to live in a certain style. The result is that the press has always wanted to write about me.

I'm not saying that they necessarily like me. Sometimes they write positively, and sometimes they write negatively. But from a pure business point of view, the benefits of being written about have far outweighed the drawbacks. It's really quite simple. If I take a full-page ad in the *New York Times* to publicize a project, it might cost $40,000, and in any case, people tend to be skeptical about advertising. But if the *New York Times* writes even a moderately positive one-column story about one of my deals, it doesn't cost me anything, and it's worth a lot more than $40,000.

The funny thing is that even a critical story, which may be hurtful personally, can be very valuable to your business. Television City is a perfect example. When I bought the land in 1985, many people, even those on the West Side, didn't realize that those one hundred acres existed. Then I announced I was going to build the world's tallest building on the site. Instantly, it became a media event: the *New York Times* put it on the front page, Dan Rather announced it on the evening news, and George Will wrote a column about it in *Newsweek*. Every architecture critic had an opinion, and so did a lot of editorial writers. Not all of them liked the idea of the world's tallest building. But the point is that we got a lot of attention, and that alone creates value.

The other thing I do when I talk with reporters is to be straight. I try not to deceive them or to be defensive, because those are precisely the ways most people get themselves into trouble with the press. Instead, when a reporter asks me a tough question, I try to frame a positive answer, even if that means shifting the ground. For example, if someone asks me what negative effects the world's tallest building might have on the West Side, I turn the tables and talk about how New Yorkers deserve the world's tallest building, and what a boost it will give the city to have that honor again. When a reporter asks why I build only for the rich, I note that the rich aren't the only ones who benefit from my buildings. I explain that I put thousands of people to work who might otherwise be collecting unemployment, and that I add to the city's tax base every time I build a new project. I also point out that buildings like Trump Tower have helped spark New York's renaissance.

The final key to the way I promote is bravado. I play to people's fantasies. People may not always think big themselves, but they can still get very excited by those who do. That's why a little hyperbole never hurts. People want to believe that something is the biggest and the greatest and the most spectacular.

I call it truthful hyperbole. It's an innocent form of exaggeration—and a very effective form of promotion.

Fight Back

Much as it pays to emphasize the positive, there are times when the only choice is confrontation. In most cases I'm very easy to get along with. I'm very good to people who are good to me. But when people treat me badly or unfairly or try to take advantage of me, my general attitude, all my life, has been to fight back very hard. The risk is that you'll make a bad situation worse, and I certainly don't recommend this approach to everyone. But my experience is that if you're fighting for something you believe in—even if it means alienating some people along the way—things usually work out for the best in the end.

When the city unfairly denied me, on Trump Tower, the standard tax break every developer had been getting, I fought them in six different courts. It cost me a lot of money, I was considered highly likely to lose, and people told me it was a no-win situation politically. I would have considered it worth the effort regardless of the outcome. In this case, I won—which made it even better.

When Holiday Inns, once my partners at the Trump Plaza Hotel and Casino in Atlantic City, ran a casino that consistently performed among the bottom 50 percent of casinos in town, I fought them very hard and they finally sold out their share to me. Then I began to think about trying to take over the Holiday Inns company altogether.

Even if I never went on the offensive, there are a lot of people gunning for me now. One of the problems when you become successful is that jealousy and envy inevitably follow. There are people—I categorize them as life's losers—who get their sense of accomplishment and achievement from trying to stop others. As far as I'm concerned, if they had any real ability they wouldn't be fighting me, they'd be doing something constructive themselves.

Deliver the Goods

You can't con people, at least not for long. You can create excitement, you can do wonderful promotion and get all kinds of press, and you can throw in a little hyperbole. But if you don't deliver the goods, people will eventually catch on.

I think of Jimmy Carter. After he lost the election to Ronald Reagan, Carter came to see me in my office. He told me he was seeking contributions to the Jimmy Carter Library. I asked how much he had in mind. And he said, "Donald, I would be very appreciative if you contributed five million dollars."

I was dumbfounded. I didn't even answer him.

But that experience also taught me something. Until then, I'd never understood how Jimmy Carter became president. The answer is that as poorly qualified as he was for the job, Jimmy Carter had the nerve, the guts, the balls, to ask for something extraordinary. That ability above all helped him get elected president. But then, of course, the American people caught on pretty quickly that Carter couldn't do the job, and he lost in a landslide when he ran for reelection.

Ronald Reagan is another example. He is so smooth and so effective a performer that he completely won over the American people. Only now, nearly seven years later, are people beginning to question whether there's anything beneath that smile.

I see the same thing in my business, which is full of

people who talk a good game but don't deliver. When Trump Tower became successful, a lot of developers got the idea of imitating our atrium, and they ordered their architects to come up with a design. The drawings would come back, and they would start costing out the job.

What they discovered is that the bronze escalators were going to cost a million dollars extra, and the waterfall was going to cost two million dollars, and the marble was going to cost many millions more. They saw that it all added up to many millions of dollars, and all of a sudden these people with these great ambitions would decide, well, let's forget about the atrium.

The dollar always talks in the end. I'm lucky, because I work in a very, very special niche, at the top of the market, and I can afford to spend top dollar to build the best. I promoted the hell out of Trump Tower, but I also had a great product to promote.

Contain the Costs

I believe in spending what you have to. But I also believe in not spending more than you should. When I was building low-income housing, the most important thing was to get it built quickly, inexpensively, and adequately, so you could rent it out and make a few bucks. That's when I learned to be cost-conscious. I never threw money around. I learned from my father that every penny counts, because before too long your pennies turn into dollars.

To this day, if I feel a contractor is overcharging me, I'll pick up the phone, even if it's only for $5,000 or $10,000, and I'll complain. People say to me, "What are you bothering for, over a few bucks?" My answer is that the day I can't pick up the telephone and make a twenty-five-cent call to save $10,000 is the day I'm going to close up shop.

The point is that you can dream great dreams, but they'll never amount to much if you can't turn them into reality at a reasonable cost. At the time I built Trump Plaza in Atlantic City, banks were reluctant to finance new construction at all, because almost every casino up to then had experienced tens of millions of dollars in cost overruns. We brought Trump Plaza in on budget, and on time. As a result, we were able to open for Memorial Day weekend, the start of the high season. By contrast, Bob Guccione of *Penthouse* has been trying for the past seven years to build a casino on the Boardwalk site right next to ours. All he has to show for his efforts is a rusting half-built frame and tens of millions of dollars in lost revenues and squandered carrying costs.

Even small jobs can get out of control if you're not attentive. For nearly seven years I watched from the window of my office as the city tried to rebuild Wollman Rink in Central Park. At the end of that time, millions of dollars had been wasted and the job was farther from being completed than when the work began. They were all set to rip out the concrete and start over when

I finally couldn't stand it anymore, and I offered to do it myself. The job took four months to complete at a fraction of the city's cost.

Have Fun

I don't kid myself. Life is very fragile, and success doesn't change that. If anything, success makes it more fragile. Anything can change, without warning, and that's why I try not to take any of what's happened too seriously. Money was never a big motivation for me, except as a way to keep score. The real excitement is playing the game. I don't spend a lot of time worrying about what I should have done differently, or what's going to happen next. If you ask me exactly what the deals I'm about to describe all add up to in the end, I'm not sure I have a very good answer. Except that I've had a very good time making them.

3

GROWING UP

THE MOST IMPORTANT INFLUENCE on me, growing up, was my father, Fred Trump. I learned a lot from him. I learned about toughness in a very tough business, I learned about motivating people, and I learned about competence and efficiency: get in, get it done, get it done right, and get out.

At the same time, I learned very early on that I didn't want to be in the business my father was in. He did very well building rent-controlled and rent-stabilized housing in Queens and Brooklyn, but it was a very tough way to make a buck. I wanted to try something grander, more glamorous, and more exciting. I also realized that if I ever wanted to be known as more than Fred Trump's son, I was eventually going to have to go out and make my own mark. I'm fortunate that my father was content to stay with what he knew and did so well. That left me free to make my mark in Manhattan. Even so, I never forgot the lessons I learned at my father's side.

His story is classic Horatio Alger. Fred Trump was born in New Jersey in 1905. His father, who came here from Sweden as a child, owned a moderately successful restaurant, but he was also a hard liver and a hard drinker, and he died when my father was eleven years old. My father's mother, Elizabeth, went to work as a seamstress to support her three children. The oldest, also named Elizabeth, was sixteen at the time, and the youngest, John, was nine. My father was the middle child but the first son, and he became the man of the house. Almost immediately, he began taking odd jobs—everything from deliveries for a local fruit store to shining shoes to hauling lumber on a construction site. Construction always interested him, and during high school he began taking night classes in carpentry, plan-reading, and estimating, figuring that if he learned a trade, he'd always be able to make a living. By the age of sixteen, he'd built his first structure, a two-car frame garage for a neighbor. Middle-class people were just beginning to buy cars, few homes had attached garages, and my father was soon able to establish a very good new business building prefabricated garages for fifty dollars apiece.

He graduated from high school in 1922, and with a

family to support, he couldn't even consider college. Instead, he went to work as a carpenter's helper for a home-builder in Queens. He was better with his hands than most, but he also had some other advantages. For starters, he was just a very smart guy. Even to this day, he can add five columns of numbers in his head and keep them all straight. Between his night courses and his basic common sense, he was able to show the other carpenters, most of whom had no education at all, shortcuts, such as how to frame a rafter with a steel square.

In addition, my father was always very focused and very ambitious. Most of his co-workers were happy just to have a job. My father not only wanted to work, he also wanted to do well and to get ahead. Finally, my father just plain loved working. From as early as I can remember, my father would say to me, "The most important thing in life is to love what you're doing, because that's the only way you'll ever be really good at it."

One year after he got out of high school, my father built his first home, a one-family house in Woodhaven, Queens. It cost a little less than $5,000 to build, and he sold it for $7,500. He called his company Elizabeth Trump & Son because at the time he wasn't of age, and his mother had to sign all his legal documents and checks. As soon as he sold his first house, he used the profit to build another, and then another and another, in working-class Queens communities like Woodhaven, Hollis, and Queens Village. For working people who'd spent their lives in small, crowded apartments, my father offered a whole new life-style: modestly priced suburban-style brick houses. They were gobbled up as fast as he could build them.

Instinctively, my father began to think bigger. By 1929, aiming at a more affluent market, he started building much larger homes. Instead of tiny brick houses, he put up three-story Colonials, Tudors, and Victorians in a section of Queens that ultimately became known as Jamaica Estates—and where, eventually, he built a home for our family. When the Depression hit and the housing market fell off, my father turned his attention to other businesses. He bought a bankrupt mortgage-servicing company and sold it at a profit a year later. Next, he built a self-service supermarket in Woodhaven, one of the first of its kind. All the local tradesmen—butcher, tailor, shoemaker—rented concessions in the space, and the convenience of having everything available under one roof made the operation an immediate success. Within a year, however, eager to return to building, my father sold out to King Kullen for a large profit.

By 1934 the Depression was finally beginning to ease, but money was still tight and so my father decided to go back to building lower-priced homes. This time he chose the depressed Flatbush area of Brooklyn, where land was cheap and he sensed there was a lot of room for growth. Once again his instincts were right. In three weeks he sold 78 homes, and during the next dozen years, he built 2,500 more throughout Queens and Brooklyn. He was becoming very successful.

In 1936 my father married my wonderful mother, Mary MacLeod, and they began a family. My father's success also made it possible for him to give to his younger brother something he'd missed himself: a college education. With my father's help, my uncle, John Trump, went to college, got his Ph.D. from M.I.T., and eventually became a full professor of physics and one of the country's great scientists. Perhaps because my father never got a college degree himself, he continued to view people who had one with a respect that bordered on awe. In most cases they didn't deserve it. My father could run circles around most academics and he would have done very well in college, if he'd been able to go.

We had a very traditional family. My father was the power and the breadwinner, and my mother was the perfect housewife. That didn't mean she sat around playing bridge and talking on the phone. There were five children in all, and besides taking care of us, she cooked and cleaned and darned socks and did charity work at the local hospital. We lived in a large house, but we never thought of ourselves as rich kids. We were brought up to know the value of a dollar and to appreciate the importance of hard work. Our family was always very close, and to this day they are my closest friends. My parents had no pretensions. My father still works out of a small, modest back office on Avenue Z in the Sheepshead Bay section of Brooklyn, in a building he put up in 1948. It's simply never occurred to him to move.

My sister Maryanne was the first born, and when

she graduated from Mount Holyoke College, she followed my mother's path at first, marrying and staying at home while her son grew up. But she also inherited a lot of my father's drive and ambition, and when her son David became a teenager, she went back to school, to study law. She graduated with honors, began with a private firm, worked for five years as a federal prosecutor in the U.S. Attorney's Office, and four years ago became a federal judge. Maryanne is really something. My younger sister, Elizabeth, is kind and bright but less ambitious, and she works at Chase Manhattan Bank in Manhattan.

My older brother, Freddy, the first son, had perhaps the hardest time in our family. My father is a wonderful man, but he is also very much a business guy and strong and tough as hell. My brother was just the opposite. Handsome as could be, he loved parties and had a great, warm personality and a real zest for life. He didn't have an enemy in the world. Naturally, my father very much wanted his oldest son in the business, but unfortunately, business just wasn't for Freddy. He went to work with my father reluctantly, and he never had a feel for real estate. He wasn't the kind of guy who could stand up to a killer contractor or negotiate with a rough supplier. Because my father was so strong, there were inevitably confrontations between the two of them. In most cases, Freddy came out on the short end.

Eventually, it became clear to all of us that it wasn't working, and Freddy went off to pursue what he loved most—flying airplanes. He moved to Florida, became a professional pilot, and flew for TWA. He also loved fishing and boating. Freddy was probably happiest during that period in his life, and yet I can remember saying to him, even though I was eight years younger, "Come on, Freddy, what are you doing? You're wasting your time." I regret now that I ever said that.

Perhaps I was just too young to realize that it was irrelevant what my father or I thought about what Freddy was doing. What mattered was that he enjoyed it. Along the way, I think Freddy became discouraged, and he started to drink, and that led to a downward spiral. At the age of forty-three, he died. It's very sad, because he was a wonderful guy who never quite found himself. In many ways he had it all, but the pressures of our particular family were not for him. I only wish I had realized this sooner.

Fortunately for me, I was drawn to business very early, and I was never intimidated by my father, the way most people were. I stood up to him, and he respected that. We had a relationship that was almost businesslike. I sometimes wonder if we'd have gotten along so well if I hadn't been as business-oriented as I am.

Even in elementary school, I was a very assertive, aggressive kid. In the second grade I actually gave a teacher a black eye—I punched my music teacher because I didn't think he knew anything about music and I almost got expelled. I'm not proud of that, but it's clear evidence that even early on I had a tendency to stand up and make my opinions known in a very forceful way. The difference now is that I like to use my brain instead of my fists.

I was always something of a leader in my neighborhood. Much the way it is today, people either liked me a lot, or they didn't like me at all. In my own crowd I was very well liked, and I tended to be the kid that others followed. As an adolescent I was mostly interested in creating mischief, because for some reason I liked to stir things up, and I liked to test people. I'd throw water balloons, shoot spitballs, and make a ruckus in the schoolyard and at birthday parties. It wasn't malicious so much as it was aggressive. My brother Robert likes to tell the story of the time when it became clear to him where I was headed.

Robert is two years younger than I am, and we have always been very close, although he is much quieter and more easygoing than I am. One day we were in the playroom of our house, building with blocks. I wanted to build a very tall building, but it turned out that I didn't have enough blocks. I asked Robert if I could borrow some of his, and he said, "Okay, but you have to give them back when you're done." I ended up using all of my blocks, and then all of his, and when I was done, I'd created a beautiful building. I liked it so much that I glued the whole thing together. And that was the end of Robert's blocks.

When I turned thirteen, my father decided to send me to a military school, assuming that a little military training might be good for me. I wasn't thrilled about the idea, but it turned out he was right. Beginning in the eighth grade I went to the New York Military

Academy in upstate New York. I stayed through my senior year, and along the way I learned a lot about discipline, and about channeling my aggression into achievement. In my senior year I was appointed a captain of the cadets.

There was one teacher in particular who had a big impact on me. Theodore Dobias was a former drill sergeant in the marines, and physically he was very tough and very rough, the kind of guy who could slam into a goalpost wearing a football helmet and break the post rather than his head. He didn't take any back talk from anyone, least of all from kids who came from privileged backgrounds. If you stepped out of line, Dobias smacked you and he smacked you hard. Very quickly I realized that I wasn't going to make it with this guy by trying to take him on physically. A few less fortunate kids chose that route, and they ended up getting stomped. Most of my classmates took the opposite approach and became nebbishes. They never challenged Dobias about anything.

I took a third route, which was to use my head to get around the guy. I figured out what it would take to get Dobias on my side. In a way, I finessed him. It helped that I was a good athlete, since he was the baseball coach and I was the captain of the team. But I also learned how to play *him*.

What I did, basically, was to convey that I respected his authority, but that he didn't intimidate me. It was a delicate balance. Like so many strong guys, Dobias had a tendency to go for the jugular if he smelled weakness. On the other hand, if he sensed strength but you didn't try to undermine him, he treated you like a man. From the time I figured that out—and it was more an instinct than a conscious thought—we got along great.

I was a good enough student at the academy, although I can't say I ever worked very hard. I was lucky that it came relatively easily to me, because I was never all that interested in schoolwork. I understood early on that the whole academic thing was only a preliminary to the main event—which was going to be whatever I did after I graduated from college.

Almost from the time I could walk, I'd been going to construction sites with my father. Robert and I would tag along and spend our time hunting for empty soda bottles, which we'd take to the store for deposit money. As a teenager, when I came home from school for vacation, I followed my father around to learn about the business close up—dealing with contractors or visiting buildings or negotiating for a new site.

You made it in my father's business—rent-controlled and rent-stabilized buildings—by being very tough and very relentless. To turn a profit, you had to keep your costs down, and my father was always very price-conscious. He'd negotiate just as hard with a supplier of mops and floor wax as he would with the general contractor for the larger items on a project. One advantage my father had was that he knew what everything cost. No one could put anything over on him. If you know, for example, that a plumbing job is going to cost the contractor $400,000, then you know how far you can push the guy. You're not going to try to negotiate him down to $300,000, because that's just going to put him out of business. But you're also not going to let him talk you into $600,000.

The other way my father got contractors to work for a good price was by selling them on his reliability. He'd offer a low price for a job, but then he'd say, "Look, with me you get paid, and you get paid on time, and with someone else, who knows if you ever see your money?" He'd also point out that with him they'd get in and out quickly and on to the next job. And finally, because he was always building, he could hold out the promise of plenty of future work. His arguments were usually compelling.

My father was also an unbelievably demanding taskmaster. Every morning at six, he'd be there at the site and he would just pound and pound and pound. He was almost a one-man show. If a guy wasn't doing his job the way my father thought it should be done—and I mean any job, because he could do them all—he'd jump in and take over.

It was always amusing to watch a certain scenario repeat itself. My father would start a building in, say, Flatbush, at the same time that two competitors began putting up their own buildings nearby. Invariably, my father would finish his building three or four months before his competitors did. His building would also always be a little better-looking than the other two, with a nicer, more spacious lobby and larger rooms in the apartments themselves. He'd rent them out quickly, at a time when it wasn't so easy to rent. Eventually, one or both of his competitors would go bankrupt before they'd finish their buildings, and my father would step in and buy them out. I saw this happen over and over.

In 1949, when I was just three years old, my father began building Shore Haven Apartments, the first of several large apartment complexes that eventually made him one of the biggest landlords in New York's outer boroughs. Because he built the projects so efficiently, my father did exceptionally well with them. At the time, the government was still in the business of financing lower- and middle-income housing. To build Shore Haven, for example, my father got a loan of $10.3 million from the Federal Housing Administration (FHA). The loan was based on what the agency projected as a fair and reasonable cost for the project, including a builder's profit of 7.5 percent.

By pushing his contractors very hard, and negotiating hard with his suppliers, my father was able to bring the project in ahead of schedule and almost $1 million under budget. The term "windfall profits" was actually coined to describe what my father and some others managed to earn through hard work and competence. Eventually such profits were disallowed.

In the meantime, however, my father put up thousands of good quality lower- and middle-income apartments of the sort that no one is building today because it's not profitable and government subsidies have been eliminated. To this day, the Trump buildings in Queens and Brooklyn are considered among the best reasonably priced places to live in New York.

After I graduated from New York Military Academy

in 1964 I flirted briefly with the idea of attending film school at the University of Southern California. I was attracted to the glamour of the movies, and I admired guys like Sam Goldwyn, Darryl Zanuck, and most of all Louis B. Mayer, whom I considered great showmen. But in the end I decided real estate was a much better business.

I began by attending Fordham University in the Bronx, mostly because I wanted to be close to home. I got along very well with the Jesuits who ran the school, but after two years, I decided that as long as I had to be in college, I might as well test myself against the best. I applied to the Wharton School of Finance at the University of Pennsylvania and I got in. At the time, if you were going to make a career in business, Wharton was the place to go. Harvard Business School may produce a lot of CEOs—guys who manage public companies—but the real entrepreneurs all seemed to go to Wharton: Saul Steinberg, Leonard Lauder, Ron Perelman—the list goes on and on.

Perhaps the most important thing I learned at Wharton was not to be overly impressed by academic credentials. It didn't take me long to realize that there was nothing particularly awesome or exceptional about my classmates, and that I could compete with them just fine. The other important thing I got from Wharton was a Wharton degree. In my opinion, that degree doesn't prove very much, but a lot of people I do business with take it very seriously, and it's considered very prestigious. So all things considered, I'm glad I went to Wharton.

I was also very glad to get finished. I immediately moved back home and went to work full-time with my father. I continued to learn a lot, but it was during this period that I began to think about alternatives.

For starters, my father's scene was a little rough for my tastes—and by that I mean physically rough. I remember, for example, going around with the men we called rent collectors. To do this job you had to be physically imposing, because when it came to collecting rent from people who didn't want to pay, size mattered a lot more than brains.

One of the first tricks I learned was that you never stand in front of someone's door when you knock. Instead you stand by the wall and reach over to knock. The first time a collector explained that to me, I couldn't imagine what he was talking about. "What's the point?" I said. He looked at me like I was crazy. "The point," he said, "is that if you stand to the side, the only thing exposed to danger is your hand." I still wasn't sure what he meant. "In this business," he said, "if you knock on the wrong apartment at the wrong time, you're liable to get shot."

My father had never sheltered me, but even so, this was not a world I found very attractive. I'd just graduated from Wharton, and suddenly here I was in a scene that was violent at worst and unpleasant at best. For example, there were tenants who'd throw their garbage out the window, because it was easier than putting it in the incinerator. At one point, I instituted a program to teach people about using the incinerators. The vast majority of tenants were just fine, but the bad element required attention, and to me it just wasn't worth it.

The second thing I didn't find appealing was that the profit margins were so low. You had no choice but to pinch pennies, and there was no room for any luxuries. Design was beside the point because every building had to be pretty much the same: four walls, common brick façades, and straight up. You used red brick, not necessarily because you liked it but because it was a penny a brick cheaper than tan brick.

I still remember a time when my father visited the Trump Tower site, midway through construction. Our façade was a glass curtain wall, which is far more expensive than brick. In addition, we were using the most expensive glass you can buy—bronze solar. My father took one look, and he said to me, "Why don't you forget about the damn glass? Give them four or five stories of it and then use common brick for the rest. Nobody is going to look up anyway." It was a classic, Fred Trump standing there on 57th Street and Fifth Avenue trying to save a few bucks. I was touched, and of course I understood where he was coming from—but also exactly why I'd decided to leave.

The real reason I wanted out of my father's business— more important than the fact that it was physically rough and financially tough—was that I had loftier dreams and visions. And there was no way to implement them building housing in the outer boroughs.

Looking back, I realize now that I got some of my sense of showmanship from my mother. She always had a flair for the dramatic and the grand. She was a very traditional housewife, but she also had a sense of the world beyond her. I still remember my mother, who is Scottish by birth, sitting in front of the television set to watch Queen Elizabeth's coronation and not budging for an entire day. She was just enthralled by the pomp and circumstance, the whole idea of royalty and glamour. I also remember my father that day, pacing around impatiently. "For Christ's sake, Mary," he'd say. "Enough is enough, turn it off. They're all a bunch of con artists." My mother didn't even look up. They were total opposites in that sense. My mother loves splendor and magnificence, while my father, who is very down-to-earth, gets excited only by competence and efficiency.

4

THE
CINCINNATI KID

Prudence Pays

IN COLLEGE, while my friends were reading the
comics and the sports pages of newspapers, I was
reading the listings of FHA foreclosures. It might
seem a bit abnormal to study lists of federally financed
housing projects in foreclosure, but that's what I did.
And that's how I found out about Swifton Village. It
was a job that I bought with my father, while I was in
college, and it was my first big deal.

Swifton Village was a 1,200-unit apartment development in Cincinnati, Ohio, and it was a very troubled
place. There were 800 vacant apartments, the developers had gone under, the government had foreclosed

and the whole deal was a disaster. But from our perspective that was great, because it gave us a terrific opportunity.

A lot of times, when you are dealing with a government agency on a foreclosure, they just want to get out of it as quickly as possible. They aren't equipped to manage it. In this case, things had deteriorated so badly that no one else was even bidding.

Today you'll find the same thing if you go out to the Sun Belt, where they built all that housing during the oil boom. Now you have huge developments with 30 and 40 percent vacancy rates. Developers are suicidal because banks are foreclosing on them. It's a great time for a smart buyer, because you can get unbelievable deals.

My father and I put in a very minimal bid for Swifton, and it was accepted. We ended up paying less than $6 million for a job which had cost twice that much to build just two years earlier. We were also immediately able to get a mortgage for what we paid, plus about $100,000, which we put toward fixing the place up. In other words, we got the project without putting down any money of our own. All we had to do was go and run it. And if we did even a halfway decent job, we could easily cover our mortgage from the proceeds of the rent.

The fact that it was such a big job appealed to my father and to me because it meant we could focus a lot of energy on it without feeling we were wasting our time. It takes almost the same amount of energy to manage 50 units as it does 1,200—except that with 1,200 you have a much bigger upside.

After we negotiated the deal, success became a matter of management and marketing. The challenge was to get the place rented, and rented to good tenants who would stay there. The tenants who were living in the project when I took over had ripped the place apart. Many of them had come down from the hills of Kentucky. They were very poor and had seven or eight children, almost no possessions, and no experience living in an apartment complex. They crammed into one-room and two-room apartments, and their children went wild. They would just destroy the apartments and wreak havoc on the property.

The tenants not only didn't care, many of them also didn't see fit to pay rent. If you pressed them, they had a tendency to take off. What we discovered is that to avoid paying rent, these people would rent a trailer, pull it up in front of their apartments at one or two in the morning, and disappear into the night with all their belongings. That was fine by me, but I wanted to make sure we got paid first. Our solution was to institute a "trailer-watch." We had someone on round-the-clock patrol.

After we got rid of the bad tenants, we set about fixing the place up to attract a better element. That required a substantial investment, almost $800,000 by the time we were done, which was a lot of money in those days. But it was more than worth it. In New York the laws prevent you from getting fair increases even when you make improvements, but in Cincinnati we were immediately able to charge and get much higher rents for the apartments at Swifton Village.

The first thing we did was invest in beautiful white shutters for the windows. That may not sound like a big deal, but what the shutters did was give a bunch of cold red brick buildings a feeling of warmth and coziness, which was important. It was also much more expensive than you'd guess, because you're talking about 1,200 units, each of which has eight to ten windows. The next thing we did was rip out the cheap, horrible aluminum front doors on the apartments and put up beautiful colonial white doors.

I made sure the whole complex was very clean and very well maintained. As I said earlier, I've always had a personal thing about cleanliness, but I also believe it's a very good investment. For example, if you want to sell a car and you spend five dollars to wash and polish it and then apply a little extra elbow grease, suddenly you find you can charge an extra four hundred dollars—and get it. I can always tell a loser when I see someone with a car for sale that is filthy dirty. It's so easy to make it look better.

It's no different in real estate. Well-maintained real estate is always going to be worth a lot more than poorly maintained real estate. That's been less true during the past few years in New York, when there's been such a fever for real estate that people buy anything. But it's a mistake to be lulled by good times. Markets always change, and as soon as there's a downturn, cleanliness becomes a major value.

We painted the hallways, we sanded and stained the

floors, we kept the vacant apartments immaculately clean, and we landscaped the grounds. We also ran beautiful newspaper ads for the project—at a time when not many people in Cincinnati were advertising real estate. People came to check us out, and the word of mouth started getting good. Within a year, the buildings were 100 percent rented.

Along the way we went through a half dozen different project managers before we found the one we wanted. We had managers who were honest but dumb, including one guy who literally painted himself into the corner of an apartment. Others were smart but didn't know the first thing about managing. Fortunately, we went through them fast, because I tend to size people up pretty quickly.

Ultimately, we got a fabulous man whom I'll call Irving. Irving was sixty-five years old and a real character. He was one of the greatest bullshit artists I've ever met, but in addition to being a very sharp talker and a very slick salesman, he was also an amazing manager. Irving was the kind of guy who worked perhaps an hour a day and accomplished more in that hour than most managers did in twelve hours. I learned something from that: it's not how many hours you put in, it's what you get done while you're working.

The problem with Irving was that he wasn't the most trustworthy guy in the world. I suspected as much from the first day, but it wasn't until I tried to put a bond on him—something I do with any employee who handles money—that my instincts were confirmed. My insurance agent called me back after running a check, and he said, "Donald, you've got to be kidding about a bond. This guy is a con man." It turned out that Irving had done all sorts of con jobs and swindles, and he'd often been in trouble with the law.

My philosophy has always been that if you ever catch someone stealing, you have to go after him very hard, even if it costs you ten times more than he stole. Stealing is the worst. But with Irving I had a dilemma: he was far and away more capable than any honest manager I had found, and so long as he was in charge, no one *under* him would dare steal. That meant I only had to keep my eye on *him*. I used to kid Irving. I'd say, "We pay you $50,000 and all you can steal." And he would act all upset.

If I'd caught him in the act, I would have fired Irving on the spot, but I never did. Still, I figure he managed to steal at least another $50,000 a year. Even so, I was probably getting a bargain.

One day I walked into the office, and one of the girls who worked there was crying. It turned out that there was something they called a funeral fund, to which they all contributed in order to buy flowers for anyone they knew who'd died. They had about $80 in the fund. When I asked the girl what she was crying about, she said, "Oh, that Irving, he stole our funeral fund."

I went to Irving and I said, "Irving, dammit, did you steal their money?" Of course he just denied it. He swore he'd get those girls, and he ranted and raved for half an hour. But I always assumed the girls were telling the truth. Irving was a classic. He had problems, but he was a classic.

I'll give you an example of how Irving worked. You've got to understand that we are talking about a short, fat, bald-headed guy with thick glasses and hands like Jell-O, who'd never lifted anything in his life beside a pen, and who had no physical ability whatsoever. What he did have, however, was an incredible mouth.

As I mentioned, in the early days we had a good number of tenants who didn't believe in paying rent. Sometimes, Irving would go out and collect himself. He'd ring the doorbell, and when someone came to the door, he'd go crazy. He'd get red in the face, use every filthy word he could think of, and make every threat in the book. It was an act, but it was very effective: usually they paid up right then and there.

One day, while Irving was on his rounds, he knocked on a door, and a little ten-year-old girl answered. Irving said, "You go tell your father to pay his f——ing rent or I'm going to knock his ass off." And he went on like that, until the girl's mother came out to see what was going on. As it happened, she was an absolutely beautiful woman.

Now Irving had a weakness for all women, and this woman was quite exceptional. So immediately, Irving started putting the move on her. He invited her out to dinner. The woman, whose husband was either a truck driver or a construction worker, had never experienced anyone like Irving and obviously didn't know what to make of him. There was no way, however, that she was interested in Irving, and finally he gave up and we left.

About an hour later, Irving and I were sitting in his office when this huge guy, a monster, maybe 240 pounds, burst through the door. He was furious that Irving had cursed in front of his daughter, and he was ready to strangle him for coming on to his wife. The guy had murder in his eyes.

I expected Irving, if he had any sense, to run for his life. Instead, he started verbally attacking the man, flailing and screaming and chopping his hands in the air. "You get out of this office," he said. "I'll kill you. I'll destroy you. These hands are lethal weapons, they're registered with the police department."

I'll never forget how the guy looked at Irving and said, "You come outside, you fat crap, I want to burn grass with you." I always loved that phrase: "burn grass." And I thought to myself, Irving is in serious trouble. But Irving didn't seem to think so. "I'd fight you any time you want," he said, "but it's unlawful for me to fight."

All you had to do was look at Irving to know those hands were hardly registered weapons. But Irving was very much like a lion tamer. You've seen these guys, maybe 150 pounds, who walk blithely into a cage where there's a magnificent 800-pound lion pacing around. If that animal sensed any weakness or any fear, he'd destroy the trainer in a second. But instead the trainer cracks his whip, walks with authority, and, amazingly, the lion listens. Which is exactly what

Irving did with this huge guy, except his whip was his mouth.

The result was that the guy left the office. He was still in a rage, but he left. Irving probably saved his own life, just by showing no fear, and that left a very vivid impression on me. You can't be scared. You do your thing, you hold your ground, you stand up tall, and whatever happens, happens.

As for Swifton Village, once Irving had it running well, I began spending less and less time there. I wasn't really needed anymore in Cincinnati. So I cut back my visits to Swifton, first to once a week, and eventually to once a month.

Early on, I'd become particularly friendly with one of the newer tenants at Swifton. He was Jewish, an older man who'd been in a concentration camp in Poland. He'd started off in America as a butcher, then bought the shop, and by the time I met him, he owned perhaps fourteen butcher shops. He and his wife had taken two apartments in Swifton and put them together, and they had a great place, and they were very happy there. I had a lot of respect for this guy, because he had street smarts, he'd been around, and he was obviously a true survivor.

One day, a number of years after we first bought the place, I was out visiting. I ran into my friend. "How are you doing, how are you feeling?" I asked. "Good, good," he replied, but then he took me aside and whispered, "Donald, you are a friend of mine and I have to tell you, sell this job." And I said, "Why?"

"Because it's going real bad—not the job but the

area. It's being surrounded by people who are so bad they will cut your throat and walk away and not even think about it. I'm talking about people who *enjoy* cutting throats.'' That was the exact expression. I never forgot it.

Now, I'm someone who responds to people I have respect for, and I listen. Again, it's instincts, not marketing studies. So I spent an extra two days in Cincinnati, and I rode around, and I saw that there was trouble brewing, that neighborhoods were getting rough.

I put the job up for sale, and almost immediately we got an offer. We'd already done very well with Swifton Village, because our debt was very small relative to the size of the complex, and our rent roll, by the end, had reached about $700,000 a year. But selling was how we made a real killing.

The buyer was the Prudent Real Estate Investment Trust. Those were the go-go days when real estate investment trusts—partnerships that invested in real estate—were very hot. The banks were loaning money to any REIT. The only problem was that many of the people running the REITs were neither knowledgeable nor competent. I called them the guys with the white bucks. They were the sort of people who'd throw money into a project in Puerto Rico without even going to see it. Eventually they'd discover that the building they thought they'd bought had never even been built.

In the case of Prudent, they sent a young man out to inspect and evaluate the property prior to making a final decision on whether to go forward with the sale. This kid was about my age, but he looked like a teenager. Frankly, I was surprised they'd entrusted such a big decision to him.

It turned out that what he wanted to do more than anything was go out for lunch. He'd heard about this restaurant in downtown Cincinnati called the Maisonette, which was supposed to be one of the five best restaurants in the country. He really wanted to eat there, and when he called to say he was coming, he asked me to make a lunch reservation. I said fine.

His flight came in a little late, about midday, and I met him, and I took him over to Swifton Village and showed him the job. We still had 100 percent occupancy at the time, and he wasn't interested in asking a lot of questions beyond that. He was anxious to get to the Maisonette. It took about half an hour to get there from Swifton, and we ended up spending about three hours over lunch, which is the opposite of the way I normally work. If I'd had only one day to look over a big job like Swifton, I'd sure as hell skip lunch and spend my time learning everything I could about what I was thinking of buying.

By the time we were done with lunch, it was almost four o'clock, and I had to take him to his plane. He returned to New York well fed and feeling great, and he strongly recommended going ahead with the purchase. He told his bosses that the area was wonderful and that Swifton was a great deal. They approved the sale. The price was $12 million—or approximately a

$6 million profit for us. It was a huge return on a short-term investment.

What happened next is that we signed a contract. By then, I could see the dark clouds clearly on the horizon. A lot of tenants had their leases coming up and weren't planning to renew. We put a clause in the contract of sale saying that all representations contained in it were as of the signing of the contract—not as of the closing, which is what's typically required. In other words, we were willing to represent that the project was 100 percent rented at the time of the contract signing, but we didn't want to make the same promise at the time of closing, three or four months down the line.

The other thing I did was to insist on a clause in the contract in which they guaranteed they'd close, or else pay a huge penalty. That was also very unusual, because in nearly every other deal, the buyer puts up a 10 percent deposit, and if he fails to close, all he forfeits is the deposit.

Frankly, the Prudent people should have been more prudent. But, as I said, the REITs were hot to trot, and they couldn't make deals fast enough. In the end, of course, it never pays to be in too much of a hurry. On the day we closed, there were dozens of vacant apartments.

5

THE MOVE
TO MANHATTAN

I HAD MY EYE on Manhattan from the time I graduated from Wharton in 1968. But at that point, the market in the city was very hot, the prices seemed very high, and I was unable to find a deal I liked—meaning a good piece of property at a price I found affordable. My father had done very well for himself, but he didn't believe in giving his children huge trust funds. When I graduated from college, I had a net worth of perhaps $200,000, and most of it was tied up in buildings in Brooklyn and Queens. So I waited. I went to work helping to run my father's business, and

I continued to spend as much time as possible in Manhattan.

The turning point came in 1971, when I decided to rent a Manhattan apartment. It was a studio, in a building on Third Avenue and 75th Street, and it looked out on the water tank in the court of the adjacent building. I jokingly referred to my apartment as a penthouse, because it did happen to be near the top floor of the building. I also tried to divide it up so that it would seem bigger. But no matter what I did, it was still a dark, dingy little apartment. Even so, I loved it. Moving into that apartment was probably more exciting for me than moving, fifteen years later, into the top three floors of Trump Tower on Fifth Avenue and 57th Street overlooking Central Park.

You have to understand; I was a kid from Queens who worked in Brooklyn, and suddenly I had an apartment on the Upper East Side.

The really important thing was that by virtue of this move I became much more familiar with Manhattan. I began to walk the streets in a way you never do if you just come in to visit or do business. I got to know all the good properties. I became a city guy instead of a kid from the boroughs. As far as I was concerned, I had the best of all worlds. I was young, and I had a lot of energy, and I was living in Manhattan, even though I commuted back to Brooklyn to work.

One of the first things I did was join Le Club, which at the time was the hottest club in the city and perhaps the most exclusive—like Studio 54 at its height. It was located on East 54th Street, and its membership included some of the most successful men and the most beautiful women in the world. It was the sort of place where you were likely to see a wealthy seventy-five-year-old guy walk in with three blondes from Sweden.

I'll never forget how I became a member. One day I called up Le Club and I said, "My name is Donald Trump and I'd like to join your club." The guy on the other end of the phone just laughed and said, "You've got to be kidding." Nobody, of course, had heard of me. The next day I got another idea, and I called back and I said to the guy, "Listen, could I have a list of your members? I may know someone who is a member." And he said, "I'm sorry, we don't do that," and he hung up.

The next day I called again and said, "I need to reach the president of the club. I want to send him something." For some reason, the guy gave me the president's name and his business number, and I called him up. I introduced myself. I said, very politely, "My name is Donald Trump, and I'd like to join Le Club." And he said, "Do you have any friends or family in the club?" and I said, "No, I don't know anybody there."

He said, "Well, what makes you think you should be admitted as a member?" I just kept talking and talking, and finally this fellow said to me, "I'll tell you what, you sound like a nice young man, and maybe it would be good to have some younger members, so why don't you meet me for a drink at Twenty-one?"

The next night we met for a drink. There was just one small problem. I don't drink, and I'm not very big on sitting around. My host, on the other hand, liked to drink, and he had brought along a friend who also liked to drink. For the next two hours, we sat there as they drank and I didn't, until finally I said, "Listen, fellas, can I help you get home?" and they said, "No, let's just have one more."

Now, I just wasn't used to that. I have a father who has always been a rock, very straight and very solid. My father would come home every night at seven, have his dinner, read the newspaper, watch the news, and that was that. And I'm as much of a rock as my father. This was a totally different world. I remember wondering if every successful person in Manhattan was a big drinker. I figured it that was the case, I was going to have a big advantage.

Finally, about ten, these guys had enough, and I practically had to carry them home. Two weeks passed, and I never heard from the president. Finally, I called him, and he didn't even remember who I was. So now I had to go through the whole thing all over again, back to 21, only this time he didn't drink as much, and he agreed to put me up for membership. He had only one misgiving. He said that because I was young and good-looking, and because some of the older members of the club were married to beautiful young women, he was worried that I might be tempted to try to steal their wives. He asked me to promise that I wouldn't do that.

I couldn't believe what I was hearing. My mother is

as much of a rock as my father. She is totally devoted to my father—they recently celebrated fifty years of marriage. That's what I grew up with, and here's this guy talking about stealing wives.

Anyway, I promised. I was admitted to the club, and it turned out to be a great move for me, socially and professionally. I met a lot of beautiful young single women, and I went out almost every night. Actually, I never got involved with any of them very seriously. These were beautiful women, but many of them couldn't carry on a normal conversation. Some were vain, some were crazy, some were wild, and many of them were phonies. For example, I quickly found out that I couldn't take these girls back to my apartment, because by their standards what I had was a disaster, and in their world appearances were everything. When I finally did get married, I married a very beautiful woman, but a woman who also happens to be a rock, just like my mother and father.

During that same period, I also met a lot of very successful, very wealthy men at Le Club. I had a good time when I went out at night, but I was also working. I was learning how the New York scene operates and I was meeting the sort of people with whom I'd eventually work on deals. I also met the sort of wealthy people, particularly Europeans and South Americans, who eventually bought the most expensive apartments in Trump Tower and Trump Plaza.

It was at Le Club that I first met Roy Cohn. I knew him by reputation and was aware of his image as a guy who wasn't afraid to fight. One night I found myself sitting at the table next to him. We got introduced, and we talked for a while, and I challenged him. I like to test people. I said to him, "I don't like lawyers. I think all they do is delay deals, instead of making deals, and every answer they give you is no, and they are always looking to settle instead of fight." He said he agreed with me. I liked that and so then I said, "I'm just not built that way. I'd rather fight than fold, because as soon as you fold once, you get the reputation of being a folder."

I could see Roy was intrigued, but he wasn't sure what the point of it all was. Finally he said, "Is this just an academic conversation?"

I said, "No, it's not academic at all. It so happens that the government has just filed suit against our company and many others, under the civil rights act, saying that we discriminated against blacks in some of our housing developments." I explained to him that I'd spent that afternoon with my father, talking to lawyers in a very prestigious Wall Street firm, and that they'd advised us to settle. That's exactly what most businessmen do when the government charges them with anything, because they just don't want bad publicity, even if they believe they can beat a phony rap.

The idea of settling drove me crazy. The fact was that we did rent to blacks in our buildings.

We wanted tenants who we could be sure would pay the rent, who would be neat and clean and good neighbors, and who met our requirement of having an income at least four times the rent. So I said to Roy, "What do you think I should do?"

And he said, "My view is tell them to go to hell and fight the thing in court and let them prove that you discriminated, which seems to me very difficult to do, in view of the fact that you have black tenants in the building." He also told me, "I don't think you have any obligation to rent to tenants who would be undesirable, white or black, and the government doesn't have a right to run your business."

That's when I decided Roy Cohn was the right person to handle the case. I was nobody at the time, but he loved a good fight, and he took on my case. He went to court, and I went with him, and we fought the charges. In the end the government couldn't prove its case, and we ended up making a minor settlement without admitting any guilt. Instead, we agreed to do some equal-opportunity advertising of vacancies for a period of time in the local newspaper. And that was the end of the suit.

I learned a lot about Roy during that period. He was a great lawyer, when he wanted to be. He could go into a case without any notes. He had a photographic memory and could argue the facts from his head. When he was prepared, he was brilliant and almost unbeatable. However, he wasn't always prepared. Even then, he was so brilliant that he could sometimes get away with it. Unfortunately, he could also be a disaster, and so I would always question Roy very closely before a court date. If he wasn't prepared, I'd push for a postponement.

I don't kid myself about Roy. He was no Boy Scout. He once told me that he'd spent more than two thirds of his adult life under indictment on one charge or another. That amazed me. I said to him, "Roy, just tell me one thing. Did you really do all that stuff?" He looked at me and smiled. "What the hell do you think?" he said. I never really knew.

Whatever else you could say about Roy, he was very tough. Sometimes I think that next to loyalty, toughness was the most important thing in the world to him. For example, all Roy's friends knew he was gay, and if you saw him socially, he was invariably with some very good-looking young man. But Roy never talked about it. He just didn't like the image. He felt that to the average person, being gay was almost synonymous with being a wimp. That was the last thing he wanted to project, so he almost went overboard to avoid it. If the subject of gay rights came up, Roy was always the first one to speak out against them.

Tough as he was, Roy always had a lot of friends, and I'm not embarrassed to say I was one. He was a truly loyal guy—it was a matter of honor with him—and because he was also very smart, he was a great guy to have on your side. You could count on him to go to bat for you, even if he privately disagreed with your view, and even if defending you wasn't necessarily the best thing for him. He was never two-faced.

Just compare that with all the hundreds of "respectable" guys who make careers out of boasting about their uncompromising integrity but have absolutely no loyalty. They think only about what's best for them and don't think twice about stabbing a friend in the back if the friend becomes a problem. What I liked most about Roy Cohn was that he would do just the opposite. Roy was the sort of guy who'd be there at your hospital bed, long after everyone else had bailed out, literally standing by you to the death.

In any case, I got to know a lot of people when I moved to Manhattan, and I got to know properties, but I still couldn't find anything to buy at a price I liked. Then, suddenly, in 1973 things began to turn bad in Manhattan. I'd always assumed the market would cool off, because everything runs in cycles and real estate is no different. Even so, I never expected things to get as bad as they did. It was a combination of factors. First, the federal government announced a moratorium on housing subsidies, which they had been giving out by the bushel, particularly in the city. At the same time, interest rates began to rise, after being so stable for so many years that it was easy to forget they could move at all. Then, to make things worse, there was a spurt of inflation, particularly in construction costs, which seem to rise even when there's no inflation anywhere else.

But the biggest problem by far was with the city itself. The city's debt was rising to levels that started to make everyone very nervous. For the first time you heard people talk about the city going bankrupt. Fear led to more fear. Before long New York was suffering from a crisis of confidence. People simply ·stopped believing in the city.

It wasn't an environment conducive to new real estate development. In the first nine months of 1973, the city issued permits for about 15,000 new apartments and single-family homes in the five boroughs. In the first nine months of 1974, the number dropped to 6,000.

I worried about the future of New York City too, but I can't say it kept me up nights. I'm basically an optimist, and frankly, I saw the city's trouble as a great opportunity for me. Because I grew up in Queens, I believed, perhaps to an irrational degree, that Manhattan was always going to be the best place to live—the center of the world. Whatever troubles the city might be having in the short term, there was no doubt in my mind that things had to turn around ultimately. What other city was going to take New York's place?

One of the pieces of property that had always fascinated me was the huge abandoned railyard along the Hudson River beginning at 59th Street and extending all the way up to 72nd Street. Every time I drove along the West Side Highway, I found myself dreaming about what could be built there. It didn't take a genius to realize that one hundred acres of undeveloped riverfront property in Manhattan had a lot of potential. But it was another story to consider trying to develop such a huge piece of property when the city was in the midst of a financial crisis.

I don't believe that you can ever be hurt by buying a good location at a low price. At the time, a lot of neighborhoods on the West Side were considered dangerous places to live. There were welfare hotels on every side street, and drug dealers in every park. I remember the *New York Times* running a long series of articles about the block between Central Park West and Columbus Avenue at 84th Street—what a tough area it was.

Even so, you didn't have to look very far to see how easily it could all change. Even on the tough side streets, like West 84th, there were magnificent old brownstones only a few steps away from Central Park. And on the avenues, especially Central Park West and Riverside Drive, there were beautiful old buildings with huge apartments and spectacular views. It was only a matter of time before people discovered the value.

One day, in the summer of 1973, I came across a newspaper story about the Penn Central Railroad, which was in the middle of a massive bankruptcy filing. This particular story said that the Penn Central trustees had hired a company headed by a man named Victor Palmieri to sell off the assets of the railroad. Among the assets, it turned out, were those abandoned yards in the West Sixties, as well as more yards in the West Thirties. The deal Victor made with the Penn Central was that each time his company managed to find a buyer for an asset, he got a percentage of the sale.

I had never heard of Victor Palmieri, but I realized immediately that he was someone I wanted to know. I called his representatives and said, "Hello, my name is Donald Trump, and I'd like to buy the Sixtieth Street yards." The simplest approach is often the most effective.

I think they liked my directness and my enthusiasm.

I hadn't built anything yet, but what I did have was the willingness to go after things that people in a better position than mine wouldn't have considered seeking.

I went to meet Victor, and we got on very well right from the start. He was a very smooth, attractive guy, an Italian who looked like a WASP. I told him how bad the 60th Street yards were, that the neighborhood was in trouble and the city was in trouble, and that I was probably crazy to be interested in the property at all. If you want to buy something, it's obviously in your best interest to convince the seller that what he's got isn't worth very much.

The second thing I told Victor was how incredibly hard it was going to be politically to get zoning approvals for such a big piece of undeveloped land. I pointed out that the community board would fight any development, and that the process of going before the City Planning Commission and the Board of Estimate would be endless.

The third thing I did, and probably the most important, was to sell myself to Victor and his people. I couldn't sell him on my experience or my accomplishment, so instead I sold him on my energy and my enthusiasm.

Victor banks on people and he decided to take a shot on me. He ended up suggesting that I develop not only the 60th Street yards but also the yards on West 34th Street. In truth, I probably oversold myself to him. I had no other choice. I was twenty-seven years old at the time, and I had never built anything in Manhattan, nor had my father. Much as Victor liked me, I don't think he could have justified going with me if he hadn't believed our company was big and powerful. We had no formal name for the company when I met Victor, so I began to call it the Trump Organization. Somehow the word "organization" made it sound much bigger. Few people knew that the Trump Organization operated out of a couple of tiny offices on Avenue Z in Brooklyn.

The other thing I promoted was our relationship with politicians, such as Abraham Beame, who was elected mayor of New York in November of 1973. My father did belong to the same Democratic club that Abe Beame came out of, and they did know each other. Like all developers, my father and I contributed money to Beame, and to other politicians. The simple fact is that contributing money to politicians is very standard and accepted for a New York City developer. We didn't give any more to Beame than a lot of other developers did. In fact, it often seemed to me that, perhaps because we knew Beame personally, he almost went out of his way to avoid any appearance that he was doing us any special favors.

Instead I spent most of the four years when Beame was mayor trying to promote the West 34th Street site for a convention center. It was by far the best site on the merits, and we eventually got nearly every big-name New York City businessman behind us. Still, Beame never came out in support of the site until a few weeks before he left office. Nor did he ever give it his official approval. It was Ed Koch, newly elected in 1978, who finally chose our site for the convention center. No one, so far as I know, has ever suggested that Donald Trump and Ed Koch are close personal friends. But that's getting well ahead of the story.

By building a close relationship with Victor from the start, I was able, in effect, to work for him, rather than to be just another buyer. That was terrific for me. For example, we drew up agreements giving me an exclusive option to purchase the 60th Street and 30th Street yards—but subject to zoning, subject to approval by the court handling the Penn Central bankruptcy, subject to everything except my having to put up any money. The Penn Central even agreed to pay my development costs. It was remarkable in a way: the seller paying for the costs of the potential buyer. Still, you have to put it into perspective. What sounds like a stupid deal today was very different at a time when no one wanted to build anything, and the city was dying.

Palmieri, in turn, helped give me credibility with the press. When he was asked by a reporter from *Barrons* why he chose Trump over others, he said, "Those properties were nothing but a black hole of undefinable risk. We interviewed all kinds of people who were interested in them, none of whom had what seemed like the kind of drive, backing, and imagination that would be necessary. Until this young guy Trump came along. He's almost a throwback to the nineteenth century as a promoter. He's larger than life."

At one point, when I was hyping my plans to the press but in reality getting nowhere, a big New York real estate guy told one of my close friends, "Trump has a great line of shit, but where are the bricks and mortar?"

I remember being outraged when I heard that, and I didn't speak to this guy for more than a year. But looking back, I can see he was right. It could all have gone up in smoke. If I hadn't managed to make one of those first projects happen, if I hadn't finally convinced the city to choose my West 34th Street site for its convention center and then gone on to develop the Grand Hyatt, I'd probably be back in Brooklyn today, collecting rents. I had a lot riding on those first projects.

On July 29, 1974, we announced that the Trump Organization had secured options to purchase the two waterfront sites from the Penn Central—West 59th Street to West 72nd Street, and West 34th Street to West 39th Street—at a cost of $62 million. With no money down. The story made the front page of the *New York Times*.

My original idea was to build middle-income housing on the sites at rents that seem ridiculously cheap today—$110 to $125 a room—but were considered moderately high at the time. I planned to seek financing from the Mitchell-Lama program, through which the city provided low-interest long-term mortgages and tax abatements to builders. The program had been initiated to encourage middle-income housing.

The month before our announcement, Victor and I and some of his people met with Abe Beame to sound him out about our development plans. Although he was encouraging, from the moment we went public he refused to take any position until our plan had been considered by city agencies, including the City Planning Commission, the Board of Estimate, and the local community boards. He was a politician, and he wanted to see which way the winds were blowing before he took a stand.

No sooner had I announced my plans publicly than other bidders for the railyards suddenly came out of the woodwork. Starrett Housing, for example, a company we were partners with on the Starrett City housing project in Brooklyn, made a bid of $150 million, contingent on financing and city approvals and all the rest. On the face of it, their bid was a lot higher than mine.

I'm the first to admit that I am very competitive and that I'll do nearly anything within legal bounds to win. Sometimes, part of making a deal is denigrating your competition. In this case, I happened to genuinely believe that the Starrett bid wasn't legitimate, that the company would never close the deal and would not be able to successfully develop the site even if the deal did go through. The fact is that anyone can bid anything, particularly when there are all sorts of contingencies. The same thing could be said about my bid, except that by then I'd put in enough time and effort to have convinced Palmieri's people that I was very serious and very committed.

In the end, I managed to convince Palmieri that it made more sense to stick with my $62 million bid than to take a flier on Starrett.

The irony is that less than a year after I announced my plans for the site—and beat my competition—the economic situation in New York City turned from bad to much worse.

In February 1975, the Urban Development Corporation, the state agency that sold bonds to finance public housing, defaulted on more than $100 million of repayment on its bonds.

In September 1975, Beame announced that because of the fiscal crisis, the city was suspending its own plans to finance the construction of virtually all new housing.

In November 1975, the state announced that it, too, was suspending any financing of lower- and middle-income housing for the next five years—including a huge number of city projects that had already received preliminary approval.

You couldn't get up in the morning without running across some new headline about the city's fiscal crisis. I can't say that any of this made me truly fearful about the city's future. Still, when it became clear that I wasn't going to get any subsidies to build housing, I decided to try a new tack.

I'd always thought that the West 34th Street site would be perfect for a new convention center. The problem was that nearly everyone else had other ideas. For starters, the city—with the support of many prominent local businessmen—had already spent more than three years studying and trying to develop another site by the Hudson River, at 44th Street. In the planning process alone, the city acknowledged, $13 million had been spent, but people I knew told me that the number was actually closer to $30 million.

Then, just weeks after the city said it wouldn't finance any new housing, Beame announced that the city was also freezing further spending on development of the 44th Street location. I immediately hired Samuel H. Lindenbaum, a talented attorney who specialized in zoning, and who had been working until then on the 44th Street site.

The other person I hired to help with the convention center was a highly dedicated woman named Louise Sunshine, who had extraordinary political connections. Louise had been the finance director for Hugh Carey when he ran for governor in 1974. She was also treasurer of the state Democratic party. At first, she worked for me for practically no pay. Later, she became an executive in our company.

But even as I was assembling a team to promote my site, the city and state were hatching their own alternative: to put the convention center in Battery Park City, opposite the World Trade Center in southern Manhattan. In my opinion, both sites—West 44th Street and Battery Park—were terrible choices. Making my case was another matter. I wanted to wage the battle in public, but I was an unknown. If I was going to attract attention for my site and win support for it, I had to raise my profile.

I decided to call my first news conference. Louise and Howard Rubenstein, a major New York public relations executive, helped attract support from several powerful people, including Manfred Ohrenstein, majority leader of the state senate, and Theodore Kheel, the labor negotiator, who was very powerful in New York politics. Kheel delivered a classic line at the press conference. "Placing the new convention center in Battery Park," he said, "is like putting a nightclub in a graveyard." For our part, we put up a huge banner that said, "Miracle on 34th Street," and I announced, before a ton of reporters, that I could build my convention center for $110 million—or at least $150 million less than the city had estimated it would cost to build at West 44th Street.

Not surprisingly, that raised some eyebrows and even got us some attention in the press. But there was scarcely an approving peep from the politicians. I discovered, for the first time but not the last, that politicians don't care too much what things cost. It's not their money.

In promoting my site, the first thing I pointed out wherever I went was how important it was to build a convention center. A lot of people were saying that the best solution, in light of the city's fiscal crisis, was to scrap the idea altogether.

To me, that was classic shortsightedness. For example, in the face of a sales drop, most companies cut back on their advertising budgets. But in fact, you need advertising the most when people aren't buying. Essentially, that's what I said about a convention center. Building one, I argued, was critical to reviving the city's image and, ultimately, to putting its economy back on track.

I also told anyone who would listen how great my

site was, and how horrible the alternatives were. I pointed out that at 44th Street the convention center would have to be built on platforms over the water, which would be more costly, more problematic, and ultimately more time-consuming. I said that the 44th Street site was too small, that there was no room to expand it, and that because it was on the water, you'd have to cross under the crumbling West Side Highway to get to it. Finally, I made a big deal out of the fact that you needed something called a nonnavigable permit to build on the 44th Street site. A nonnavigable permit, which I became an expert about very quickly, is the federal approval required to build on certain waterways, and getting it requires an act of Congress.

I was just as rough on the Battery Park site, which was an even more ridiculous location at the absolute southern tip of the city. I pointed out how remote it was from midtown, how far from hotels and entertainment, and how inconvenient to public transportation. I also circulated a state study which concluded that building a convention center at Battery Park would require major reconstruction of the West Side Highway leading to it, as well as the addition of at least 2,000 new hotel rooms.

Most of all, I talked about what a wonderful location I had on West 34th Street. It was on the right side of the highway—the eastern side—which meant it was easily accessible. It was closer to subways and buses than the alternative sites. I continued to make the case that the center could be built more cheaply on my site, without dispossessing any tenants. Also, because my site was so big, there was plenty of room for expansion in the future. When a group of graduate students in a class taught by City Councilman Robert Wagner did a little study that rated our site the best, I managed to get hold of it and immediately christened it the Wagner Report. Its namesake wasn't thrilled.

Before long, I had everything going for me except the support of a few absolutely key people. Abe Beame was at the top of the list. Once he gave up on West 44th Street, Beame got behind Battery Park, and no matter how many great arguments I came up with for my site, he wouldn't budge. Another major opponent was John Zuccotti, a deputy mayor under Beame. He began going around town bad-mouthing my site. The reason, I'm convinced, was that he didn't want to admit that he'd wasted several years of his life and millions of dollars of public money on a location that never made sense in the first place. And that's exactly what I said publicly. I accused him of being self-serving and petty and a half-dozen other things. He got pretty riled up. The battle received a lot of media attention, and ultimately, I think, it was good for my site. It became just another way to promote my site's many advantages.

In the end, we won by wearing everyone else down. We never gave up, and the opposition slowly began to melt away. In 1977 Beame appointed yet another committee to study the alternative sites, and it concluded that we did have the best site. On that basis, Beame finally gave us his support—although not his signature—just before leaving office at the end of the year.

In January of 1978, Ed Koch took over as mayor and decided to do his own study. I figured we were back to square one. But things moved fast and once again our site came out ahead. Finally, in April 1978, the city and state announced that they had decided to purchase the 34th Street site and build the convention center there. It was a victory for me, but more symbolically than financially. For all the time I'd invested, I earned much less than I deserved—and nowhere near enough to justify the effort financially.

As my deal with the Penn Central was structured, I was paid total compensation of about $833,000 based on the $12 million price for the site that the city negotiated with Penn Central. In the end I offered to forgo my fee altogether, if the city would agree to name the convention center after my family. I've been criticized for trying to make that trade, but I have no apologies. There wouldn't be a new convention center in New York today if it hadn't been for the Trumps.

More important, the city would have saved a fortune by letting me build the center, which I very much wanted to do. Instead, Ed Koch decided, by some logic I could never understand, that because I'd helped arrange the sale of the property, it was a conflict for me to be the builder as well. Eventually, I offered the city a deal that, frankly, was ridiculous for me. I said I would bring the entire job in for less than $200 million, and that if there were any overruns, I'd pay for them myself. You won't find many builders willing to put themselves on the line that way.

Instead, the city and state decided to oversee the job—and the result was perhaps the most horrendous construction delays and cost overruns in the history of the building business. A man named Richard Kahan was put in charge of the Urban Development Corporation, and ultimately it was his job to oversee the convention center project. Richard Kahan is a nice man, but he had visions of being the next Robert Moses. It wasn't clear that he had the experience or the talent.

One of the first things Kahan did was to hire I. M. Pei as his architect. I. M. Pei is a man with a terrific reputation, but in my view he often chooses the most expensive solution to a problem—and is virtually uncontrollable. Immediately, Pei decided to design a space frame for the center—a structural system that any professional builder will tell you is one of the most difficult to build and is especially vulnerable to cost overruns. This is particularly true when you're dealing with the sort of huge space frame they needed for a convention center.

From the very start, I told Kahan and his people that it was critical to build a parking garage simultaneously. How can you have a convention center without parking? They told me that a garage would hold up the city's environmental-impact approval. "Look," I said to them, "those approvals are only going to be tougher to get later, and at the very least you should begin a separate filing for the garage now, so you can at least start the process." They ignored me, and now they have no parking, and no prospect of building any in the near future.

The choice of where to put the entrance was equally ill-considered. If you put the entrance at the west, the whole center faces the Hudson River, which is a beautiful view. Instead, they built the entrance on the eastern side of the building—facing the traffic on Eleventh Avenue.

As I watched all these mistakes being made, I became very angry and frustrated. In 1983, when it was clear the construction of the convention center was already a disaster of delays and overruns, I wrote a letter to William Stern, who by then had replaced Richard Kahan as president of the Urban Development Corporation. For a second time I offered, this time for no fee at all, to oversee the project and to assure that it would get completed quickly and without further cost overruns.

My offer was refused—and a disaster eventually turned into a catastrophe. By the time the convention center was finally finished last year, it was four years behind schedule—and at least $250 million over budget. When you add interest—the carrying costs for all those years of construction—the total cost was probably $1 billion, or $700 million over budget.

The construction was a terrible disgrace, and all the worse because no one raised a fuss about it. When I was invited to attend opening-day ceremonies in 1986, I refused. What happened at the convention center is that the city and state took a great piece of property and a great project and ruined it through terrible planning and ridiculous cost overruns. Even if the convention center is ultimately a success, it can never earn back all the money that was unnecessarily squandered to build it.

The funny thing about devoting so much time and energy to the 34th Street site is that I never considered it anything to compare with the 60th Street yards. The problem was that developing 60th Street proved even more difficult than promoting 34th Street. The community opposition was stronger, the zoning was more complicated, and the banks were highly reluctant to finance a huge residential housing project in a city still teetering on the verge of bankruptcy.

In 1979 I reluctantly let my option on the 60th Street yards expire so that I could concentrate on other deals that seemed more immediately promising.

The first one, fittingly, was with Palmieri and the Penn Central—for the purchase of the Commodore Hotel.

6

GRAND HOTEL

Reviving 42nd Street

URING THE PERIOD when I was trying to make something happen with the two West Side yards, I got more and more friendly with Victor Palmieri and his people. One day, late in 1974, I was in Victor's office, and I said to him, half-jokingly, "Listen, now that I've got the options on the two yards, what other properties does the Penn Central own that I can buy for nothing?"

"As a matter of fact," said Victor, "we have some hotels you might be interested in."

It so happened that the Penn Central owned several old hotels within a few blocks of each other in midtown: the Biltmore, the Barclay, the Roosevelt, and the Commodore. The first three were at least moderately successful, which meant buying them was likely to cost more money than I wanted to spend. The only one in real trouble was the Commodore, which had been losing money and defaulting on its property taxes for years.

As it turned out, that was the best news Victor could have given me. I decided very quickly that the Commodore, in the heart of New York at 42nd Street and Park Avenue, next to Grand Central Station, had potentially the best location of any of the four hotels.

I still remember walking over to look at the Commodore the day Victor first mentioned it to me. The hotel and the surrounding neighborhood were unbelievably run-down. Half the buildings were already in foreclosure. The brick façade of the Commodore was absolutely filthy, and the lobby was so dingy it looked like a welfare hotel. There was one of those sleazy flea markets operating on the ground floor with a bunch of boarded-up storefronts on either side and derelicts lying in the doorways. To most people, it would have been a very depressing scene.

But as I approached the hotel, something completely different caught my eye. It was about nine in the morning, and there were thousands of well-dressed Connecticut and Westchester commuters flooding onto the streets from Grand Central Terminal and the subway stations below. The city was on the verge of bankruptcy, but what I saw was a superb location. Unless the city literally died, millions of affluent people were going to keep passing by this location every day. The problem was the hotel, not the neighborhood. If I could transform the Commodore, I was sure it could be a hit. Convenience alone would assure that.

I went back and told Victor I was interested in making a deal for the Commodore. He was pleased, because everyone else considered it a loser. I also went to my father and told him I had a chance to make a deal for this huge midtown hotel. At first, he refused to believe I was serious. Later, he told a reporter that his initial reaction to my idea was that "buying the Commodore at a time when even the Chrysler Building is in receivership is like fighting for a seat on the *Titanic*."

I wasn't naïve. I saw potential, but I also recognized a downside. I could envision a huge home run, but I also knew that failing could bury me. From the very first day I went to work on the deal, I tried to keep my risk to an absolute minimum, and financially, I succeeded. But as the months went by, the deal became more and more complicated and difficult. I kept investing more time and more energy, and the stakes rose for reasons unrelated to money. I could talk big for only so long. Eventually I had to prove—to the real estate community, to the press, to my father—that I could deliver the goods.

The Commodore deal was basically a juggling act, but a much trickier one than I originally imagined. First, I had to keep Palmieri's people believing I was their best bet to buy the hotel, while trying to avoid, for as long as I could, putting down any cash. At the same time, I had to convince an experienced hotel operator to come in with me before I actually had a deal, knowing that such a partner would give me more credibility with the banks when I went to seek financing. And even a great partner wasn't enough. I also had to try to persuade city officials that it was in their interest to give me a totally unprecedented tax break. That savings, I knew, would make it far easier to prove to the banks that the numbers for my hotel made sense—at a time when they were loathe to lend money even for projects in good neighborhoods.

The funny thing is that the city's desperate circumstances became my biggest weapon. With Palmieri, I could argue that I was the only developer around who would even consider buying a loser hotel in a decaying neighborhood in a dying city. With the banks, I could point to their moral obligation to finance new developments as a way to help get the city back on its feet. And with city officials, I could legitimately argue that in return for a huge tax abatement, I'd be able to create thousands of new construction and service jobs, help save a neighborhood, and ultimately share with the city any profits the hotel earned.

In the late fall of 1974, I began talking seriously with Palmieri about a deal. Eight or nine months before, the Penn Central had invested $2 million on a renovation of the Commodore that was the equivalent of applying a coat of wax to a car that's just been in a major accident. Even after the renovation, the Penn Central was projecting a huge loss for 1974, and that didn't even include the $6 million that the hotel already owed in back taxes. The Commodore was a terrible cash drain on a bankrupt company.

In a short time we came up with a basic structure for a deal. In simple terms, I would take an option to purchase the hotel at a price of $10 million, subject to my being able to get tax abatement, financing, and a hotel company partner—subject, in other words, to my putting the entire deal together before I made the purchase. In the meantime, I would put down a nonrefundable $250,000 for an exclusive option. There was just one problem: I wasn't too eager to fork over even $250,000 on a deal that was still very much a long shot. In 1974, $250,000 was a huge sum of money for me. So I stalled. Contracts were drawn up, but I had my lawyers find plenty of little legal points to argue back and forth over. In the meantime, I went to work to try to put the rest of the deal together.

What I needed first, I decided, was a really fantastic design—one that would get people excited. I set up a meeting with a young, talented architect named Der Scutt. We met at Maxwell's Plum on a Friday night, and right away I liked Der's enthusiasm. When I told him what I had in mind, he immediately started making sketches on one of the menus.

The key thing, I told Der, was to create something that looked absolutely brand-new. I was convinced that half the reason the Commodore was dying was because it looked so gloomy and dark and dingy. My idea, from the beginning, was to build a new skin directly over the brick—bronze, if it could be done economically, or glass. I wanted a sleek, contemporary look, something with sparkle and excitement that would make people stop and take notice. And it was obvious to me that Der understood what I had in mind.

After we ate, I took Der and another friend back to my apartment, the tiny studio I was still living in on Third Avenue, and I asked him what he thought about my furniture. Some people would just have said, "Fantastic, great," but Der didn't do that. "There's too much of it," he said, and he started moving furniture around, and even pushed several pieces out into the hallway. When he finished, he'd managed to make the apartment look much bigger, which I liked.

I hired Der and paid him to come up with sketches that we could use in our presentations to the city and to banks. I also told him to make it appear that we'd spent a huge sum on the drawings. A good-looking presentation goes a long way.

By the spring of 1975, we were pretty far along on a design. Then, one evening in the middle of April, Der called to tell me that he'd been fired from the architectural firm he worked for, Kahn & Jacobs/Hellmuth, Obata & Kassabaum. I knew he hadn't been getting along with his bosses. At the same time, I didn't want to hold up the project. I needed the resources and the prestige of a big firm to do a job this size, and I figured it was going to be a while before Der made a new association. But he formed an association very quickly with a firm named Gruzen & Partners, and I was able to use the situation to my advantage. The Obata group desperately wanted to keep the job, and so, of course, did Der. The competition gave me an opportunity to negotiate a lower architectural fee, which I did. In the end I went with Der, and paid him a very modest fee. I also told him that doing this job would pay off big in the end. "This is going to be a monumental project," I said. "It's going to make you into a star." Der wasn't thrilled about his fee, but later he admitted that I'd been right about the impact that doing the Hyatt—and subsequently Trump Tower—had on his career.

During this same period, early 1975, I began to look for an operator for the hotel. The truth was that I knew nothing about the hotel business. I've learned a lot since then, and today I operate my own hotels. But at the time, I was only twenty-seven years old, and I'd hardly even slept in a hotel. Nonetheless, I was trying to buy this monster building, 1,500,000 square feet, and proposing to create a 1,400-room hotel—the largest since the construction of the New York Hilton twenty-five years earlier. It seemed clear that I needed an experienced operator. I also figured it probably had to be one of the large chains, and I wasn't totally wrong. The chains may not be very exciting, but they do give you access to a national reservations system, good referral business, and basic management expertise.

From the start, Hyatt was at the top of my list. Hilton seemed a little backward and old, Sheraton didn't excite me for much the same reasons, and Holiday Inns and Ramada Inn didn't have enough class. I liked the Hyatt image. Their hotels had a modern look, light and clean and a little glossy, and that was what I had in mind architecturally for the Commodore. In addition, Hyatt was very strong on conventions, which I thought could be a big business for a hotel in the Grand Central area.

I also liked Hyatt because I thought I might have more leverage with them in making a deal. Chains like Hilton and Sheraton already had hotels in New York City, and they weren't necessarily hungry to build new ones, particularly with the city in the dumps. Hyatt, on the other hand, was very successful in other cities but still had no flagship presence in New York City, and I'd heard they wanted one very badly.

In late 1974 I called up the president of Hyatt, a guy named Hugo M. Friend, Jr., and we arranged to meet. I wasn't terribly impressed with Skip Friend, but it turned out that I was right about Hyatt's desire for a New York flagship, and we began to discuss a partnership on the Commodore. Fairly rapidly, I made a tentative deal with him, full of contingencies. I was very happy and very proud of myself. Then two days later I got a call and Skip said, "No, I'm sorry, we can't do the deal that way." This became a pattern. We'd negotiate new terms, shake hands, a few days would go by, and the deal would suddenly be off again. Finally, a guy I'd become friendly with at Hyatt, a high-level executive, called. "I'd like to make a suggestion," he said. "I think you should call Jay Pritzker and deal with him directly."

I'd barely heard of Pritzker, which tells you something about how young I was at the time. I knew, vaguely, that the Pritzker family owned a controlling interest in Hyatt, but that was about all. My Hyatt friend explained that Pritzker was the guy who really ran the company. Suddenly it dawned on me why my deals kept coming apart: if you're going to make a deal of any significance, you have to go to the top.

It comes down to the fact that everyone underneath the top guy in a company is just an employee. An employee isn't going to fight for your deal. He's fighting for his salary increase, or his Christmas bonus, and the last thing he wants to do is upset his boss. So he'll present your case with no real opinion. To you, he might be very enthusiastic, but to his boss he'll say, "Listen, a guy named Trump from New York wants to make such and such a deal, and here are the pros and cons, and what do you want to do?" If it turns out his boss likes the idea, he'll keep supporting you. But if the boss doesn't like it, the employee will say, "Yes, I agree, but I wanted to present it to you."

By now it was the early spring of 1975, and I called Jay Pritzker, and he seemed happy to hear from me. Hyatt was based in Chicago, but Pritzker told me he was coming to New York the next week, and we should meet. Could I pick him up at the airport? I didn't go around in limousines at the time, so I picked him up in my own car. Unfortunately it was a very hot day, and it was extremely uncomfortable in the car. If it bothered Jay, though, he didn't show it. I realized right then that Jay is very focused when it comes to business. He can be fun-loving when he's relaxed, but mostly he's tough and sharp, and he plays very close to the vest. Fortunately I had no problem with that, so we got along pretty well. The other thing about Jay is that he doesn't much trust people in business, which is the way I tend to be. We were wary of each other, but I think there was also a mutual respect from the start.

We managed to make a deal in a short time. We agreed to be equal partners. I'd build the hotel and Hyatt would manage it once it was built. More important than coming to a tentative agreement was the fact that from then on I was able to deal directly with Jay when difficulties arose. To this day, though we've had our disagreements, the partnership is strong because Jay and I can talk straight to one another.

On May 4, 1975, we called a joint press conference and announced that we'd agreed, as partners, to purchase, gut, and fully renovate the Commodore—assuming we could get financing and tax abatement. The announcement of the partnership with Hyatt, coupled with Der's preliminary drawings and rough construction-cost estimates, finally gave me some ammunition to bring to the banks. By then I had hired Henry Pearce, a real estate broker with a special expertise in financing. Together, we went calling.

Henry Pearce was the head of a firm called Pearce, Mayer, and Greer, and he was a fantastic guy. He was in his late sixties, but he had more energy than most twenty-year-olds, and he was unrelenting in his quest for financing for this job. His persistence helped, and so did his age. We'd go in together to see these very conservative bankers, most of whom had never heard of Donald Trump. In many ways I was much more conservative than Henry, but it reassured these bankers to see me alongside this white-haired guy with whom they'd been dealing forever.

Our pitch was very much the one I made when I first met Victor Palmieri. I would talk about the great Trump Organization and all we had done. I would push very hard the fact that we built on time and on budget, because I knew that the banks were scared to death of cost overruns, which can kill even a good loan. We would show these bankers drawings and scale models of this huge gleaming new hotel I planned to build. We would talk about how the job was going to turn the neighborhood around, how it would create thousands of jobs. We would go on and on about the fantastic, incomparable Hyatt Company, and we'd even mention the great tax abatement we hoped to get from the city. This last point would usually stir some interest, but unfortunately we were in something of a Catch-22. Until we had our financing in place, the city wasn't interested in seriously discussing tax abatement. And without tax abatement, the banks weren't very interested in talking about financing.

Eventually we decided to take a new tack. Realizing that the positive approach wasn't working, we tried to play to their guilt and their fear and their sense of moral obligation. Forget us, we'd say; you owe it to New York. The city is in trouble, but it's still a great city, and it's our city, and if you don't believe in it, if you won't invest in it, how can you expect it to turn around? If you lend millions of dollars to Third World countries and suburban-shopping-mall magnates, don't you also owe some obligation to your own city?

Nothing seemed to work. On one occasion, we found a bank that seemed ready to say yes. Then, at the last moment, the guy in charge raised some trivial technical issue that just killed the whole deal. This guy was what I call an institutional man, the type who has virtually no emotion. To him it's purely a job, and all he wants to do is go home at five and forget about it. You're better off dealing with a total killer with real passion. When he says no, sometimes you can talk him out of it. You rant and you rave, and he rants and raves back, and you end up making a deal. But when a machine says no, it's very tough. We gave this guy every argument in the world, and after listening, he didn't flinch and he didn't move. He just said very slowly and steadfastly, "The answer is no, Donald. No. No. No." After that experience, I remember saying to Henry, "Let's just take this deal and shove it." But Henry refused to give up. He and Jerry Schrager, my lawyer, kept me going, and we continued to push.

It was increasingly clear that the only way I was going to get financing was if the city gave me tax abatement. My hope rested in a program called the Business Investment Incentive Policy, which the city adopted in early 1975. It was designed, in a bad market, to encourage commercial development by providing tax abatements to developers. In the middle of 1975, I decided to approach the city, even though I hadn't found financing. To most people, that would have been ridiculous. I took it one step further. I went in and asked for the world—for an unprecedented tax abatement—on the assumption that even if I got cut back, the break might still be sufficient. In a funny way, it was like a high stakes poker game in which neither side has very strong cards so both are forced to bluff. By this point, I almost couldn't afford to walk away from the deal if I wanted to maintain any credibility. The city, meanwhile, was more desperate than ever to encourage development.

I first made my case to the city in October 1975, and it was direct. The Commodore was losing money and deteriorating fast. The Grand Central neighborhood was turning into a slum. The Hyatt hotel chain was ready to come to New York, but there was no way we could afford to put up millions to build a new hotel unless the city gave me some relief on property taxes.

The city's economic development people agreed to structure a program in which we'd effectively be partners. The city would give me a total abatement of property taxes for forty years. In return, I would pay the city a yearly fee, and a share of any profits the hotel made. The mechanism was fairly complicated. First, I would buy the Commodore from the Penn Central for $10 million, $6 million of which would immediately go to the city to pay off the back taxes. Then I would sell the hotel to the city for one dollar and they would lease it back to me for ninety-nine years. My rent, paid in lieu of all property taxes, would begin at $250,000 a year and rise by the fortieth year to $2.7 million. Also, I would pay the city a percentage of the profits. At the end, I'd be paying the equivalent of full property taxes based on the hotel's assessed value as of the time we were making our deal.

The whole arrangement was subject to approval by the city's Board of Estimate, which met to consider it for the first time in late December 1975. A week before the meeting, I went to Victor Palmieri and explained that if he wanted the city to take our abatement seriously, we had better make it clear that the Commodore was in deep trouble and that it might not survive much longer. He agreed with me. On December 12, Palmieri announced that the Penn Central had lost another $1.2 million on the Commodore during 1975, was anticipating worse losses for 1976, and as a result intended to close the hotel permanently no later than June 30, 1976.

Two days later, there was another significant announcement, which I hadn't anticipated. Portman Associates, a company that had spent the past two years trying to get financing for a huge new hotel across town in Times Square, revealed that it was scrapping the project because it had been unable to get bank support. In a way, that was bad for me, because I needed all the evidence I could get that investing in New York made sense. On the other hand, in dealing with the city, I could point to the Portman fiasco as clear proof that the only chance I had to get financing was if they gave me my tax abatement.

Early in 1976, the Board of Estimate decided to switch the structure of the tax-abatement program. Instead of my selling the hotel to the city and then leasing it back, I would do the whole deal through the state's Urban Development Corporation. The reasons were technical, but actually the change was advantageous to me. Unlike the city, the UDC has the power of condemnation, meaning the statutory right to evict quickly and efficiently—something that a private developer can spend months or even years trying to do.

By April, however, the Board of Estimate still hadn't considered my tax abatement, and opposition to it had begun to intensify. The loudest chorus came from other hotel owners. Albert Formicola, head of the city's Hotel Association, argued that the tax abatement would give me an unfair advantage competing against the other hotel owners in the city who paid full property taxes. The head of the Hilton, Alphonse Salamone, said he could understand a ten-year tax abatement, but that everyone ought to compete as equals after that. Even Harry Helmsley, who was more successful and less envious than most of my competitors, said he thought the deal was a little excessive. Just before the Board of Estimate vote, three city councilmen held a news conference in front of the Commodore to denounce the deal. I didn't take it personally. They were politicians. They sensed an issue that might play with the voters and the press, so they jumped on the bandwagon.

I worried about the growing opposition, but publicly my posture was to take the offensive and concede nothing to my critics. When a reporter later asked me why I got a forty-year tax abatement, I answered, "Because I didn't ask for fifty."

The basic case against us was that the city was

giving me too rich a deal. The length of the tax abatement was only part of it. In addition, critics said, there shouldn't be a cap on the profits I shared with the city. Also, if my maximum rent was going to be equivalent to the full property-tax assessment as of 1974, then that number should at least be adjustable, so that it could take into account the possibility that real estate values—and assessments—might rise over the years.

If I'd been the city official in charge of negotiating with me, I might have made those same arguments. But while other hotel owners were great at carping, not one of them made an alternative offer for the Commodore. Admittedly, most everyone assumed I had an exclusive option on the property—and it helped that the city didn't dispute that. Several months earlier, a city official had requested that I send along a copy of my option agreement with the Penn Central. I did—but it was signed only by me, and not the railroad, because I had yet to put down my $250,000. No one even noticed that until almost two years later, when a reporter doing a story on the deal called the city and asked to see the original agreement.

Two weeks before the Board of Estimate was scheduled for the third time to vote on my plan, an alternative offer finally was made for the Commodore. It came from a company that owned a bunch of low-rent hotels in bad neighborhoods. If the city could get title to the Commodore, these people said, they'd be willing to buy it, put up a couple of million dollars toward a renovation, share all profits with the city, and forgo a cap. Because it was a half-baked offer from a questionable group, I think it actually helped my case. The last thing the Commodore needed was a second-rate renovation by a third-rate hotel operator.

The clincher, I'm convinced, came from Palmieri and Penn Central. The one thing that nobody wanted was to see the Commodore shut down and boarded up. On May 12, Palmieri announced that the Penn Central was going to close the Commodore permanently in six days—exactly one day before the Board of Estimate had scheduled, for the fourth time, a vote on my tax abatement. Immediately, the critics called the announcement a pressure tactic. I can't say I was unhappy about the timing, but the fact was that the Penn Central had revealed six months earlier its plans to close the hotel by summer. In the meantime, occupancy had dropped from 46 percent the previous year to 33 percent. Moreover, losses for the full year of operation in 1976 were projected at $4.6 million.

On May 19, all the local papers carried front-page stories about the last tenants moving out of the Commodore, the hundreds of employees who were now looking for work, and the dread that local shopowners were feeling in anticipation of a boarded-up hotel. The stories certainly didn't hurt me. On May 20, the Board of Estimate voted unanimously—8 to 0—to give me the full tax-abatement program I'd sought. Over the course of the forty years, that abatement will save me tens of millions of dollars. The battle was more than worth it.

Whatever my critics may have felt, a *New York*

Times editorial ten days later made my case better than I could have. "The alternative," said the editorial, "is the Commodore boarded up and in tax arrears. Beyond the tax loss, this would be a visual wound and a serious depressant for one of the city's prime areas."

But incredibly, getting the tax abatement still didn't convince the banks we had a viable enterprise. When you look back, it seems almost hard to believe that the banks could doubt our numbers. What it shows you is how bad things were. In 1974, the Commodore was charging an average of $20.80 a night for a room, and as long as occupancy remained above 40 percent, the hotel nearly broke even. In our entirely new hotel, we projected charging an average of $48 a night for our rooms, with an average occupancy rate of 60 percent. Those were hardly great numbers, but the banks insisted we were being too optimistic. As it turned out, by the time we opened our doors in September 1980, the city had turned around, and we were able to charge $115 for a single room, with an average occupancy of more than 80 percent. By July 1987, we'd raised the room rate to $175, and now we average almost 90 percent occupancy.

In the end, we got our financing from two institutions. The first was Equitable Life Assurance Society, which, in addition to its other businesses, owns a lot of real estate. George Peacock, the head of Equitable Real Estate, agreed to put up $35 million for the Grand Hyatt, primarily because he and his people thought it would be good for the city. The other institution was the Bowery Savings Bank, which happened to have its headquarters right across the street from the Commodore and agreed to lend $45 million. Their motivation was practical: they didn't want to see their own neighborhood go to hell.

I could have saved millions and millions of dollars just by refurbishing the old Commodore rather than creating a brand-new building. Indeed, almost everyone fought against my spending the extra money on a major renovation. From the day we went public with our plans to cover the Commodore's brick façade with an entirely new curtain wall of highly reflective glass, critics and preservationists were furious. They were outraged that I wasn't making some attempt to fit in with the architecture in the rest of the neighborhood—the classical look of Grand Central Station and the ornamented limestone-and-brick office buildings up and down the block.

In my view, staying with that look would have been suicide. I said to these critics, "Hey, fellas, do me a favor and don't tell me about these great monuments, because the Chrysler Building is in foreclosure, the neighborhood is a disaster, and it's obvious something's not working. If you think I'm going to leave the façade of the old Commodore the way it is, you're crazy. There's no way."

It's strange how things can turn around. Many of the same critics and preservationists who hated the original concept of my building now love it. What they discovered is that by choosing this highly reflective glass, I've created four walls of mirrors. Now when you go across 42nd Street or go over the

Park Avenue ramp and look up at the Grand Hyatt, you see the reflection of Grand Central Terminal, the Chrysler Building, and all the other landmarks, which otherwise you might not have noticed at all.

The other new element that had a dramatic effect was the lobby. Most hotel lobbies in New York are dull and unexciting. I was determined to make ours an event, a place people wanted to visit. We chose a luxurious brown paradisio marble for the floors. We used beautiful brass for the railing and columns. We built a 170-foot glass-enclosed restaurant pitched out over 42nd Street, which no one had ever done before. I'm convinced that if I'd left the Commodore the way it was—old and dull and nondescript—it would have had absolutely no impact, and it wouldn't be doing the business it is doing today.

The Grand Hyatt opened in September 1980, and it was a hit from the first day. Gross operating profits now exceed $30 million a year. Hyatt's job was to manage the hotel, so my role was essentially over. But the fact is I still had a 50 percent interest, and I'm not exactly the hands-off type. That caused some problems at the start. I would send over one of my executives, or more often my wife, just to see how things were going, and Hyatt wasn't happy about that. One day I got a call from the head of all the Hyatt Hotels, Patrick Foley, and he said, "Donald, we have a problem. The manager of the hotel is going nuts, because your wife comes by, and she'll see dust in the corner of the lobby and call over a porter to clean it up. Or she'll see a doorman in a uniform that's not pressed, and she'll tell him to get it cleaned. Unfortunately, my manager happens to be a guy who has a problem with women to start off with. But in his defense, he's running a hotel with 1,500 employees, and there's got to be a chain of command or else a business like this just doesn't work.''

So I said to Pat, ''I understand what you're saying, and I agree with you that it's a real problem, but as long as I own fifty percent of the building, I'm not going to walk in and make believe everything's fine if it isn't.'' Pat suggested we meet the following week. I wanted to work this out because I like Pat, and I respect him, and I think he is an extraordinary executive. Pat has one of those great Irish personalities. He'll walk through the Hyatt Regency in Washington, D.C., or West Palm Beach, Florida, and he'll know everyone's name, he'll remember their families, he'll kiss the chef, tell the porter he's doing a great job, say hello to the lifeguard and the maids. By the time he leaves an hour later, everyone feels uplifted, like they're ten feet tall.

So I met with Pat, and he said, ''I've decided what to do. I'm going to change managers. I'm going to put in one of my best guys. He's Eastern European, like your wife. He's also very flexible, and they'll get along great. That way, she can come in and talk to anyone she wants, and everyone will be happy.''

Sure enough, Pat made the switch, and then his new manager did something brilliant. He began to bombard us with trivia. He'd call up several times a week, and he'd say, ''Donald, we want your approval to change the wallpaper on the fourteenth floor" or "We want to introduce a new menu in one of the restaurants" or "We are thinking of switching to a new laundry service." They'd also invite us to all of their management meetings. The guy went so far out of his way to solicit our opinions and involve us in the hotel that finally I said, "Leave me alone, do whatever you want, just don't bother me." What he did was the perfect ploy, because he got what he wanted not by fighting but by being positive and friendly and solicitous.

As successful as our partnership has turned out to be, there was one small clause in the deal that I think may be even more valuable than my half-ownership of the Grand Hyatt. It's something called an exclusive covenant, and its effect is to permanently prohibit Hyatt from building competing hotels in the five boroughs of New York without my permission.

I first tried to get the covenant from Jay Pritzker at the time we made our deal, but he refused. Jay is a smart guy, and he wasn't about to foreclose the future expansion of his hotel chain in one of the biggest cities in the world. We finally got to the closing, and just before we all sat down, I was alone with an executive from the bank. I pointed out that this was a rather big and risky investment the bank was making, and that one way to further protect the loan might be to insist on a restrictive covenant, so that Hyatt couldn't throw up a second hotel two years later, right down the street. The banker saw the implications immediately. He stormed into the room where the Hyatt people were sitting, and he said, "Hey, fellas, we're putting up tens of millions of dollars, which is a lot of money, and we're not going to make this loan unless we get a covenant from Hyatt saying you won't open up any other hotels in New York.''

I was taking a chance, because right then and there the whole financing could have fallen through. But what I had going for me was that Jay Pritzker wasn't at the closing. The executive representing Hyatt tried to reach Jay, but it turned out he was off in Nepal, mountain climbing, and he couldn't be reached. Meanwhile, the bank gave Hyatt one hour to make a decision, or that was the end of the financing. While we were waiting, I wrote up a covenant myself. In effect, it said that Hyatt can't open any competing hotels in the New York area, including the two airports. The only exception is the right to build one small luxury hotel—which I don't believe would be economically feasible anyway. And before the hour was up they agreed to sign the document I'd written.

I now have in my will a clause describing the importance of that restrictive covenant, just on the chance that one of my heirs happens not to be that sharp. What I don't want, after I'm gone, is for some nice, smooth person from Hyatt to come to one of my heirs and say, "Listen, you wouldn't mind if we threw up a little noncompetitive hotel at Kennedy Airport, would you?" The simple fact is that Hyatt would love to build more hotels. By retaining the right to say yes or no, I own something very valuable.

I've already seen the proof. A. N. Pritzker, a wonderful man who was the patriarch of his family and who died recently, used to call me frequently when he came to New York. A.N. and his son Jay were very different men. What they had in common was brilliance, but where Jay keeps very much to himself, A.N. was extremely effusive and outgoing, almost a teddy bear. They were a perfect combination. A.N. built the foundation of the company from nothing, and he got the banks to back him not because he had great assets but because they loved him. Now the company has a huge base, and Jay, who is a much cooler personality, doesn't need the banks to love him. He can be very tough and they still want to do business with him.

Anyway, A.N. would come to New York, and he'd call and he'd say "Hi ya, Don, I'm here visiting, and I'd love to stop over and just say hello to you for a couple of seconds." And I'd say, "A.N., I know what you're doing. You want to build a hotel someplace in New York, don't you?" And he'd say, "I'd love you to let us do that, Don, because it's not going to hurt you, and it's good for us, and it's good for everyone." And when A.N. would do that, I'd find some way of changing the subject, because I liked him so much that I never had the heart to say no to him directly.

There are very few people I feel that way about. A.N. died in 1986, and I happened to have an extremely important business meeting in my office on the day of his funeral in Chicago. It was a deal I very much wanted to make, and I'd been planning it for months, and people were flying in from all over to be there. But I canceled the meeting in order to go to

Chicago, and as it turned out, I was never able to make that particular deal. I have no regrets. There are some people in your life you just want to pay your respects to, no matter what it involves. And in the end, I think one reason my partnership with Hyatt has remained so strong—beside the fact that the hotel has been so successful—is that I always felt such affection for A. N. Pritzker.

7

TRUMP TOWER

The Tiffany
Location

IT WAS NOT an auspicious start, my meeting with Franklin Jarman.

From the time I took an apartment in Manhattan in 1971 and began walking the streets, the site that excited me the most was the eleven-story building at 57th Street and Fifth Avenue that housed Bonwit Teller. The main attraction was location, but in addition, it was on an unusually large piece of property. In my mind, that combination made it perhaps the greatest single piece of real estate in New York City. There was the potential to build a great building in a prime location.

Bonwit was owned by Genesco, a company founded in the late 1950s by a gentleman named W. Maxey Jarman, who built it into a real high-flying conglomerate. Maxey started off with a shoe company, and then he began buying other shoe companies, and eventually he moved into retail stores, purchasing Tiffany and Henri Bendel, and Bonwit Teller. But then, in the mid-1970s, a tremendous battle began to take shape between Maxey and his son, Franklin. They were both strong guys with their own ideas and they both wanted control. It became so bitter that they finally came to blows at a stockholder meeting. Since I am so close to my father, I found the whole thing hard to believe, but the bottom line was that Franklin finally managed to push his father out and take over. And so, in 1975, it was Franklin I called to discuss my interest in Bonwit.

At the time, I really had no track record. I was trying to get the Grand Hyatt off the ground, and I was still fighting for my convention center site, and nothing had yet gelled. But for whatever reason, Franklin Jarman was willing to see me. We met, and I told him straight out that I would love to buy the Bonwit Teller store and building. I knew this was a tough sell, so I tried to find ways to make the deal sound more attractive. I suggested, for example, that I would build above his store, and that he could keep it open during construction. That's not really feasible, but the point was that I would have done almost anything to get that piece of property.

Even before I'd finished my pitch, I could see from the look on Franklin's face that he thought this was perhaps the most preposterous thing he had ever heard. When I was done, he said to me, very politely, but also very firmly, "You've got to be crazy if you think there's any way we'd ever sell this incredible site." We shook hands and I left, believing that under no circumstances would I or anybody else ever purchase this property. It was a dead issue.

Even so, I didn't give up. I began writing letters to Franklin Jarman. First, I wrote to thank him for seeing me. A couple of months later, I wrote to ask if he might reconsider. When I got no answer and a few more months had gone by, I wrote again and said I'd love to drop by and see him again. More time passed, and I wrote another letter, suggesting a whole new way to make the deal. I was relentless, even in the face of the total lack of encouragement, because much more often than you'd think, sheer persistence is the difference between success and failure. In this case, Franklin Jarman never budged from his original position. But as it happened, the letters I wrote eventually did have an impact.

Almost three years passed after my first meeting with Franklin. During that time, Genesco began to experience very serious financial problems. I didn't give any of it a second thought until one evening in June 1978, when I picked up *Business Week* magazine and read an article about a management change at Genesco. The banks, trying to save the company from declaring bankruptcy, had insisted that a new chief executive be put in charge. The man's name was John Hanigan, and he was something of a turnaround artist.

He'd just successfully saved AMF-Brunswick, which had been ready to go down the drain. His specialty was something called pruning, which is just a nice way of saying that he took companies apart. In other words, he'd sell, sell, sell the assets, get rid of the debt, and pay off the banks. The key, for a guy like Hanigan, was that he came to companies without any emotional attachment to its people or its products. As a result, he had no trouble being ruthless. He was a tough, smart, totally bottom-line-oriented guy.

At nine sharp, the morning after I read the article, I called Genesco, and I got Hanigan on the phone. He'd just begun his new job, but to my surprise, he said, "I'll bet I know what you're calling about."

"You do?" I said.

And he said, "Yeah, you're the guy who has been writing all those letters about wanting to buy Bonwit Teller. When would you like to meet?"

"As soon as possible," I said.

He said, "Can you be here in half an hour?"

It just shows you that sometimes making a deal comes down to timing. Somebody else might have called him a few days or a few weeks before me, and the whole thing could have turned out differently. Instead, I went to see him, and we had a very good meeting. It was clear that the company needed cash very badly and very quickly, and that he had no reluctance about selling Bonwit, or any other asset, for that matter. It was like a giant garage sale. By the time I left, I thought there was a good chance we'd make a deal very quickly.

Then something funny happened. Jack Hanigan suddenly refused to take my phone calls. I must have called him ten or fifteen times over a period of the next several days, but I never got through. I figured that some other bidder had come along, and that in any case I was in trouble. I asked Louise Sunshine to speak to her friend Marilyn Evans, whose husband, David, owned a shoe company that he'd sold to Genesco several years before. He'd become a fairly large stockholder in Genesco, and that gave them some clout. Marilyn said they'd speak to Hanigan on my behalf, and almost immediately he called me back. I never found out what the delay had been about, but Hanigan suggested we have another meeting. This time I brought my lawyer, Jerry Schrager, and we were able to make a deal. It was really quite simple. Genesco owned the Bonwit building but not the underlying land. For the land, they had a lease with twenty-nine years left to run. I agreed to buy the building and their land lease for the sum of $25 million.

In my mind, that was just a first step. In order to put up the building I had in mind, I was going to have to assemble several other adjacent pieces—and then seek numerous zoning variances. That's often the situation in New York real estate, but in this case I was dealing with an exceptionally prestigious, visible site, which meant every move I made was going to be unusually difficult, and very carefully scrutinized.

My most immediate problem was trying to keep the deal secret. I was convinced that if anyone got wind of the fact that the Bonwit site was up for sale before I signed a contract, I'd never make the deal. Once the Bonwit store went on the open market, everyone in the world was going to be after it, and the asking price would go right through the roof. That's why, after I'd shaken hands with Jack, I said to him, "Listen, I'd like to draw up a quick, simple letter of intent that says that I've agreed to buy the property for $25 million, and you've agreed to sell it—subject only to the drawing of reasonable documents. That way, neither of us can walk away from the deal." To my surprise, Jack said, "Well, that sounds reasonable." Now Jack is a very smart man, but he wasn't a New York guy, and he didn't realize how hot this property was—so valuable that even in the middle of a depression, there'd still be people lined up to buy it.

Jerry and I drew up the letter of intent right then and there. Jack read it, and the only change he made was to stick in a clause making the sale subject to approval by his board of directors. When he handed it back to me, I said to him, "Listen Jack, I can't live with that clause. In three or four weeks, you might tell your board of directors not to approve the deal, and that would defeat the whole idea of this letter of intent." Then I asked whether he needed approval from the board of directors to sell the store. He said he didn't, and I said, "Let's just take this one clause out." He gave it a little thought and finally he agreed. I left the meeting with a deal—and something on paper to confirm it.

Once I had the letter of intent from Jack Hanigan—but before I had a contract—I went to see a man named Conrad Stephenson at the Chase Manhattan Bank. My father had always done his business with Chase, and so I figured that was the best place to go first for the $25 million I needed to make the Bonwit purchase. I explained the deal to Connie—that I was buying the Bonwit building and their land lease, which had twenty-nine years left to run, and that I hoped to put up a great skyscraper on the site. Immediately he said, "Unless you own the underlying land, that's not a long enough lease to justify financing." In other words, he was reluctant to put up money for me to purchase a site that twenty-nine years later—when my lease ran out—could be taken over by the owner of the underlying land. But I'd taken that into consideration. I said to Connie, "Look, I've got two alternatives, and I think either one could work."

The first one, I told him, was to do a very inexpensive conversion into an office building, with retail on the ground floor. Because I'd be paying such a low rent through the remainder of the lease—$125,000 a year, which was peanuts, even then—I was confident I'd be able to pay off my mortgage and still make a nice profit over the next thirty years. But Connie wasn't totally convinced, and even I considered the first option my worst-case scenario.

What I really wanted to do, I explained, was to purchase not only the building and the lease but also the underlying land. Then, I said, I could build a big building without risk of losing it at lease expiration. When I told Connie that the owner of the underlying land was the Equitable Life Assurance Society, he got excited for the first time. That, we both agreed, gave me a leg up, since I already had a great relationship with Equitable. They'd put up a big percentage of the financing for the Hyatt, and by this time the hotel was under construction, things were going very well, and everyone was feeling terrific about the deal.

The next thing I did was to set up a date to see George Peacock, the head of Equitable Real Estate. It was September 1978, just a month since I'd first sat down with Jack Hanigan. George and I met and I told him I was in the process of purchasing the Bonwit lease, for which Equitable owned the land, and that I saw a chance to forge a partnership that could be very good for both of us. I would contribute my lease, I said, if they would contribute their land. Together, as fifty-fifty partners, we'd build a great new residential and office building on this incredible site.

Equitable could have chosen simply to hold on to the site until the Bonwit lease ran out, and then own it outright. But the downside, I pointed out to George, was that then they would have to settle for a meager annual rent from a lease negotiated long before the value of New York real estate had begun to escalate. I also told George that my other option was to renovate the existing building and earn a more modest but still decent profit over the next thirty years. In truth, I was no longer certain that I could get financing for such a deal, but I didn't want him to think that a partnership with Equitable was my only option. Then he'd just feel free to drive a much harder bargain with me. Fortunately, George took to the idea of a partnership almost immediately. He was skeptical that I'd get the zoning necessary to build the huge building I had in mind, but he'd also seen what I'd achieved with the Commodore. By the time I left his office, he'd given me a commitment—subject to my delivering on my promises. Once again, I found myself juggling provisional commitments.

My next move was to use my first two commitments—for the Bonwit lease and the Equitable land—to try to get a third, from Tiffany. Specifically, I wanted to buy the air rights above Tiffany, which was directly adjacent to the Bonwit site at the corner of 57th and Fifth. By purchasing those rights I'd get something called a merged zoning lot, which would allow me to build a much larger building. Unfortunately, I didn't know anyone at Tiffany, and the owner, Walter Hoving, was known not only as a legandary retailer but also as a difficult, demanding, mercurial guy. Even so, I'd always admired Hoving, because everything he'd ever touched had turned to gold. When he ran Lord and Taylor, it was the best, and when he ran Bonwit Teller, it was the best, and so long as he ran Tiffany, it was the best. I'd seen him at parties, and he was a man with impeccable manners, perfect white hair, beautifully tailored suits, and an imperial style. If you were casting a movie about the president of Tiffany, Walter Hoving would get the part.

I decided to be very direct. I called Hoving on the phone and introduced myself. I was very polite and very respectful, and he agreed to see me. By this time Der Scutt had done a scale model of the building I hoped to build, as well as one for an alternative building, in the event that I didn't get Tiffany's air rights. I brought both models to the meeting. I said to Hoving, "Look, I want to buy your air rights, because that will allow me to build a much better building that you yourself will like much more. By selling me air rights, you will preserve Tiffany forever. No one will ever be able to build over it, and therefore no one will ever try to rip it down." The other reason to sell, I told Hoving, was that if I didn't have his air rights, for technical reasons the city would require me to put in lot-line windows—tiny little windows with wire mesh, which would look absolutely horrible, rising up fifty stories directly over Tiffany. With his air rights, on the other hand, I'd be permitted to put in beautiful picture windows on the side of the building overlooking Tiffany.

At that point I showed Hoving the two models—one a magnificent building, which is essentially the design of Trump Tower today, the other my hideous alternative. "I'm offering you five million dollars," I said to Walter Hoving, "to let me preserve Tiffany. In return you're selling me something—air rights—that you'd never use anyway."

Hoving had been at Tiffany almost twenty-five years. He'd built it into an incredible success, and naturally he took great personal pride in his creation. I was playing to that, and it worked. He immediately liked my concept. "Look, young man," he said, "I am going to make a deal with you at the price you've suggested. I just hope that you do as nice a job as you say you will, because I want to be proud of it. In the meantime, I have one small problem. I'm going away with my wife for a month, and I won't have time to devote to this until I get back."

Immediately I started to get nervous. I said, "Gee, Mr. Hoving, that's a big problem, because if I have your air rights, I can build a totally different building, and that's the basis on which I'm going to seek my zoning variance. If for some reason you change your mind while you're away, I'll have done a great deal of architectural work and zoning work which I'll just have to throw out."

Walter Hoving looked at me as if I'd insulted him. "Young man," he said, "perhaps you didn't understand. I shook your hand. I made a deal with you. That's that." I was speechless. You have to understand where I was coming from. While there are certainly honorable people in the real estate business, I was more accustomed to the sort of people with whom you don't want to waste the effort of a handshake because you know it's meaningless. I'm talking about the lowlifes, the horror shows with whom nothing counts but a signed contract.

With Walter Hoving, I realized, I was dealing with a totally different type—a gentleman who was genuinely shocked at any suggestion that he might renege on a deal. He also had a way of talking down, so that he actually made me feel a little guilty for even suggesting that anything could possibly go wrong in our deal.

As it happened, Walter Hoving went away, and no sooner had he left than Philip Morris made a deal to buy the air rights over Grand Central at a price far in excess of what I'd agreed to pay for the Tiffany air rights, which were in a much better location. Then, during that same month, several more air-rights deals were made, also for very big numbers. Quite simply, New York City was recovering, and the real estate market was beginning to go through the roof. I knew Hoving was honorable, but I couldn't help worrying about how he was going to feel when he heard about those other deals.

Several days after he returned, we met to talk over some points in our deal. Sure enough, even as we sat down, two of his executives began to try to talk him out of making the deal by pointing out what had happened in the market. I was upset, but I could see very quickly that Hoving was even more upset. "Gentlemen," he said, "I shook hands with this young man over a month ago. When I make a deal, that's the deal, whether it's a good one or a bad one. And I trust I won't have to explain myself again." That was the end of that.

Later, I heard that Hoving went even a step further. During this same period he'd apparently decided to make another deal, much bigger than the one with me: to sell Tiffany to the Avon Corporation. I thought Avon was a rather second-rate buyer for a classy store like Tiffany. On the other hand, they'd offered to pay such an inflated price that I couldn't blame Hoving for agreeing to sell. However, as one of the conditions of its purchase, Avon wanted Hoving to agree not to go through with the air-rights deal with me. Hoving, I heard, stood totally firm. If Avon had a problem with the air-rights deal, he told their executives, then they didn't have to buy his store. They dropped the demand and bought the store, and my deal went through.

Walter Hoving was just a totally honorable, totally classy man. That's exactly what made him such a brilliant retailer, and it's why Tiffany has never been the same since he left. I'll give you a small example. Hoving had a policy at Tiffany that when his best customers came in, they could pick out what they wanted, sign for it, and be billed later. It was very simple and very elegant. No sooner did Avon take over than their team of accountants started instituting new policies, including the introduction of little blue plastic Tiffany credit cards. That was fine, except that all of a sudden Tiffany's best customers were told that they, too, had to use the little plastic cards. It was not only stupid, it was self-defeating. You want your best customers to feel special.

Before very long, Hoving, who'd agreed at first to stay on as a consultant, got fed up and left. That just made things worse. As long as Hoving ran Tiffany, for example, you'd never see peddlers out front on the street, selling fake watches and cheap jewelry, blocking pedestrians, and degrading Fifth Avenue. Whenever Walter Hoving saw a peddler, he'd go to his people, and he'd start screaming, in his dignified manner, "How dare you let them do that?" And within minutes, the peddler would be gone. But as soon as Hoving left, a dozen street peddlers immediately set up shop in front of Tiffany, and they haven't moved since. However, I learned a lesson from Walter Hoving. I now employ some very large security people who make absolutely sure that the street in front of Trump Tower is kept clean, pristine, and free of peddlers.

Once I got Tiffany's air rights, there was just one more parcel I needed. Adjacent to Tiffany's along 57th Street and leased by Bonwit was a tiny site, perhaps 4,000 square feet, that was critical if I was going to build the building I had in mind. Under the zoning regulations, you're required to have a minimum of thirty feet of open space—a rear yard—behind any building. Without this last piece, I would have been forced to chop the rear yard out of the building we'd already designed, and that would have been a disaster.

The piece I wanted was owned by a man named Leonard Kandell. By buying the overall Bonwit lease, I effectively controlled the site, but once again, my problem was a short lease. It had less than twenty years to run and also included provisions that made any zoning changes practically impossible. Fortunately, Leonard Kandell, like Hoving, is a totally honorable man. Leonard began in real estate by buying apartment buildings in the Bronx in the thirties and forties. But unlike most small landlords, he decided to get out when he saw rent control coming. He sold all his buildings and came to Manhattan, where he began buying up leaseholds on prime property—meaning the land under buildings. As the market rose, Leonard became very rich, and with none of the problems of having to run the buildings himself. Meanwhile, the landlords who stayed in the Bronx went down the tubes, because, sure enough, rent control proved to be a disaster for them.

One reason I'd left Brooklyn and my father's business was to escape rent control, and so from the start Leonard and I had an affinity. My problem was that Leonard wasn't a seller. It wasn't a matter of price, or that he had any particular attachment to his 57th Street parcel. It was simply that Leonard didn't sell *anything*, on the theory that in the long run, land prices in Manhattan were headed in only one direction and that was up. He was exactly right, of course, and though we got along fine, Leonard wouldn't budge. Then one day I discovered an unexpected bonus in my Tiffany deal. I was reviewing my air-rights contract when I came across a clause that gave Tiffany an option to purchase the adjoining Kandell property within a certain time frame.

I said to myself, Holy Christmas, this could give me a lever to make a deal with Leonard. So I went back to Walter, and I said, "Listen, you're never going to buy that Kandell site, so would you mind if I also bought your option, as part of my deal?" Walter agreed, we put it into my deal, and immediately I exercised the option. At first, Leonard took the position that I didn't have the right to exercise the option because it belonged to Tiffany and therefore was nontransferable. Leonard may have been right but it was also possible, in a litigation, that I would win the right to exercise the option.

When I pointed this out to Leonard, we sat down together, and in no more than twenty minutes, we made a deal that was good for both of us. I agreed to withdraw my exercise of the option, and in return, Leonard agreed to extend my lease on the site from twenty years to one hundred years, which was long enough to make it financeable. He also rewrote the lease to eliminate any prohibitions against rezoning. And while I agreed to pay a slightly higher rent, it was still very low for a long lease on such a prime site. Leonard and I shook hands, and we've remained very good friends.

It's funny how things turn around. Leonard is an older man, and in the past couple of years, he's begun giving thought to his heirs and his estate. Early in 1986, he called and said he'd like to make me a gift of a 15 percent interest in the land under the Ritz Carlton hotel on Central Park South, which is one of his more valuable holdings. In addition, he gave me control over the disposition of the land when the hotel's lease comes up in approximately twenty-five years. His purpose, Leonard told me, was to put the land in the hands of someone he thought would get the most value from it—which in turn would benefit his heirs, who retain a majority ownership. Leonard is a very generous man and he is also very smart. I'll be fighting like hell for the Kandell family.

By the time I got the Kandell site on 57th Street, it was December 1978, and I was in a delicate situation. I'd pieced together everything I needed, I'd managed to keep the deal completely secret, but I still had no contract with Genesco. As 1979 began, my lawyers were still discussing a few final points with the Genesco lawyers, and we expected to sign contracts no later than February. But in mid-January, word finally began to leak out to the real estate community that Genesco might be making a deal to sell the Bonwit site. Just as I'd predicted, Genesco was immediately besieged with interested buyers for the property, among them wealthy Arabs with oil-boom money to burn. And sure enough, Genesco suddenly began trying to back out of the deal. Even as our contract was being prepared, it became clear that if Genesco could find a way to break the deal, it would.

It was then that I thanked my lucky stars I'd gotten that one-page letter of intent from Jack Hanigan. Without it, there was zero chance my deal would have gone through. I'm not at all sure the letter would have proved legally binding, but at the very least I could have litigated it and held up any sale of the Bonwit property for several years. Naturally, I let Genesco know I fully intended to do just that if they reneged on my deal. With creditors breathing down their necks, Genesco, I knew, didn't have a lot of time.

On the morning of January 20 I got a call that proved to be a blessing. It was from Dee Wedemeyer, a reporter from the *New York Times*, who wanted to know if it was true that I was about to make a deal with Genesco to buy the Bonwit building. Genesco, still seeking a way out, had declined to give Wedemeyer any comment. But I decided to take a calculated risk. I'd tried very hard to keep the deal as secret as possible until I had a signed contract, because I didn't want to prompt a bidding war. But now the rumors were circulating, and I had a seller who was balking. So I confirmed for Wedemeyer that I'd reached an agreement with Genesco for the property—and that because I anticipated building a new tower on the site, Bonwit would most likely be closed within the next several months.

My idea was to put public pressure on Genesco to live up to their agreement. What I didn't calculate was a secondary benefit. No sooner did Wedemeyer's article appear the next morning than all of Bonwit's best employees began heading over to Bergdorf Goodman, Saks Fifth Avenue, and Bloomingdale's to look for new jobs. Suddenly Bonwit began losing its best people in droves, and it was becoming almost impossible to run the store. That, I believe, was the straw that broke Genesco's back. Suddenly, they stopped balking. Five days after the *New York Times* article appeared, we signed our contract. The company's desperation saved my deal.

On the other hand, desperation can be a double-edged sword. Because Genesco needed cash so badly, and so quickly, they insisted on a very unusual contract. In a typical real estate deal, you put down a 10 percent deposit when you sign a contract, and the remaining 90 percent at closing. Instead, Genesco demanded that I put down 50 percent at contract—$12.5 million—and the other half at closing. My lawyers advised me not to agree to such a demand. The way they saw it, there was a reasonable risk that the company might go bankrupt before we ever got to closing. If that happened, a bankruptcy judge—who has powers you wouldn't believe—might choose to take my deposit and use it to pay off other creditors. For me to put so much money at such risk, my lawyers said, was totally imprudent.

I looked at it another way. I wasn't thrilled about putting $12.5 million on the line, but at the same time I believed that the more cash I gave Genesco, the more money they'd have to pay off debts—and keep their creditors at bay. Also, my period of risk would be relatively short, since it was in our mutual interest to close the deal as quickly as possible. The time between contract and closing is often six months or more. In this case, we set it at sixty days.

In addition, I already had a good deal of time and money invested in the deal. As far back as August, following my first meeting with Jack Hanigan, I'd begun working on plans for the site, and I'd started negotiating with the city for zoning. Actually, within minutes of leaving Jack Hanigan's office, I had called Der Scutt and asked him to meet me at the Bonwit site. When he got there, I pointed to the building, and I asked him what he thought. It was obviously a super location, he said, but what did I have in mind for it?

"I want to build the most fantastic building in New York," I told Der, "and I want you to get working right away, because I want to know how big a building I can legally build."

From the start, size was a top priority. With such a great location, the more apartments I could build, the better the return I could hope to get on my investment. Moreover, the higher I could go, the better the views—

and the more I could charge for the apartments. A guy named Arthur Drexler, from the Museum of Modern Art, put it very well when he said, "Skyscrapers are machines for making money." Drexler meant it as a criticism. I saw it as an incentive.

From the start, everyone I talked with was skeptical that I could get approval to build a huge glass skyscraper along a stretch of Fifth Avenue filled with short, old, limestone and brick buildings. I'd heard the same thing about the Hyatt, of course, and so I didn't take the warnings too seriously. Even putting commercial considerations aside, I felt a tall building would be much more striking than a short one. Very quickly, Der got caught up in my enthusiasm. When someone complained at a community board hearing that the building we had in mind was too tall and would block too much light, Der answered, only half kidding, "If you want sunlight, move to Kansas."

For any new building, the permissible height is determined by something called Floor Area Ratio (FAR). Specifically, the total square footage of a building can be no more than a certain multiple of the square footage of the building lot. It was possible to get some bonuses, but on this lot, for example, the absolute maximum FAR was 21.6. Naturally, that's what I intended to go after. I knew it was going to be an uphill battle. When Der did his first computations, using just the Bonwit site without Tiffany's air rights or the Kandell parcel, he determined that our maximum FAR was 8.5—which he said translated into a twenty-story building with 10,000 square feet of usable space per floor. Immediately, I told him to transform it into a forty-story building with 5,000 square feet per floor. Not only would that give me apartments with better views, it would also mean fewer apartments per floor, which is another luxury for which buyers will pay a premium.

Of course I had no intention of settling for a low FAR. For starters, my FAR would increase substantially when I acquired the Tiffany air rights. In addition, developers can get extra FAR by providing certain amenities that the City Planning Commission deems desirable. On this site, for example, I could get a bonus by building residential units instead of just offices, on the theory that office buildings create far more pedestrian traffic and congestion. In addition, I could get a bonus by building a public area for pedestrians—something called a through-block arcade— on my ground floor. I could get a third bonus by building more than the minimum retail space required by law. And I could get a final bonus by building a public park within the shopping area and arcade.

Eager for every advantage I could get, I began talking to Der about designing an atrium with several levels of shopping. As a business, a retail atrium seemed a long shot. Enclosed shopping malls have been a hit all across the country, but they've almost never succeeded in New York City. The typical suburban mall is clean, controlled, safe, and antiseptic, which is exactly why most people feel so comfortable in them. New Yorkers, on the other hand, seem to thrive on gritty street life and are quite happy to do business with street vendors.

But the way I figured it, even if the atrium wasn't terribly successful, the bonus I'd get for building it—several extra floors in my residential tower—would more than make up for its cost. It wasn't until much later, when I began to see how magnificently it was turning out, and when we started to attract the best stores in the world as tenants, that I realized the atrium was going to be something special, a hit on its own terms.

In the early stages, I focused more of my attention on the design of the building itself. I wanted to create something memorable and monumental, but I also knew that without a unique design, we'd never get approval for a very big building. The standard four-sided glass box just wasn't going to fly with city planning. Der went to work. He probably did three to four dozen drawings, and as we went along, I picked the best elements from each one.

At first, we started out with a glass tower built on a rectangular limestone base, but that just didn't look good. Later, we tried a design with three exterior glass elevators. That appealed to me, but it turned out that they'd use up far too much of our saleable interior space. Finally, Der came up with the concept of a series of terraces stepped back from the street to the height of the adjacent Tiffany building. My wife, Ivana, and I agreed that the setbacks created a certain compatibility and gave our building a less bulky feeling than it would have with straight sides, like most skyscrapers have. On the higher floors, we settled on a sawtooth design, a zig-zag effect that gave the building twenty-eight different sides, as if you took the steps of a staircase and turned them on their side.

The design was obviously going to be more expensive to execute than something more standard, but the advantages seemed obvious. With twenty-eight surfaces, we'd be creating a striking, distinctive building. Also, the multiple sides would ensure at least two views from every room, and in the end, that would make it possible to charge more for the apartments. To me, we were creating the best of all possible worlds. It was a great-looking design, but it was also very saleable. To hit a real home run, you need both.

The next challenge was to have the design approved by the city—which meant, among other things, getting zoning variances. In one key case, we were able to prevail simply by using logic. The zoning law required that we build a ground-floor through-block arcade that ran north-south, meaning from 57th Street to 56th Street. That would have meant putting the entrance to the building on 57th Street, rather than on Fifth Avenue, and the latter was obviously more prestigious. We simply pointed out to city planning that the IBM Building, between our site and Madison Avenue, already had a north-south through-block arcade, so that ours would be redundant. By running our arcade on a west-east axis, we could connect from Fifth Avenue through to IBM's atrium, and therefore all the way out to Madison Avenue. Remarkably, everyone agreed that was the best solution. The result was that we got the variance that allowed us to create our spectacular entrance on Fifth Avenue.

What the city balked at, from the very start, was the size of the building we were proposing—seventy stories high, with square footage at the maximum 21.6 FAR. As early as December 1978, even before I'd closed my deal with Bonwit, city planning let us know that they considered our proposed building too big. They said they intended to oppose letting us use bonuses to increase our FAR and that they were very concerned about the issue of compatibility with the smaller, surrounding buildings on Fifth Avenue.

Fortunately, by the time I closed my deal in early 1979 and we entered into serious discussions with city planning, I had some ammunition of my own. For starters, I could have chosen to build something called an "as of right" building—one that doesn't require any variances. Much the way I'd done earlier with Walter Hoving, I had Der prepare a model of the "as of right" building to show city planning. It was hideous: a thin little four-sided box going straight up eighty stories, cantilevering over Tiffany's. We took the position that if the city wouldn't approve the building we wanted, we were prepared to build "as of right"—and we showed them the model and the renderings. Naturally, they were horrified. I'm not sure they believed we'd ever build it, or even that it was buildable, but there was no way they could be sure.

The next thing I was able to use in my favor—unexpectedly—was Bonwit Teller itself. At first, I assumed I'd just tear down the store and that would be the end of it. But very shortly after I'd signed my deal for the site, another company, Allied Stores Corporation, made a deal with Genesco to purchase the twelve remaining Bonwit Teller branches in locations ranging from Palm Beach, Florida, to Beverly Hills, California. Soon after that, the president and CEO of Allied, a terrific retailing executive named Thomas Macioce, approached me.

Allied itself had been very close to bankruptcy when Macioce took it over in 1966. But over the next ten years, he'd transformed it into one of the strongest retailing companies in the country. Macioce explained to me that while several of the Bonwit stores he'd just purchased were quite successful, he felt it was critical to continue to have the flagship Bonwit in Manhattan. And ideally, he said, he'd like to keep the store at 57th Street and Fifth Avenue, not only because it had been there for fifty years, but also because the location was unbeatable.

I told Tom, right off, that there was no way I could give Bonwit nearly as much space as it previously had. On the other hand, I said, I could give him good space, fronting on 57th Street, and connected directly through to the atrium I intended to build on my ground floor. I showed him my plans, and in a very short time, we were able to strike a deal.

It was very good for Tom, because we signed a long-term lease, at a rent-per-square-foot far below what I later got for other retail space in the building. But it was also very good for me. I leased 55,000 square feet to Allied—giving them a store less than one quarter the size of the original Bonwit—for an annual rent of $3 million, plus a percentage of their profits. I'd paid $25 million to purchase Bonwit's lease and building, and with a 10 percent mortgage, my carrying costs were approximately $2.5 million a year. In other words, I was paying out $2.5 million to own the site, and getting $3 million back from Allied for leasing them a small portion of the total space. That meant I had a profit of $500,000 a year and owned the land for nothing—all guaranteed before I even began construction. Better yet, since I was giving the new Bonwit only a small portion of my site, I could rent the rest to other retailers.

But perhaps best of all, what I got in Bonwit was a store the city very much wanted to keep in New York. I was able to make a very simple, very strong case to the people at the City Planning Commission. If you want Bonwit to return to Fifth Avenue, I told them, you're going to have to give me my zoning.

Even with that, my approval was far from a sure thing. The local community board opposed such a tall building. As a ploy, they suggested a six-month moratorium on new buildings, to study whether the area was already overbuilt. A Committee to Ban the Building Boom sprang up. As soon as that happened, politicians had a knee-jerk reaction: they latched on to the cause.

Looking back, I don't think politics or leverage made a critical difference one way or the other. I'm absolutely convinced that it was the architecture itself that won us our approval. And perhaps no one had a more powerful influence than Ada Louise Huxtable, then the chief architecture critic of the *New York Times*.

I took a calculated risk by inviting Huxtable to look at our model and renderings before the City Planning Commission voted on our zoning. The power of the *New York Times* is just awesome. It is certainly one of the most influential institutions in the world, and I recognized that anything Huxtable wrote would have enormous impact. Moreover, I knew that she was hostile to skyscrapers in general, and that she almost always preferred old and classical to new and glitzy. But by the middle of 1979, I was worried about whether I was going to get my zoning. I figured that Huxtable couldn't make things worse, and that if I got lucky, she might write something that would help.

In early June, Huxtable came to see our plans. On Sunday, July 1, the *Times* Arts and Leisure section carried her "Architecture View" column about Trump Tower. It was titled "A New York Blockbuster of Superior Design." That headline probably did more for my zoning than any single thing I ever said or did. The funny thing was that Huxtable spent the first half of her review complaining that our building was too big and suggesting that I had used "every trick in the book to maximize its size." But, interestingly, she didn't blame me so much as she did the city, for zoning laws that she said encouraged developers to do what I'd done. And then, at the end, she gave us several terrific lines. "A great deal of care has been lavished on its design," she wrote, adding, "It is undeniably a dramatically handsome structure."

In October, the planning commission unanimously approved our zoning. The commission said it would have preferred a masonry façade for Trump Tower, as more compatible with neighboring buildings, but added that they didn't insist, in light of the fact that I would be providing "extraordinary public amenities." In the end, we negotiated an FAR of 21, barely less than the 21.6 maximum. I settled for just two fewer floors than I'd originally sought. That gave me the equivalent of a sixty-eight-story building, including the huge double-ceilinged six-level atrium, which made Trump Tower the tallest residential building in the city. At the same time, the city took Huxtable's comments about the zoning laws to heart. Responding to the way I'd used bonuses and air rights to create a much bigger building, the city amended its zoning laws to prevent others from doing the same thing in the future.

Once I had my zoning, the next challenge was getting the tower built. It wasn't going to be cheap. When you build above a certain height, construction costs rise almost geometrically, simply because it becomes so much more costly to do everything, from reinforcing the infrastructure to bringing up piping. On the other hand, because I had such a prime location, I felt I could afford it. If I did the job right, I'd be able to charge such a premium that the extra cost would be irrelevant.

In October 1980, Chase Manhattan agreed to provide financing for the construction of Trump Tower. I made a deal with HRH Construction to be my general contractor. The budget for the whole job—acquisition of the land, construction, carrying charges, advertising, and promotion—was slightly more than $200 million. The person I hired to be my personal representative overseeing the construction, Barbara Res, was the first woman ever put in charge of a skyscraper in New York. She was thirty-three at the time, she'd worked for HRH, and I'd met her on the Commodore job, where she'd worked as a mechanical superintendent. I'd watched her in construction meetings, and what I liked was that she took no guff from anyone. She was half the size of most of these bruising guys, but she wasn't afraid to tell them off when she had to, and she knew how to get things done.

It's funny. My own mother was a housewife all her life. And yet it's turned out that I've hired a lot of women for top jobs, and they've been among my best people. Often, in fact, they are far more effective than the men around them. Louise Sunshine, who was an executive vice president in my company for ten years, was as relentless a fighter as you'll ever meet. Blanche Sprague, the executive vice president who handles all sales and oversees the interior design of my buildings, is one of the best salespeople and managers I've ever met. Norma Foerderer, my executive assistant, is sweet and charming and very classy, but she's steel underneath, and people who think she can be pushed around find out very quickly that they're mistaken. Ivana, my wife, is a great manager who treats her employees very well, but she's also very demanding and very competitive. Her employees respect her because they know she's pushing herself as hard as she's pushing them.

We began demolition of the Bonwit building on March 15, 1980, and almost immediately I found myself in the middle of a major controversy over the two bas-relief Art Deco sculptures that were a decorative feature of the exterior of the building. All during 1979, long after I'd announced my plans and begun negotiating for zoning, no one expressed any interest in those friezes. No representative from zoning, from landmarks preservation, or from any community arts group ever suggested saving them. Finally, in mid-December of 1979, shortly before I was to begin construction, I got a call from someone at the Metropolitan Museum of Art, asking if I'd consider donating the friezes, and certain iron grillwork. I said that if the friezes could be saved, I'd be happy to donate them to the museum.

What happened was that we began the demolition, and when it came time to take down the friezes, my guys came to me, and they said, "Mr. Trump, these are a lot heavier than we thought, and if you want to try to save them, we're going to have to add special scaffolding for safety's sake, and it's going to take at least several weeks." My carrying charges on the construction loan for this project were enormous—not to mention the extra construction costs of delaying the job. I just wasn't prepared to lose hundreds of thousands of dollars to save a few Art Deco sculptures that I believed were worth considerably less, and perhaps not very much at all. So I ordered my guys to rip them down.

What I didn't count on was the outrage this would create. The following day, the *New York Times* ran a front-page picture of the workmen demolishing the sculptures, and the next thing I knew I'd become a symbol of everything evil about modern developers. A *Times* editorial described the demolition as "a memorable version of cash flow calculations outweighing public sensibilities" and went on to say that "obviously big buildings do not make big human beings, nor do big deals make art experts."

It was not the sort of publicity you like to get. Looking back, I regret that I had the sculptures destroyed. I'm not convinced they were truly valuable, and I still think that a lot of my critics were phonies and hypocrites, but I understand now that certain events can take on a symbolic importance. Frankly, I was too young, and perhaps in too much of a hurry, to take that into account. The point is that despite what some people may think, I'm not looking to be a bad guy when it isn't absolutely necessary.

Ironically, the whole controversy may have ended up being a plus for me in terms of selling Trump Tower. The stories that appeared about it invariably started with sentences like: "In order to make way for one of the world's most luxurious buildings . . ." Even though the publicity was almost entirely negative, there was a great deal of it, and that drew a tremendous amount of attention to Trump Tower. Almost immediately we saw an upsurge in the sales of apartments. I'm not saying that's a good thing, and in truth it probably says something perverse about the culture we live in. But I'm a businessman, and I learned a lesson from that experience: good publicity is preferable to bad, but from a bottom-line perspective, bad publicity is sometimes better than no publicity at all. Controversy, in short, sells.

So, it turned out, does glamour. Even before we started construction, I'd begun to realize that the atrium could prove to be one of the most dazzling parts of Trump Tower. At first we just set out to make it an attractive setting for retailers, but when I saw the final drawings and the model, I realized it could be truly spectacular. I also decided I would spend whatever it took to assure that it lived up to its potential.

Perhaps the best example is the marble. Originally I thought of using the brown paradisio that had been so successful for the lobby of the Grand Hyatt. But in the end, I became convinced that what was great for a hotel lobby wasn't necessarily right for a retail-shopping atrium. Der, Ivana, and I looked at hundreds of marble samples. Finally, we came upon something called Breccia Perniche, a rare marble in a color none of us had ever seen before—an exquisite blend of rose, peach, and pink that literally took our breath away. Of course it was incredibly expensive—in part because it was a very irregular marble. When we went to the quarry, we discovered that much of the marble contained large white spots and white veins. That was jarring to me and took away from the beauty of the stone. So we ended up going to the quarry with black tape and marking off the slabs that were the best. The rest we just scrapped—maybe 60 percent of the total. By the time we were finished, we'd taken the whole top of the mountain and used up much of the quarry. Next, I made sure to get the finest craftsmen to cut and lay the marble, because unless your workmen are the best, you get jagged edges, poor matching, and asymmetry, and then you've lost the whole effect.

That effect was heightened by the fact that we used so much marble—on the floors and for the walls six full floors up. It created a very luxurious and a very exciting feeling. Invariably, people comment that the atrium—and the color of the marble particularly—is friendly and flattering, but also vibrant and energizing— all things you want people to feel when they shop: comfortable, but also pumped up to spend money.

Of course, the marble was only part of it. The whole atrium space was very dramatic and different. Rather than making the railings out of aluminum, which is cheap and practical, we used polished brass, which was much more expensive but also more elegant, and which blended wonderfully with the color of the marble. Then we used a lot of reflective glass, particularly on the sides of the escalators. That was critical, because it made a fairly small core space look far larger and more dramatic. The sense of spaciousness was further enhanced by the fact that we used only two structural columns in the entire atrium. The result is that no matter where you stand, you get an unimpeded view and a sense of great openness.

The third element that adds to the drama of the

atrium is one I actually fought against at first: making the entrance from Fifth Avenue unusually large. Zoning regulations required only a fifteen-foot width, and I didn't want to lose any more retail space that fronted on Fifth Avenue than I had to. However, the city pushed very hard for a thirty-foot width, and finally, reluctantly, I went along. It cost me some very valuable retail square footage, but now I think that what I got instead—a spectacular entrance—was more than worth it. I give the City Planning Commission full credit for that.

The last key element in the atrium was the waterfall that runs along the eastern wall. It's nearly eighty feet high, and it cost almost $2 million to build. Most of my people at first favored putting paintings on the walls. To me that was old-fashioned, unoriginal, and just not very exciting. As it turned out, the waterfall proved to be an art form in itself, almost a sculptured wall. Also, it attracts far more attention than we'd have gotten if we'd put up even some very wonderful art. If most malls succeed in part because they're so safe and homogeneous, I'm convinced that the Trump Tower atrium succeeds for just the opposite reasons. It's larger than life, and walking through it is a transporting experience, almost as if you're in a wonderland.

We tried to create a version of that feeling in the apartments themselves. The most dramatic element we had to offer, of course, was the views. Since the residential units didn't start until the thirtieth level, most were higher than the surrounding buildings, which meant they had views to the north of Central Park, to the south of the Statue of Liberty, to the east of the East River, and to the west of the Hudson. In addition, the sawtooth design of the building gave all the major rooms in the apartments views in at least two directions. And then, to make sure we took the best advantage of those views, we built huge windows, virtually from floor to ceiling. I would have made the windows all the way from floor to ceiling, but I was told that unless there is at least some base below a window, some people get vertigo.

The funny thing is that the inside of the apartments was less important than a lot of the other elements. We quickly discovered that the sort of buyer who spends $1 million for a two-bedroom pied-à-terre, or $5 million for a four-bedroom duplex, is going to hire his own designer, gut the apartment, and rebuild it to fit his own tastes.

In the end, the reason that we were able to charge unprecedented prices for the apartments was something beyond any specific luxuries we provided. It was the fact that—through some blend of design, materials, location, promotion, luck, and timing—Trump Tower took on a mystical aura. A lot of buildings can be successful, but I'm convinced that only one, at any given time, can achieve the blend of qualities necessary to attract the best buyers and command the top prices.

Before Trump Tower, the last building to achieve that mystique had been Olympic Tower, on 51st Street off Fifth Avenue, built in the 1970s. The key ingredient was the fact that Aristotle Onassis owned it. At the time, Onassis was living an amazing life. He was married to Jackie Kennedy and was the ultimate jet-setter with mansions around the world, a huge yacht, and even his own island, Skorpios. He was very rich and very hot, and while Olympic Tower wasn't a particularly exciting or attractive building, it was the right product done by the right guy at the right time. It absolutely stole the top of the market from another luxury building that went up around the same time, the Galleria on East 57th Street.

As it turned out, Trump Tower also stole the market from one potentially major competitor. Long before I made my deal for the Bonwit site, another developer announced plans to build a huge condominium tower above the Museum of Modern Art, just off Fifth Avenue at 53rd Street. By all rights it should have been a fantastic success. The connection with the museum was very prestigious, the location was good, the architect, Cesar Pelli, was a big name, and the developer made it clear that he would spare no expense to build the best.

However, Trump Tower far outsold Museum Tower. First of all, although we got started later on construction, we began selling apartments in Trump Tower around the same time that Museum Tower did. From the start, I could see we had some advantages. Obviously, we had a better location on Fifth Avenue. But in addition, the shape of Museum Tower wasn't inspiring. The facade, with its multicolored glass, wasn't unusually striking, and the lobby was just another

My father, Fred Trump, in a recent photograph.

With my sisters and brothers in 1951. *Left to right:* me, Freddy, Robert, Maryanne, and Elizabeth.
HENRY KERN PHOTOGRAPHERS

At age twelve, inspecting the foundation for a six-story building in Queens, New York.
FREDERICK SCHROEDER

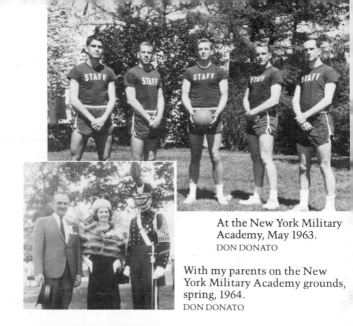

At the New York Military Academy, May 1963.
DON DONATO

With my parents on the New York Military Academy grounds, spring, 1964.
DON DONATO

Graduation photo, June 1964.
DON DONATO

Leading the New York Military Academy contingent up Fifth Avenue during the Columbus Day parade, October 1963. This was my first real glimpse of prime Fifth Avenue property.
DON DONATO

Ivana as a top fashion model in Montreal, Canada, 1975.

With Ivana on our honeymoon in Acapulco, 1977.

TOP: In 1975, at age twenty-nine, proposing a convention center for New York City on the 34th Street railyards, for which I held an option. Success arrived in 1978, when the city and state chose my site over others that had been considered. MARIANNE PERNOLD

LEFT: Explaining to reporters why my site—the 34th Street railyards—was the best location for New York City's convention center, June 1976. BILL MARK

RIGHT: With architects Jordan Gruzen and Der Scutt, answering questions about the convention center at Hilton Hotel press conference, June 1976. BILL MARK

Standing on beautiful clean newly made ice—the first in six years—after successfully turning around the city's stalled reconstruction of the Wollman Rink in Central Park, October 1986.
TED THAI/TIME MAGAZINE

Ribbon-cutting at the reopening of the Wollman Rink, November 13, 1986. *Left to right:* Toller Cranston, Michael Seibert, Judy Blumberg, Debbi Thomas, Dorothy Hamill, Scott Hamilton, Borough President David Dinkins, Robert Douglas of the Chase Manhattan Bank, me, Commissioner Henry Stern, Mayor Koch, Aja Zanova-Steindler, Dick Button, Jayne Torvil, Christopher Dean, Robin Cousins, Peggy Fleming.

Burning the mortgage after
having raised more than $100,000
to save Mrs. Annabel Hill's
Georgia farm from foreclosure,
December 23, 1986.

With Bob Hope and Ivana,
October 1986.

In the vanguard of the Vietnam Veterans Memorial ticker-tape
parade up Broadway, May 1985. I feel strongly about supporting
veterans and was proud to help underwrite both the parade and
the Vietnam Veterans Memorial constructed in downtown
Manhattan.
©1985 CHASE ROE

Signing running back Herschel Walker to play for
the New Jersey Generals, September 23, 1983.

At the Human Resources Center Twentieth Anniversary
Celebrity Sports Night, May 29, 1986.

With Mayor Ed Koch and my father, Ivana, and my mother, Mary Trump, at City Hall.
HOLLAND WEMPLE

Fifth Avenue ticker-tape parade that I put together to honor Dennis Conner and the crew of the yacht *Stars and Stripes* for recapturing the coveted America's Cup and bringing it home from Australia. The parade brought over 500,000 New Yorkers out to cheer the victorious crew on a bitter cold day in February 1987.

With friend and partner Lee
Iacocca at a recent reception.

Shooting a scene with Valerie
Bertinelli for CBS's highly
successful miniseries *I'll Take
Manhattan*, July 1986.
BOB GREENE/CBS PHOTO

Being greeted by President and Mrs. Reagan, 1986.
OFFICIAL WHITE HOUSE PHOTOGRAPH

*To Donald Trump
With best wishes,*

Nancy + Ronald Reagan

New York City's Jacob Javits Convention Center constructed at the West 34th Street railyards. I offered to oversee the construction, but the city and state went ahead on their own. Not surprisingly, the project came in years late and hundreds of millions of dollars over budget.

With the St. Moritz on one side of the avenue and Trump Parc on the other, the Trump Organization now controls twin towers flanking the Avenue of the Americas at Central Park South.

LEFT: Model of Trump Plaza, a 175-unit residential tower located near Bloomingdale's at 61st Street and Third Avenue on New York's Upper East Side.
BAEHR

RIGHT: Model of Trump Parc, generally considered the highest-priced, fastest-selling condominium in New York, containing luxurious apartments with vast terraces and all-marble baths. Adjacent to Trump Parc is 100 Central Park South, an elegant prewar building comprising 80 rental apartment units.
©WOLFGANG HOYT/ESTO

Model of the Grand Hyatt Hotel. This 34-story, 1,406-room luxury convention hotel is a $100 million development located on 42nd Street between Lexington and Park avenues, adjacent to Grand Central Station.

Grand Central Terminal restoration we carried out in 1979 during the construction of the adjoining Grand Hyatt Hotel.

Model of Trump Tower, flagship of the Trump Organization, located on Fifth Avenue and 56th Street adjacent to Tiffany. The 68-story building contains some of the most exclusive residential, retail, and office space in New York, and its 6-story pink marble atrium *(inset above)* with an 80-foot waterfall has made it a New York City landmark.

ABOVE: Model of Trump Plaza Hotel and Casino on the Boardwalk, Atlantic City's tallest hotel and one of the most successful hotel-casinos anywhere.
BAEHR

ABOVE: October 23, 1986, the luckiest day of my life. During construction of a 2,700-car garage at the Trump Plaza Hotel and Casino in Atlantic City, the boom of a huge crane reached out too far to pick up a 22-ton beam; the crane toppled over, and a large section of the garage collapsed. Minutes before the accident, at least a hundred workers were on the site. The crew had just left for a coffee break, and no one was hurt.

RIGHT: A model of the $320 million Trump's Castle Hotel and Casino located at the Marina in Atlantic City, New Jersey. Under construction at this massive development is a major new tower containing a ballroom and super-luxury suites, and a spectacular 600-slip marina complex.

LEFT: My controlling interest in Resorts International includes the Taj Mahal in Atlantic City, scheduled for completion in September 1988, which will be the largest hotel-casino anywhere in the world, with a casino floor of approximately 120,000 square feet.

ABOVE: Mar-a-Lago, our winter home in Palm Beach, Florida, was designed by Joseph Urban in the mid-twenties for Marjorie Merriweather Post, the Post cereal heiress. This magnificent 118-room home sits on property that stretches from the Atlantic Ocean on the east to Lake Worth on the west and comprises 20 acres of perfectly landscaped lawns, a 9-hole golf course, citrus groves, a greenhouse and cutting garden, guest houses, staff quarters, tennis courts, and a swimming pool. It is considered one of the most valuable parcels of land in the United States.

RIGHT: Trump Plaza of the Palm Beaches, a 260-unit deluxe condominium on the Intercoastal Waterway in Florida, with spectacular views of Lake Worth and the Atlantic Ocean.

TOP: Displaying one of the early conceptual designs of Television City. ©1987 THOMAS VICTOR

ABOVE: West Side railyards, the largest undeveloped waterfront tract in Manhattan, encompassing approximately 100 acres and stretching from West 59th Street to West 72nd Street along the Hudson River—the projected site for Television City. On this site will be both the world's tallest building and the most advanced television production complex, approximately 8,000 residential units, a major retail concourse, and more than 13 acres of beautifully landscaped recreational space, including a waterfront promenade. COPYRIGHT SKYVIEWS SURVEY INC.

lobby. Finally, Museum Tower was marketed poorly. Their ads were dull, there was no attempt to create excitement, and it came off as just an average building.

By contrast, we took our strengths and promoted them to the skies. From day one, we set out to sell Trump Tower not just as a beautiful building in a great location but as an event. We positioned ourselves as the only place for a certain kind of very wealthy person to live—the hottest ticket in town. We were selling fantasy.

The one market we didn't go after was old-money New Yorkers, who generally want to live in older buildings anyway. On the other hand, we could appeal to several other categories of wealthy people.

Obviously, we were a natural choice for people connected with show business, in the sense that we'd created something very glamorous. Foreigners were another big market—Europeans, South Americans, Arabs, and Asians. Practically speaking, we offered them an immediate advantage. At the time we began selling Trump Tower, it was virtually the only condominium in New York. To buy an apartment in a condominium, all you need is the purchase price. To buy a cooperative—which is what most buildings in New York were at the time—you need approval from its board of directors, who have ridiculous, arbitrary powers, including the right to demand all kinds of financial data, social references, and personal interviews. Then they can reject you for any reason they choose, without explanation. It's a license to discriminate. The worst part is that many people on these co-op boards get their kicks from showing off their power. It's absurd and probably illegal, but it happened to be great for Trump Tower. Many wealthy foreigners didn't have the proper social references for these cooperatives, or didn't want to put themselves through the scrutiny of a bunch of prying strangers. Instead, they came to us.

I still remember the morning, just before we began selling apartments, when one of my salespeople rushed into my office. "Mr. Trump," she said, "we're in trouble. Museum Tower just announced its prices, and they're much lower than ours." I thought for a minute, and I realized that actually the opposite was true: Museum Tower had just done itself damage. The sort of wealthy people we were competing for don't look for bargains in apartments. They may want bargains in everything else, but when it comes to a home, they want the best, not the best buy. By pricing its apartments lower than ours, Museum Tower had just announced that it was not as good as Trump Tower.

A lot of people think that we set out to attract celebrities to Trump Tower, or that we hired a fancy public relations firm to promote the building. The truth is that we never hired anyone to do public relations, and every star who bought an apartment— Johnny Carson, Steven Spielberg, Paul Anka, Liberace, and many others—came to us. Nor did I give any of them special deals. Other developers cut prices to attract stars and celebrities, but to me that's a sign of weakness. What really means something is when a celebrity is willing to pay full price for an apartment.

If any press story about a celebrity helped promote Trump Tower, I suspect it was one about a sale that never actually occurred. Shortly after we began selling apartments, I got a call from a reporter asking whether or not it was true that Prince Charles had purchased an apartment in Trump Tower. It so happened that this was the week when Prince Charles and Lady Diana had gotten married, and they were, at that moment, the most celebrated couple in the world. Our policy was not to comment about sales, and that's what I told this reporter. In other words, I refused to confirm or deny the rumor. Apparently, the reporter then decided to call Buckingham Palace. By this time, the royal couple had left for their honeymoon and they were out on the yacht *Britannia*, so the Buckingham Palace spokesman said just what I had: they couldn't confirm or deny the rumor.

That was all the media needed. In the absence of a denial, the story that the royal couple was considering buying an apartment in Trump Tower became front-page news all over the world. It certainly didn't hurt us, but I had to laugh to myself. Just a month earlier, Prince Charles had come to New York for a visit, and the IRA had come out in force to protest. As Prince Charles walked into Lincoln Center for a concert one evening, hundreds of protestors stood outside, hissing and screaming and throwing bottles. It had to be a frightening experience for him, and I can't imagine it left Prince Charles with a great desire to take an apartment in New York City. Also, while Trump Tower is a great building, I suspect Prince Charles would find it very hard to get used to *any* apartment after growing up in Buckingham Palace.

With so much demand, our marketing strategy was to play hard to get. It was a reverse sales technique. If you sit in an office with a contract in your hand, eager to make the first deal that comes along, it's quite obvious to people that the apartments aren't in demand. We were never in a rush to sign a contract. When people came in, we'd show them the model apartments, sit down and talk, and, if they were interested, explain that there was a waiting list for the most desirable apartments. The more unattainable the apartments seemed, the more people wanted them.

As demand grew, I kept raising the prices—twelve times in all. We started out selling for much more than Olympic Tower, which until then had been the most expensive building in New York. Within a short period, we'd almost doubled the price for the best apartments on the highest floors. People were buying two-bedroom apartments for $1.5 million, and before we finished construction, we'd sold a huge majority of the apartments.

The cycles of buyers at Trump Tower became something of a barometer of what was going on in the international economy. At first, the big buyers were the Arabs, when oil prices were going through the roof. Then, of course, oil prices fell and the Arabs went home. In 1981, we got a sudden wave of buyers from France. I wasn't sure why, but then I realized the reason was that François Mitterrand had been elected president, and anyone smart and wealthy realized immediately that Mitterrand was going to hurt the French economy. It wasn't just that he was a socialist, and that he began nationalizing companies, it was also that he turned out to be a dangerous man. What can you say about a guy who goes around selling nuclear technology to the highest bidder? It's the lowest anyone can stoop.

After the European cycle, we got the South Americans and the Mexicans, when the dollar was weak and their economies still seemed fairly strong. Then, when inflation set in, their currencies were devalued, and their governments tried to restrict the outflow of cash, that cycle ended.

During the past several years, we've had two new groups buying. One is American—specifically, Wall Street types, brokers and investment bankers who've made instant fortunes during the bull market frenzy. It's ridiculous, when you think about it. You get stockbrokers, barely twenty-five years old, who suddenly earn $600,000 a year because clients they've never met call up and say, "I'll take fifty thousand shares of General Motors." The broker pushes a button on a computer and, presto, he's got a huge commission. As soon as the stock market falls out—which it will, because it too runs in cycles—most of these guys will be out on the street looking for work.

The other new buyers are the Japanese. I have great respect for what the Japanese have done with their economy, but for my money they are often very difficult to do business with. For starters, they come in to see you in groups of six or eight or even twelve, and so you've got to convince all of them to make any given deal. You may succeed with one or two or three, but it's far harder to convince all twelve. In addition, they rarely smile and they are so serious that they don't make doing business fun. Fortunately, they have a lot of money to spend, and they seem to like real estate. What's unfortunate is that for decades now they have become wealthier in large measure by screwing the United States with a self-serving trade policy that our political leaders have never been able to fully understand or counteract.

Because the 263 apartments in Trump Tower proved to be so desirable, I decided to keep a dozen or so off the market, much the way a hotel operator always holds a few choice rooms free for emergencies. It was a way of keeping options open—particularly my own. Originally, I decided to take one of the three penthouse triplexes on the top floors—about 12,000 square feet in all—for my family. We moved in at the end of 1983. I had offers as high as $10 million for each of the two apartments adjoining mine, but I resisted selling them, figuring I might ultimately want more space myself.

It proved true sooner rather than later. In the middle of 1985, I got an invitation from Adnan Khashoggi, a Saudi Arabian and a billionaire at the time, to come to his apartment in Olympic Tower. I went, and while I didn't particularly go for the apartment, I was impressed by the huge size of its rooms. Specifically, it had the biggest living room I'd ever seen. I had plenty of space in my triplex, but I figured, What the hell? Why shouldn't I have exactly the apartment I wanted—particularly when I built the whole building?

I decided to take over one of the other apartments on the top three floors and combine it with mine. It has taken almost two years to renovate, but I don't believe there is any apartment anywhere in the world that can touch it. And while I can't honestly say I need an eighty-foot living room, I do get a kick out of having one.

Successful as we were in selling the Trump Tower apartments to the top buyers, we did at least as well in attracting the best retailers to the atrium. It began when Asprey, a London-based store that sells the finest crystal, jewelry, and antiques, selected the atrium for its first branch store in two hundred years of operation. At first, they took a small store in the atrium. Business was so good that they have since expanded to a much larger space. Quality, of course, attracts more quality. The next thing we knew we had leases with many of the world's top retailers—Asprey, Charles Jourdan, Buccellati, Cartier, Martha, Harry Winston, and many others.

It didn't hurt, of course, that in April 1983, just after the atrium opened, we got a good review from Paul Goldberger, who by then had replaced Ada Louise Huxtable as architecture critic of the *Times*. The review was headlined ATRIUM IN TRUMP TOWER IS A PLEASANT SURPRISE. It began by saying, in effect, that other critics had been wrong. The atrium, Goldberger wrote, "is turning out to be a much more pleasant addition to the cityscape than the architectural oddsmakers would have had it." The review went on to say that the atrium "may well be the most pleasant interior public space to be completed in New York in some years. It is warm, luxurious and even exhilarating—in every way more welcoming than the public arcades and atriums that have preceded it in buildings like Olympic Tower, the Galleria, and Citicorp Center."

That review had two positive effects. First, it reinforced the feeling among the retailers in the atrium and the people who'd purchased apartments in Trump Tower that they'd made the best choice. But second, and more important, it helped bring more shoppers to the atrium. They, of course, were ultimately the key to its success.

The odd thing is that no one could ever quite believe that the atrium was a commercial success. From the day it opened, false rumors circulated. One was that while it was obviously a tourist attraction, no one really bought anything there. Another was that the European retailers stayed only because their stores functioned as high-visibility loss-leaders. Still other stories had it that the stores on the ground floor did well, but those on the upper floors did not. As late as 1986, a *New York Times* reporter came to see me, obviously prepared to do a hatchet job on the atrium. Instead, he did his reporting and ended up writing a front-page business-section story about the atrium's extraordinary success.

Typically, a suburban mall has a turnover of at least a third of its original tenants during the first several years. Trump Tower lost only a handful of its stores during the first three years. More important, no sooner does a tenant leave than he is replaced by one of the fifty retailers we have on our waiting list. Stores with the most expensive merchandise in the world have prospered in the atrium.

Not every quality retailer has found the location appropriate, of course. The best example is the experience of Loewe, the leather-goods retailer, which was among the atrium's first tenants. Loewe had beautiful merchandise. But it turned out that while a wealthy woman might pay thousands of dollars for a piece of jewelry or an evening gown at a shop next door, she was not willing to shell out $3,000 for a pair of Loewe's leather pants, no matter how soft and buttery they might feel. So Loewe's didn't do well. But in the end, everyone came out okay. Asprey, which was doing very well next door, took over Loewe's space. Loewe, therefore, got out of a long-term lease, Asprey got an additional 4,600 square feet it very much wanted, and I got a great new lease.

One last element helped make the Trump Tower deal a huge home run, and that was something called a 421-A tax exemption. Ironically, getting my 421-A ended up taking me longer than it had to assemble the site and complete the entire construction of Trump Tower.

The city enacted the 421-A law in 1971, to encourage residential development. In return for improving a site, developers were entitled to an exemption from real estate taxes over a ten-year period. Every two years the exemption decreased by 20 percent. Everyone who applied for the 421-A exemption got it, almost as a matter of course. Then I came along with Trump Tower.

There was no question that I was entitled. I was proposing to take a ten-story building in a state of disrepair and to build in its place a multiuse sixty-eight story $200 million tower. Unlike the tax abatement I'd gotten on the Grand Hyatt, where I was forgiven all taxes, the 421-A program wouldn't exempt me from taxes currently being paid on the site—but it would exempt me from additional taxes attributable to an increased assessed value on the site. Who could argue that I wouldn't be improving and better utilizing the site with Trump Tower?

Ed Koch could, for one. And the reason had nothing to do with the merits of my case. It was all politics. Koch and his deputies sensed an opportunity they couldn't resist: to position themselves as consumer advocates taking on a greedy developer. From a public relations perspective, I was vulnerable. It was quite obvious that Fifth Avenue wasn't exactly a marginal neighborhood, and that I'd probably succeed with Trump Tower even if I didn't get a tax exemption.

But in my mind, none of that had any bearing on my legal right to a 421-A exemption. In December 1980, I applied for a 421-A for the first time. A month later, I met with Tony Gliedman, commissioner of the city's Department of Housing, Preservation and Development, to make my case in person. In March, Gliedman and the HPD turned my application down.

I called Koch and told him I thought the ruling was

unfair, that I wasn't about to give up, and that the city was going to waste a huge amount of money litigating a case I'd eventually win.

In April 1981, I filed something called an Article 78 proceeding in state supreme court, seeking to have the city's ruling overturned. The court found in my favor, but an appellate court reversed the ruling, so I took my case to the state's highest court, the court of appeals. In December 1982—nearly two years after my original application—the court of appeals ruled 7-0 that the city had improperly refused me an exemption. But instead of simply ordering the city to expedite my exemption, the court told the city to reconsider my request. They did—and turned me down again.

By now I was so outraged that the cost of the litigation was beside the point. We refiled an Article 78, and exactly the same scenario unfolded. We won in supreme court, got overturned at the appellate level, and ended up again before the court of appeals. My lawyer, Roy Cohn, did a brilliant job, arguing before seven justices without so much as a note. This time, the court again ruled unanimously that we were entitled to our exemption—and ordered the city to provide it without further delay.

That was just the icing on the cake. By this time, Trump Tower was an unqualified success. It had given me visibility and credibility and prestige. It was also a great success financially. The way I figure it, the entire project—including land, construction costs, architecture fees, advertising and promotion, and finance charges—cost approximately $190 million. The sales of apartments have so far generated $240 million—meaning that even before including revenues from the stores and offices, we have earned a profit of approximately $50 million on Trump Tower. I also earned more than $10 million in commissions as a sales agent for apartments in Trump Tower. Finally, the rent from office space and the retail atrium generates many millions more a year—almost all of it profit.

Ultimately, Trump Tower became much more than just another good deal. I work in it, I live in it, and I have a very special feeling about it. And it's because I have such a personal attachment that I ended up buying out my partner, Equitable, in 1986. What happened is that Equitable put a new guy in charge of its New York real estate operation. One day this fellow called me up and said, "Mr. Trump, I've just been looking over the books, and I'd like you to explain why we're spending so much on the maintenance of Trump Tower." We were, in fact, spending nearly $1 million a year, which is almost unheard of. But the explanation was very simple. When you set the highest possible standards, they're expensive to maintain. As one simple example, my policy was to have all of the brass in the atrium polished twice a month. Why, this fellow asked, couldn't we save some money by polishing once every couple of months?

At first I was civil. I tried to explain that one of the key reasons for the success of the atrium is that it was so impeccably well-run. I also said I had no intention of changing our policy, and I suggested to this executive that perhaps he ought to take a day to think about whether he really wanted to push it. He called me back twenty-four hours later, and he said he'd thought about it and he did want to go ahead with cutbacks. That was probably the end of my partnership with Equitable. Much as I liked Equitable, I wasn't about to tamper with something so successful just to save a few bucks. To do that would have been totally self-destructive.

I was upset, but I was also philosophical. I went to my friend George Peacock, the head of real estate at Equitable, and I explained that we had a problem, and that there didn't seem to be a way out of it. Therefore, I wanted to buy out Equitable's share. In a short time we made a deal, and I now own Trump Tower outright. After we'd signed the contracts, I got a letter from George Peacock, who ended by saying, "As with most things in life, time calls for change and it is best to accept that fact. Nevertheless, I shall always be proud of my involvement in the creation of Trump Tower and fondly remember how we worked to bring it about."

I was very happy to get that letter. It was a classy way to conclude a partnership that had been a class act from the start.

8

GAMING

The Building
on the Boardwalk

THE FIRST TIME the economics of the casino gaming business really came home to me was one day late in 1975. I was driving along in my car, to yet another meeting about the Commodore Hotel deal, when a news report came on the radio. Hotel employees in Las Vegas, Nevada, the announcer reported, had just voted to strike. Among other consequences, the stock price of Hilton Hotels, which owned two casinos in Las Vegas, had dropped tremendously. By this time I knew something about the hotel business, but I was still stunned. How was it possible that the stock of a company that owned at least a hundred hotels worldwide could be hurt so badly by a strike against just two of them?

When I got back to my office, it took only a small amount of research to find out the answer. Hilton, it turned out, owned more than 150 hotels worldwide, but its two casino hotels in Las Vegas accounted for nearly 40 percent of the company's net profits. By comparison, a hotel such as the New York Hilton—one of the biggest in Manhattan and one I'd always assumed was a huge success—accounted for less than 1 percent of overall Hilton profits. It was a sobering thought. For nearly two years, I'd been working day and night to try to build my own huge hotel on 42nd Street. I wasn't getting my approvals, I wasn't getting my financing, and it seemed highly likely that the whole deal was going to fall through. Now, for the first time, it occurred to me that even if I finally got the hotel built and it became a major success in the greatest city in the world, it still wouldn't be nearly as profitable as a moderately successful casino hotel in a small desert town in the Southwest.

By this point I had invested a great deal of time in the Commodore deal, and I tend not to give up on something I've started. But what I did, shortly after I heard that radio report, was take a trip down to Atlantic City. A year earlier, a referendum to legalize gambling throughout the state of New Jersey had been badly defeated. Now a new initiative was on the 1976 ballot, to legalize gambling solely in Atlantic City.

It certainly seemed worth checking out. I've never had any great moral problems with gambling because most of the objections seem hypocritical to me. The New York Stock Exchange happens to be the biggest casino in the world. The only thing that makes it different from the average casino is that the players dress in blue pinstripe suits and carry leather briefcases. If you allow people to gamble in the stock market, where more money is made and lost than in all the casinos of the world put together, I see nothing terribly different about permitting people to bet on blackjack or craps or roulette.

To me, the key questions about legalizing gambling in Atlantic City were economic. Was the timing right, was the price of entry reasonable, and did the area make sense as a location? Atlantic City is 120 miles from New York City on the south shore of New Jersey, and once upon a time it was a great resort and convention center. But when the convention business shifted to bigger cities in warmer climates, Atlantic City fell on hard times. I wasn't prepared for how badly things had deteriorated. It seemed almost like a ghost town, with burned-out buildings, boarded-up stores, and the feeling of despair you sense immediately in places where a lot of people are out of work.

Ironically, the prospect of legalized gambling had already sent Atlantic City land values soaring, particularly along the Boardwalk by the ocean. Speculators—everyone from large public companies to fly-by-night con men—had moved in like vultures. Families living in tiny homes that they couldn't have sold a year earlier for $5,000 suddenly found themselves being offered $300,000, $500,000, and even $1 million.

It was a little ridiculous, and I decided not to be one of the speculators. I didn't like the idea of putting up a lot of pure risk money. Say, for example, I paid $500,000 to buy a piece of property before the referendum. If it failed, my $500,000 investment would drop in value to almost nothing the next day. If the referendum passed, that same piece of land might cost me $2 million, but I thought it was a better bet to pay more for a sure thing. The economics of a successful casino operation are so strong that paying a little more for a good site would eventually prove to be a small expense.

Sure enough, the referendum passed in November 1976 and was signed into law by the middle of 1977. By then, however, the Grand Hyatt project was finally moving forward and the price of land in Atlantic City had become more astronomical than I had anticipated. Just as I'd done five years earlier in Manhattan when prices seemed too high, I decided to stay on the sidelines a little longer. I knew that if I was patient and kept my eyes open, a better opportunity would eventually arise.

Nearly three years passed, but finally, in the winter of 1980, I got a call from an architect I had looking out for me in Atlantic City. He told me that a certain prime piece of Boardwalk property I'd always been interested in might be available. The timing couldn't have been better. For one thing, the first wave of euphoria about the casino business had passed, and times were tougher. A few casinos—Resorts, Golden

Nugget, Caesars—were doing terrific business, but the more recent ventures had run into all kinds of problems.

Bally, the newest casino in town, had come in at least $200 million over budget. The Tropicana facility, owned by Ramada Inn, was experiencing severe construction delays and enormous overruns. Bob Guccione of *Penthouse* had announced plans to build a Boardwalk casino, only to find after acquiring a site that he couldn't get financing. Hugh Hefner's plans for a Playboy hotel-casino fell apart after he was turned down for a license by the Casino Control Commission. A half dozen lesser-known players had come riding into town with great plans, only to be derailed by trouble with financing and licensing, or intimidated by the huge cost of building a hotel-casino.

Atlantic City's reputation had also been hurt by corruption charges growing out of the FBI's Abscam sting operation. In 1980, the vice-chairman of the Casino Control Commission, Kenneth MacDonald, resigned after admitting that he'd been in the room when a $100,000 bribe was passed to a local politician by potential investors looking for help in getting a casino license. To make matters still worse, the winter of 1980 had been particularly harsh—freezing cold and so windy that in January and February you could barely stand up on the Boardwalk.

Suddenly, a city that had been very hot for several years turned very cold, literally and figuratively. No one was talking about building any more new casinos. It seemed possible that the gaming business in Atlantic City was going to prove to be seasonal at best—

enough to sustain only a few casinos. In my view, however, that translated into an opportunity. The worst of times often create the best opportunities to make good deals.

The two-and-a-half-acre piece of property that I got the call about was at the center of the Boardwalk, just off the main road leading into town from the Atlantic City Expressway. In addition, the site was directly alongside the convention center, the largest space available for conventions and major entertainment— and a potential funnel into any casino built next door. I was convinced that there was no better casino site in town. Perhaps not coincidentally, it had already proved to be one of the most difficult to assemble.

By 1980, everyone and his uncle had tried, and the result was a legal mess—fragmented ownership, overlapping agreements, disputes over options, liens on individual parcels, and warring factions. The status of the site seemed almost impossible to comprehend, much less to untangle. Every lawyer and real estate broker I spoke with told me flat out that if I really wanted to build a casino in Atlantic City, I'd be far better off purchasing a site that was already assembled. I listened to the advice, but I wasn't convinced.

First of all, I always believe in going after the best location, if you can get it at a reasonable price. Secondly, I have an almost perverse attraction to complicated deals, partly because they tend to be more interesting, but also because it is more likely you can get a good price on a difficult deal.

Had I tried to assemble the same site back in 1976,

the story probably would have been very different. At that point, I had yet to build anything in New York, and no one really knew who I was. But by 1980, with the Hyatt under construction, and the Trump Tower project announced, I had a much higher profile and a lot more credibility. When you're negotiating with people who've been promised the world a half dozen times and gotten nothing, credibility is critical.

The site consisted of three large parcels, each one owned by a different investment group, as well as a half dozen small homes owned by individual immigrant families. The key to putting the deal together was making every parcel in the deal contingent on my getting all of the others. The only chance of building the great facility I envisioned was to put together the whole site. The last thing I wanted to do was invest a lot of money and then find myself squeezed at the end by one holdout owner who understood the value of controlling the final piece in a puzzle.

That's what happened to Bob Guccione, on the site next door. To this day, underneath the rusting frame of an unfinished building there remains a single-family home that Guccione never managed to purchase. Even if he'd gotten financing, he would have had a problem. Imagine spending $300 million or $400 million on a gleaming, glamorous new facility—but building it around a rotting five-room shack.

Instead, I set out to leverage my credibility. I told the owners of the sites that I was prepared to make a fair deal, and that unlike all the others before me, I was going to follow through. I pointed out that I had a

strong track record when it came to developing property. I also suggested that I might be the only person
around who still had the inclination to put this deal
together at all. If they couldn't come to an agreement
with me, I said, they might be sitting on their property
for many years to come.

The major part of the deal was for the three large
parcels on the site. The groups that owned them were
known as SSG, Magnum, and Network III, and I
negotiated with the principals of each group myself.
Rather than trying to purchase the pieces outright, I
sought very long leases with options to purchase at a
later date. My strategy was to keep my up-front
investment down, and also to avoid seeking major
financing at a time when banks were wary about
Atlantic City. In the case of leases, I could carry the
costs myself. My pitch was very simple: I was prepared to buy them out, quickly and cleanly. They, in
turn, had to cooperate with me and with each other, so
that all closings could be simultaneous. They also had
to drop the lawsuits they were waging against each
other over prior attempts to jointly sell or lease the
land. I did not want to get involved, down the road, in
a legal morass.

The properties I bought outright were the individual
homes. I hired local people to negotiate on my behalf,
because many of those we were negotiating with were
immigrants who spoke very limited English and weren't
used to dealing with outsiders. Other developers had
paid up to $1 million for tiny plots in strategic loca-
tions. Because times had turned bad, I was able to

purchase nearly all of the houses at much more modest prices.

By July 1980, we had all the pieces in place. I remember closing day very well. We had arranged simultaneous closings, beginning on a Friday afternoon, in the offices of one of our attorneys in Atlantic City. The closings went on around the clock—it took twenty-eight hours before everything was signed and sealed. At that point, we had a roomful of people almost delirious from exhaustion—but I controlled the best site in Atlantic City.

Before I could move forward, I still had to get financing, architectural approvals, and licensing as a casino operator. More important, I had to decide whether the timing was right to undertake this huge project. Fortunately, I didn't feel pressed to make any quick decisions. It was true that I had several million dollars invested—including lawyers' fees, preliminary architectural drawings, staff costs, and purchase and lease of land. But I was very confident that if I wanted to turn around and sell my assembled site to someone else, I'd get a great deal more for it than I'd put in. There are always buyers for the best.

In the meantime, my first priority was to get licensed by the Casino Control Commission. I'd followed Atlantic City closely enough to know that the licensing process could be very long, very difficult, and very unpredictable.

Playboy and Hugh Hefner, for example, were turned down for a license because the company had allegedly paid a bribe twenty years earlier in order to get a liquor license for the Playboy Club in Manhattan. When Hefner testified in New Jersey, he took the position that he'd actually been shaken down for a payment, and that neither he nor Playboy had ever been charged with a crime. Even so, his license was denied. The state official who cross-examined Hefner said afterward that several commissioners hadn't liked Hefner's demeanor and style on the witness stand. I don't believe he helped his cause when he walked into the hearing in Trenton, New Jersey, with blazing pipe, silk suit and shirt, and a blond bombshell at his side. The licensing process is very subjective; if his savvy daughter, Christie, had been involved at the time, perhaps the outcome would have been different.

Much more serious allegations of connections with organized crime had been raised against several other applicants. Caesars and Bally were among them, but nonetheless, they both eventually got licensed. What became clear to me, as I watched the licensing process, was a pattern of something I call bloodletting: in exchange for a license, applicants were regularly being forced to offer up at least one sacrificial lamb. At Caesars World, it was the Perlman brothers, who had to resign from the company, and at Bally it was William O'Donnell. But unlike a large public company, I couldn't afford to sacrifice anyone. I had to demonstrate an absolutely unblemished background.

The first thing I did was hire a lawyer to represent me. Nick Ribis was originally recommended by the Newhouse family, for whom he'd done a lot of work. I have great respect for the Newhouses, and when I met

Nick, I liked his style. He was probably thirty at the time, but he looked years younger. The first thing I said to Nick was "Look, I'm just not sure a lawyer as young as you are can handle a big project like this." Nick wasn't thrown. "To tell you the truth, Mr. Trump," he said, "I've never had a client as young as *you* who could afford my bill."

Nick and I agreed immediately on a strategy. I'd hold back on any construction until we got a decision on licensing.

In every previous situation, companies who purchased or assembled sites in Atlantic City had begun the licensing process and construction concurrently. Licensing could take as long as construction, and the sooner the casino got built, the faster it could start earning money. It's perfectly logical—so long as your licensing comes through in the end. But unlike these other companies, I didn't want to put several hundred million dollars at risk in the meantime. Also, I didn't want to be in a weak negotiating position with the Casino Control Commission. Once you've begun investing huge sums of money, it's very hard to say no to anything they ask for. Waiting to get a decision on licensing meant paying carrying costs on my land a little longer, and postponing profits, but it seemed more than worth it. To this day not many people or companies are willing to go through the nightmare of licensing in New Jersey, which gives Nevada a big advantage in attracting new investors.

My strongest card was the fact that construction of new casinos in Atlantic City had come to a complete standstill. State and city officials, I knew, were hungry for new evidence that Atlantic City was still a good investment. Because my credibility as a major builder had been established, I was confident that state and local officials would be receptive to my constructing a major casino-hotel in Atlantic City. I didn't want to be in the position of pleading with anyone. At the very least, I wanted to deal as one among equals, all with an interest in making the project work.

By this time, I'd brought my brother Robert aboard to work with me on the project. Unlike me, Robert decided after graduating from college to work on Wall Street—perhaps as a way of getting out from under the family shadow. He started in corporate finance at Kidder Peabody. Three years later, he moved to Eastdil Realty, and for the next five years did corporate real estate finance work. Finally he moved to Shearson Loeb Rhodes, where he set up a real estate finance group and ran it very successfully, until he joined me. I think both of us always assumed that eventually he'd come back to the family business.

Atlantic City was the perfect opportunity. I was looking at a potential investment of $200 million, in a town 120 miles from New York City, where I couldn't possibly be hands-on every day. What I needed was someone totally competent, totally honest, and totally loyal to oversee the project. There is nothing to compare with family if they happen to be competent, because you can trust family in a way you can never trust anyone else. I called Robert one evening in May 1980, we talked for several hours in my apartment, and by the next day, he'd agreed to take over day-to-day responsibility for Atlantic City. Among other things, that meant we'd both go for licensing.

On a February morning in 1981, Robert, Nick Ribis, and I drove to New Jersey for a meeting with the attorney general of New Jersey and the head of gaming enforcement. I was very respectful, but I was also very blunt. I said that I was prepared to make a major investment in New Jersey—my own money, not corporate money—and that I'd already invested several million dollars on my Boardwalk site. What concerned me, I said, was that New Jersey had acquired a reputation for making it very difficult for any developer to do business in the gaming area. Licensing investigations had dragged on for eighteen months and more. Much as I wanted to build a great casino on the great site I'd assembled, I said, I had a very successful real estate business in New York and I was more than willing to walk away from Atlantic City if the regulatory process proved to be too difficult or too time-consuming. The bottom line, I concluded, was that I didn't intend to invest any more money—or to begin any construction—until I got a decision one way or the other on my licensing.

The attorney general said to me, "No, Mr. Trump, you're not right about New Jersey. The licensing process can work here efficiently. I can't give you any promises about the outcome of your investigation. We may find out that you're not licensable. What I can promise is that if you cooperate fully, we'll give you an answer one way or the other in six months." Then he turned to his director of gaming enforcement and said, "Isn't that true?"

The director tried to walk a tightrope. "Well, we'll do our best," he said, "but it may take a year."

At that point, I jumped back in. "Well, if it takes a year," I said, "then I'm out of here. I'm prepared to cooperate fully, but I'm not going to sit around twiddling my thumbs waiting for answers." The attorney general nodded, and his director agreed. It was clear that six months was our timetable, and they would try very hard to meet it.

The next thing we did was to sit down with the members of the Casino Control Commission staff. In order to build a casino, you need approval on everything from room size to casino layout, from the number of restaurants to the size of the health club. Our intention was to provide the regulators with detailed building plans and architectural drawings well in advance of our construction, so that before we got started building, they'd have a chance to review our plans and tell us what changes they wanted.

Other operators—experienced in running casinos, but not in building them—hadn't bothered with this sort of planning. In a rush to get their facilities up and open, many began construction before they got final approvals—only to have the regulators show up and say, "No, this room is too small," or "No, this slot machine needs to be there instead of here." From long experience, I know that midconstruction changes are extremely costly and perhaps the key reason so many major projects suffer huge cost overruns.

With so many regulators and regulations to satisfy, we had one major advantage: the fact that we are not a bureaucracy. In most large public corporations, getting an answer to a question requires going through seven layers of executives, most of whom are superfluous in the first place. In our organization, anyone with a question could bring it directly to me and get an answer immediately. That's precisely why I've been able to act so much faster than my competitors on so many deals.

Sure enough, the gaming division concluded its investigation and issued its report on October 16, 1981, nearly six months from the day they began. They had lived up to their word. Better yet, both Robert and I got an absolutely clean bill. The Division of Gaming Enforcement recommended licensing both of us.

My actual licensing hearings weren't scheduled for several months after the enforcement division report was complete. In the meantime, we managed to get all the necessary approvals for our construction. Among them was permission from the city to build a skyway connection between our facility and the convention center next door. One consequence was that we could build part of our facility over the road and thus end up with one of the biggest hotels in town on one of the smaller sites. Unlike the owners of many of the Boardwalk hotels, we oriented our rooms and restaurants to the ocean. With such beautiful views available, why not take maximum advantage of them?

The second issue we worked on was financing—

which was hardly a given. Most banks had an unwritten policy against making loans in the gaming business, because gaming had an unsavory reputation. My problem, ironically, was almost the opposite. Our reputation among banks was very good, but when it came to the gaming business, we had no track record at all. My solution was to try using that to our advantage. Better to lend to a reputable company with a clean slate, I'd say, than to an experienced gaming operator with a questionable reputation. Also, I said, because we were proven developers and builders, we were in a far better position than most casino companies were to assure any lender that we'd come in on time and on budget.

Manufacturers Hanover, which had helped finance the Grand Hyatt, was among the banks that had a vague policy against making loans in the gaming business. Nonetheless, they agreed to provide me with funding because of our successful relationship in building the Hyatt. I wasn't thrilled about the terms they were offering us, but it was hard for me to complain: I was lucky to get financing at all.

On March 15, 1982, with provisional financing in place and all my architectural and building plans approved, I went to Trenton, New Jersey, for licensing hearings before the Casino Control Commission. Hearings for other companies had sometimes dragged on for six to eight weeks. Shortly after 10:15 A.M. I took the stand. I testified for seventeen minutes. Just before noon, the commissioners voted unanimously to license both Robert and me, as well as our corporate entity, the Trump Plaza Corporation. I was finally on my way.

Then something totally serendipitous happened. One morning in June, I got a call at my office from a man named Michael Rose. I was impressed. I'd never met the man, but I knew that he was the chairman of Holiday Inns. I picked up the phone, and Rose introduced himself. He was very pleasant, and he said he'd like to come up from Memphis to see me.

I didn't even ask the reason. A guy in Rose's position doesn't suggest a meeting unless he's got something worth talking about. Also, I was fairly sure I knew his agenda. I assumed he was interested in buying a property I'd purchased a couple of years earlier, the Barbizon-Plaza Hotel on Central Park South and Avenue of the Americas. I knew Holiday Inns had been looking for a prestigious location in New York City, and I'd let the word out in the real estate community that I might consider selling the Barbizon for the right price.

A week later, Mike Rose came to see me. Robert and Harvey Freeman joined us. Rose was an impressive-looking guy, tall, well-dressed, and very much the gentleman. I launched right into a pitch about what a great piece of property the Barbizon was, an incredible location, a piece of the rock, nothing like it, how smart he was to come and see me about it. While I really didn't want to sell it, I said, perhaps I could be convinced in this case. For ten minutes I just ranted and raved while Mike Rose, the chairman of Holiday Inns, sat and listened very politely without saying

anything. Finally, looking a little embarrassed, he said
to me, "I don't think you understand, Donald. I'm not
interested in the Barbizon-Plaza. I'm interested in
being your partner in Atlantic City. That's what I'm
here to talk about."

I like to pride myself on rolling with the punches. I
had never thought of a partner in Atlantic City, but I
jumped right back in and started talking with the same
enthusiasm about our plans there. I said that we had
the best site on the Boardwalk, that we'd designed the
best facility, that we had our approvals and financing
in place, and that we planned to be open for business
in less than two years.

Two things intrigued me immediately about Holiday
Inns. First, the company had a lot of gaming experience. Second, they had the ability to finance the deal
themselves, which could take me off the hook personally. What wasn't clear to me was why Rose might be
interested in a partnership. Holiday already owned one
successful casino in Atlantic City, Harrah's at the
Marina. I knew they were interested in a Boardwalk
casino, but they had already bought a very costly
Boardwalk site, and I'd just assumed that's where
they'd build.

Nonetheless, I decided to play a little coy. After all,
he'd come to see me. "Listen, Mike," I said, "I have
my financing. I have my license, and I have my
approvals. Frankly, I don't need a partner. But what is
it exactly that you have in mind?"

Rose explained that he was interested in my site by
virtue of its location, but more important, because of

my reputation as a builder who came in on time and on budget. Like most other casino operators, Holiday had experienced endless problems in construction and had run over budget by tens of millions of dollars on Harrah's Marina. Rose particularly liked the idea, he said, that we were already under construction. The point, Rose concluded, was that Holiday simply couldn't justify major overruns to stockholders a second time. Making a deal with us, he said, seemed like a good way to marry their management expertise with our ability as builders.

Rose had a specific deal in mind. We'd build the hotel, they'd manage it, and we'd split the profits fifty-fifty. In addition, he said, they'd put up $50 million of their own money toward construction and reimburse me immediately for approximately $22 million of my expenses up to that point. We also agreed they'd take over responsibility for financing and use the Holiday Inns guarantee to get us a very prime rate. As a final inducement to make the deal, Rose said that Holiday would guarantee me against any operating losses for a period of five years from the date the casino opened and pay me a large construction fee.

This was almost too good to believe. Several times, I looked over at Robert and Harvey just to see if perhaps I was missing something. They just smiled. By the time Mike Rose left my office, we had shaken hands on the basic elements of a partnership in Atlantic City. It was still subject to the drawing of documents, and to approval from his board of directors. I assumed that they'd exact some concessions along the way. But as long as the basic concept remained intact—no downside for me and a 50 percent share of the upside—it was an extraordinary deal. Better yet, I still believed I was about to enter into a partnership with a quality company, run by highly competent casino and hotel operators. After all, I thought, what the hell did I know about running a huge casino-hotel anyway?

Once we'd finished our negotiations, the final step was approval of the deal by Holiday's board of directors. In many situations, board approval of management initiatives is merely a formality. In this case, I worried that Rose might use his board to help him get out of the deal, or at least force changes in it.

Rose scheduled his annual board of directors meeting in Atlantic City so that the board would have an opportunity to see the proposed site and also to assess our progress in construction. It was the latter that worried me, since we had yet to do much work on the site. One week before the board meeting, I got an idea.

I called in my construction supervisor and told him that I wanted him to round up every bulldozer and dump truck he could possibly find, and put them to work on my site immediately. Over the next week, I said, I wanted him to transform my two acres of nearly vacant property into the most active construction site in the history of the world. What the bulldozers and dump trucks did wasn't important, I said, so long as they did a lot of it. If they got some actual work accomplished, all the better, but if necessary, he should have the bulldozers dig up dirt from one side of the site and dump it on the other. They should keep doing that, I said, until I gave him other instructions.

The supervisor looked a little bewildered. "Mr. Trump," he said, "I have to tell you that I've been in business for a lot of years and this is the strangest request I've ever gotten. But I'll do my best."

One week later, I accompanied top Holiday Inns executives and the entire board of directors out to the Boardwalk. It looked as if we were in the midst of building the Grand Coulee Dam. There were so many pieces of machinery on this site that they could barely maneuver around each other. These distinguished corporate leaders looked on, some of them visibly awed. I'll never forget one of them turning to me, shaking his head, and saying, "You know, it's great when you're a private guy, and you can just pull out all the stops."

A few minutes later, another board member walked over to me. His question was very simple. "How come," he said, "that guy over there is filling up that hole, which he just dug?" This was difficult for me to answer, but fortunately, this board member was more curious than he was skeptical. The board walked away from the site absolutely convinced that it was the perfect choice. Three weeks later, on June 30, 1982, we signed a partnership agreement.

Our budget was $220 million—$50 million from Holiday directly, $170 million on a loan they guaranteed— and that included everything: carrying costs, construction, operating expenses, and required cash reserves. We projected completion in May 1984, but I was confident we could finish ahead of schedule, and even under budget, based on how carefully we'd done our planning.

One way we stood to save money was from something known as value engineering. Say, for example, that your architect shows you a certain door he wants to use, which has four hinges on it. Before you approve the door, you have your engineer look at it, and perhaps he says, "Look, you only need two hinges to hang that door, or three if you want to do a really good job." So you eliminate one ten-dollar hinge, and you multiply that times 2,000 doors, and the saving on that one tiny item comes to $20,000. Another good example was the installation of the cooling towers for our air-conditioning system. Originally our architects placed them on the roof of the hotel tower. Through value engineering we determined that we'd save a lot of money by installing them on a lower section of roof, just seven floors up, because that roof could be poured much sooner. In turn we'd be able to start all the piping and electrical work for the air-conditioning six months earlier.

The second way we saved money was by producing very complete plans, so that contractors could bid on every aspect of the job. When you have incomplete drawings, a smart contractor will often come in and underbid the job just to get it, knowing he'll be able to more than cover his costs through the change orders that inevitably occur as plans become more complete.

The final thing that helped us keep costs down was the state of the construction industry in Atlantic City in the spring of 1982. The only casino still under construction by then was the Tropicana, and thousands of local construction workers were either out of work or about to be. That gave us a lot of leverage with contractors, who had to either cover a certain overhead or go out of business. I wasn't looking to force these guys to make such bad deals that they'd lose money. On the other hand, I was in a position to negotiate very reasonable prices.

I got the building finished right on schedule for a May 14 opening. That meant we'd be able to take advantage of the Memorial Day weekend, traditionally the three biggest days of the year for the casino business in Atlantic City. I also came in slightly under the original budget, at $218 million. It represented the first casino-hotel in Atlantic City ever built on time and on budget.

On May 14, the casino opened to a public response that exceeded my wildest expectations. It was a major media event attended by thousands of people, including most of New Jersey's principal officials. The governor, Thomas Kean, was the main speaker, and he was extremely generous in praising what we had accomplished. His praise was echoed by Richard Goeglein, then president of Harrah's, who told the crowd that for us to have completed such a huge facility on time and on budget was "a near miracle in this day and age."

The moment we opened the doors, thousands of people poured in. Everyone was hungry to check out the newest game in town. In a matter of minutes, they were lined up three and four deep at the tables and the slot machines.

It is public knowledge, of course, that Holiday Inns and I had many, many disagreements over the management of the facility. But under the agreement I finally made to buy out Holiday's share, I am precluded from saying anything in detail about those conflicts. While my attorneys unanimously believe that I would win any legal battle over my First Amendment rights on this issue, that's just not the way I do business. As far as I'm concerned, a deal is a deal, and I live up to what I've agreed to, even if I don't believe I'm technically obligated by any specific contractual provision.

Suffice it to say that my ultimate buyout of Holiday Inns' share of our casino-hotel in February 1986 was one of my most savored transactions.

One reason that I particularly liked owning the facility myself—rather than with any partner—has to do with the value of depreciation. Depreciation is the percentage of the total value of a building that an owner is permitted to deduct each year from his taxable earnings. The rationale is that money spent to maintain a building—to offset its normal wear and tear—shouldn't be taxable.

Put simply, depreciation permits you to pay lower taxes on your earnings. For example, if the cost of our facility in Atlantic City was $400 million and we were permitted to depreciate at the rate of 4 percent a year, that would mean we could deduct $16 million from our taxable profits each year. In other words, if we earned a pretax profit of $16 million, our earnings, after depreciation, would actually be reported as zero.

Most shareholders and Wall Street types only look at the bottom line, which shows a profit reduced by depreciation. As a result, corporate managers don't like depreciation much. It only makes them appear less successful. But I don't have to please Wall Street, and so I appreciate depreciation. For me the relevant issue isn't what I report on the bottom line, it's what I get to keep.

The best part of the deal, however, was the facility I now owned outright. Merely by running it myself, I felt certain, I could earn a far bigger profit. In addition, I planned to build new suites and restaurants.

Financing, of course, now became my responsibility. The prime rate had been around 14 percent when I first started looking at property in Atlantic City. By mid-1986, it had dropped to 9 percent. My problem with bank financing, even at these lower rates, was that I'd still be required to put myself personally on the line for the money. I didn't find that appealing.

As a result, I decided to seek public financing for the project, through a bond issue. The downside was that I'd have to pay a higher interest rate to attract buyers, but the upside was that once the issue sold out, I wouldn't be personally liable. In the end, Bear Stearns was able to sell an offering for $250 million— which not only covered the $50 million cash due to Holiday but also permitted me to pay off the $170 million mortgage on the building and left me the money to build a suitable parking facility. Interest payments on the financing came to just above $30 million a year. That was about $7 million a year more than I'd have paid for bank financing, but to me it was money well spent. By relieving me of personal financial liability, it assured I'd sleep better at night.

During this same period, I hired a new general manager for the facility, which I had renamed Trump Plaza Hotel and Casino. I looked first at my best competitors. At the time, Stephen Hyde was executive vice president and chief operating officer under Steve Wynn at the Golden Nugget. Before that, he'd worked at the Sands and at Caesars, both top casinos. When I asked people in town to name the best casino executives, Hyde was always at the top of the list. As soon as we met, I understood why. He had a lot of gaming experience, he was a very sharp guy and highly competitive, but most of all, he had a sense of how to manage to the bottom line. A lot of managers focus on maximizing revenue since that's what gets reported publicly most often. The smarter guys understand that while big revenues are great, the real issue is the spread between the revenues and costs—because that's your profit.

No sooner had I hired Steve than we turned around and hired away a dozen of the best people who'd worked for him over the years, including Paul Patay, the number-one food-and-beverage man in Atlantic City. I have a very simple rule when it comes to management: hire the best people from your competitors, pay them more than they were earning, and give them bonuses and incentives based on their performance. That's how you build a first-class operation.

In 1985, the first full year of operation under Harrah's management, the facility earned a gross operating profit of approximately $35 million before interest, taxes, and depreciation. For 1986, Harrah's projected a gross operating profit of $38 million. Based on the first five months during which they continued to manage the facility, they were running just slightly under projections.

We took over on May 16. For the full year, our gross operating profit was nearly $58 million, or $20 million more than Harrah's had projected. This was despite the fact that in June we closed down our existing parking lot to begin construction on the new garage. We're estimating that by 1988 our gross operating profit will reach $90 million.

By all rights, that should be the end of the story. However, success running the Boardwalk facility with my own management made me see a broader opportunity. Specifically, I started to look around at other possible deals to buy companies that owned casinos. Holiday Inns was an obvious target. Even after selling me the Boardwalk facility, they still owned three other casinos—one in Atlantic City and two in Nevada—as well as nearly a thousand hotels around the world.

As a result, in mid-August, two months after buying them out in Atlantic City, I began purchasing stock in Holiday. By September 9, I'd purchased nearly 5 percent of the company, or some one million shares. At that point, I had two basic options: One was to hold the stock as an investment. The other was to go for control.

I had no doubt the company was undervalued. For one thing, because they owned so much real estate, they were entitled to large write-offs for depreciation. Therefore they reported net profits far below what they were actually able to retain. On the basis of a stock price of $54 a share in early August 1986, I was in a position to purchase effective control of the company for not much more than $1 billion. In one scenario, for example, I would sell off all of the noncasino hotels—perhaps for as much as $700 million—and retain just the three casino-hotels, which by themselves were worth nearly that much.

No sooner did word get out that I'd begun accumulating Holiday Inns stock than its price started to rise. I assume arbitrageurs were buying up the stock, figuring that either I'd make a move for control, or someone else would. By early October, the price of the stock had reached 72.

On Wednesday, November 11, I heard from Alan Greenberg of Bear Stearns that Holiday was restructuring the company to fend off any potential hostile bid and was going to borrow $2.8 billion in order to pay an immediate $65-a-share dividend to the shareholders. The stock jumped to 76. Without hesitation, I told Alan to sell, and he agreed. I still believe I could have overcome any barriers Holiday tried to put in my way, but I just wasn't particularly eager to spend my life in the court with these guys. The alternative—earning a huge profit on my investment without any battle—

seemed far more appealing. By the end of the week I'd sold my entire stake in Holiday Inns—meaning that in just eight weeks, I earned a profit of many millions of dollars. Looked at another way, I earned back from my Holiday Inns stock much of the money I'd paid them just three months earlier to buy their share of my casino in Atlantic City.

Obviously, I can't complain. Perhaps no one was better rewarded by Holiday than I was. But, in a way, I got something even more valuable than money from the experience: a first-hand view of corporate management in America.

9

WYNN-FALL

The Battle
for Hilton

I N MY WILDEST FANTASY, it never occurred to me
that I would someday purchase the huge casino-
hotel that the Hilton Hotels Corporation began
building in Atlantic City in 1984. To the contrary, I
watched with some dismay the progress of construction. I hardly relished another tough competitor in
town, especially when the Boardwalk hotel I owned with
Harrah's wasn't performing well even against the existing
competition. Worse yet, it was quite obvious that Hilton—
after several years of indecision about Atlantic City—
was finally going all-out with a major facility.

To me, Hilton was a hard company to figure. It was

founded in 1921 by Conrad Hilton, who built it into
one of the great hotel chains in the world. His son
Barron joined the company in the 1950s, and of course
it was only a matter of time before he took over. It had
nothing to do with merit; it's called birthright. In
1966, Conrad finally retired, and Barron was named
chief executive. It's not easy to make your own mark
on a company your father founded and built into a
huge success. Some sons opt out altogether and don't
even try to compete. Others are content to manage
what their fathers have already built. A few sons set
out to outdo their fathers at the same game, and that
may be the toughest thing of all, particularly when the
father's name is Conrad Hilton.

Barron's first major responsibility, back in 1959,
was to run Hilton's Carte Blanche credit card business, which they'd just bought. He screwed it up and
Carte Blanche lost millions of dollars over the next six
years. Hilton finally threw in the towel in 1966 and
sold out to Citibank. In 1967, Barron convinced his
father to sell Hilton's international hotel division to
TWA in exchange for TWA stock, which was selling
for about $90 a share. There was just one problem:
OPEC. Almost immediately, oil prices started going
through the roof, which devastated the airlines. Within
eighteen months, TWA stock had dropped by half, and
by 1974, it was down to $5 a share. Until Carl Icahn
took control of the company and turned it around
recently, the stock was worth far less than it should
have been. On the other hand, the international hotels
that Hilton sold, which were recently sold again for

close to $1 billion, did great business. They earned about $70 million in 1983—almost as much as Hilton earned from all its American hotels the same year. That's partly because Hilton, resting on its past reputation, had lost considerable ground in the luxury market to more aggressive competitors such as Marriott and Hyatt. The once-great Hilton name ceased being synonymous with the best in hotels.

Barron Hilton did make one decision that proved successful: getting into casino gambling. In 1972 Hilton purchased two Nevada casinos for about $12 million—the Las Vegas Hilton and the Flamingo Hilton. Together, the two casinos began to account for a growing percentage of Hilton's profits—30 percent in 1976, 40 percent in 1981, and 45 percent, or some $70 million, in 1985.

Despite that success, Barron couldn't seem to make up his mind about Atlantic City. Hilton purchased a site at the Marina around the time gambling was legalized, began moving forward, stopped suddenly, and then started again half-heartedly. By the time Hilton finally committed to construction in 1984, most of its major Nevada competitors—including Bally, Caesars, Harrah's, Sands, and the Golden Nugget—already had their facilities up, operating, and earning huge profits in Atlantic City.

I have to say this much for Hilton: having finally made the commitment, it left no doubt it was going all-out. With an eight-acre site, one of the biggest in town, Hilton was determined to build on a grand scale—a huge, majestic entrance, ceilings thirty feet high, a 3,000-car self-park garage. Hilton described the project in its annual report as "the largest undertaking in our history." With a casino of some 60,000 square feet, and a 615-room hotel above it, the facility was comparable in size to Harrah's at Trump Plaza—which at the time was one of the largest in town. The difference was that Hilton's master plan included a second-phase expansion, to some 100,000 feet of casino space, and more than 2,000 guest rooms.

Hungry to start recouping its investment as soon as possible, Hilton began construction at the same time it filed for a gaming license. As I explained earlier, the risk of getting turned down for a license midway through construction was the reason I'd gone after licensing first. But everyone else had done it Hilton's way, and I could understand Hilton's confidence about licensing.

For starters, it was already licensed in Nevada. In addition, at a time when virtually no other construction was going on in Atlantic City, Hilton was making a huge investment in a mostly undeveloped part of town. Perhaps most important, in a business scarcely known for attracting boy scout companies, the Hilton name was about as all-American as you could hope to find. The licensing process seemed like little more than a formality for Hilton.

The problem was that the Hilton people got a little too smug and full of themselves. They assumed they were doing Atlantic City a favor by coming to town, when in fact the licensing authorities see it just the opposite way. The burden of demonstrating suitability for a license rests entirely with the applicant, no matter who it is. Hilton took the view that it was entitled to a license. It was a critical mistake.

I began to hear rumblings that Hilton was in trouble early in 1985. Atlantic City is a very political town, and everyone who does business there knows that. Hilton, trying to be smart, hired a very political lawyer. On the face of it, that seemed like a savvy move. However, according to people I knew who were familiar with the Hilton licensing hearings, it may have backfired.

The second mistake Hilton made was ignoring the experience of previous applicants. Playboy, for example, had been turned down for a license three years before. The reason, at least in part, was its past associations with a lawyer named Sidney Korshak, who supposedly had a history of organized-crime connections. For ten years he'd also been on retainer to Hilton at $50,000 a year to help negotiate labor disputes. I have no idea whether Korshak is a good guy or a bad guy, but the only issue that matters is pleasing the commissioners. They'd made it very clear that they didn't like Korshak. Instead of quietly severing the tie, Hilton kept Korshak on his retainer right up until the Division of Gaming Enforcement raised specific objections to him in mid-1984.

Virtually the next day, Hilton fired Korshak. Barron later acknowledged to the commission that he'd taken the action only because "we know how strongly you people feel about the matter." That was the worst thing he could have said. As one of the commissioners who voted against licensing Hilton put it later, "The corporation apparently didn't get religion until it was pounding on the pearly gates of licensure."

It didn't help when Barron later testified that Korshak had never interceded on Hilton's behalf to prevent certain unions from striking Hilton's hotels. Within weeks of that testimony, Korshak wrote Barron a letter, which he released to the media. It described in great detail exactly the work he'd done for Hilton in Las Vegas. It also included copies of letters Barron Hilton had written thanking Korshak for his efforts. The end of Korshak's letter was devastating. "You have caused me irreparable harm," he wrote Barron, "and as long as I live I will never forget that. When did I become a shady character? I imagine when you were having difficulty getting a license in Atlantic City."

Hilton might have survived everything if Barron himself had taken the licensing hearings more seriously. Instead he virtually ignored them. One of the few times he saw fit to show up in New Jersey was for his own testimony before the Casino Control Commission. Nor were any of his top corporate executives there for most of the hearings.

On February 14, 1985, I was in my office when I got a phone call from a guy named Al Glasgow, who publishes a newsletter about the gaming industry called *Atlantic City Action*. Al is a true Damon Runyon character who lives and breathes gaming. He knows as much as anyone in town about who's doing what to whom. "Did you hear about Hilton?" Al asked. I said, "No, what?" And he said, "They just got turned down for a license."

I thought he was kidding at first. Approval requires the concurrence of four commissioners. Hilton won a majority, but as was the case with Hugh Hefner, 3–2 in favor was a loss, not a win. In any case, Al said he suspected there was a possibility Hilton might just decide to put the facility up for sale rather than try to fight for a rehearing.

Hilton was scheduled to open the hotel in less than twelve weeks. They'd already hired more than a thousand employees, and they were adding at the rate of approximately a hundred people a day. By opening day, they'd have approximately four thousand people on the payroll. With that payroll and no income coming in, you're talking catastrophe, no matter how big the company. At the very least, Hilton was under severe time pressure to get an appeal heard by the commission. Even so, I assumed that with more than $300 million already invested, they were going to do whatever they could to try to get licensed.

After talking with Glasgow, and a few other people in Atlantic City, I decided to call Barron Hilton out in California. As much as anything else, it was a condolence call. You couldn't help feeling sorry for the man. "Hi, Barron, how are you?" I said. Not surprisingly, Barron replied, "Not well, not well at all." "I can imagine," I went on, "because what happened is just too bad." "I've got to tell you, Donald," he said, "that I didn't expect it, it caught me totally by surprise." I told him that the move had caught everyone by surprise, and the conversation just went on like that.

Before hanging up, I got to the business part of the

call. "Look, Barron," I said, "I have no idea what you want to do with this facility, but if for some reason you're thinking of selling it, I'd be interested in buying it, if the price is right." Barron said he'd keep that in mind, and he thanked me for calling. I think he genuinely appreciated it. I also figured that was as far as things would get. Hilton already had plans to file for a rehearing, and I still believed that the commission would eventually reverse its decision.

At the beginning of March I got a call from a friend named Benjamin Lambert, who runs Eastdil Realty. I'd first met Lambert ten years before, when I was just beginning to look for a hotel-chain partner for the Commodore Hotel deal. He made some suggestions, and over the years, Ben and I worked on several deals together. We had our disagreements, but the bottom line was that we were friends. As it happened, Ben was a member of Hilton's board of directors. In the weeks after Hilton was turned down for a license, we talked a few times about the situation. Ben believed Hilton ought to seriously consider selling.

On this occasion, Ben was calling to invite me to a party he was holding for the Hilton board at his townhouse, prior to their annual meeting that week in New York. As he put it, "It's not an inopportune time for you and Barron to meet about current events."

The board, it turned out, was deeply split about how to handle the Atlantic City situation. The Casino Control Commission had just agreed to the rehearing Hilton had requested on licensing. Nonetheless, several board members, including Ben, believed that it made more sense to sell the facility immediately, if the right buyer could be found. Their argument was that if the commission didn't reverse itself and grant Hilton a license, the consequences could be truly disastrous for the company. By that point, a couple of months down the line, they'd be carrying several thousand employees. Worse, by selling the hotel under pressure, they might get a bad price.

I went to the party, and Ben introduced me to Barron, whom I'd never met in person. We ended up walking out to the garden and talking alone together. Once again the conversation was nonspecific. Mostly, Barron vented his frustration about Atlantic City, while I listened sympathetically. Barron is wary and reserved by nature. He's not the kind of guy who makes impulsive decisions, so I played it very low-key. We got along very well, and afterward I heard from Ben that Barron felt very comfortable with me. There are times when you have to be aggressive, but there are also times when your best strategy is to lie back.

Very shortly after that, Steve Wynn of the Golden Nugget decided to make a full-scale assault on Hilton, seeking control of the company. It was probably the best thing that could have happened to me. If it hadn't been for Wynn, I seriously doubt that Barron Hilton would ever have made a deal with me or anyone else for his Atlantic City hotel-casino.

On April 14, Wynn wrote Barron a letter offering to buy a block of stock, amounting to 27 percent of the entire Hilton company, for $72 a share. At the time, the stock was trading for approximately $67 a share.

Wynn also said he was prepared, if his initial offer was accepted, to pay the same $72 per share to all Hilton shareholders.

Ironically, Wynn could never have gone after the company at all if it hadn't been for Conrad Hilton. When Conrad died in 1979, he totally screwed Barron. There is no nicer way to say it. The assumption had been that Conrad would pass on his near-controlling interest in the company to Barron—or at the very least that he'd spread it among family members.

Instead, Conrad Hilton used his will to disenfranchise his children and grandchildren. At the time of his death, Conrad's stock in Hilton was worth perhaps $500 million. But Conrad believed very strongly that inherited wealth destroys moral character and motivation. I happen to agree that it often does.

To me, it makes sense to put money in trust for your children, so they don't inherit millions of dollars when they turn twenty-one. But Conrad took that view to a ridiculous extreme. He left Barron a token number of shares of stock, and he left each of his grandchildren a piddling $10,000 each. Nearly all the rest of his wealth—specifically his 27 percent share of the Hilton Corporation—he left to the Conrad N. Hilton Foundation. He ordered most of the earnings from the stake to be used to support the charitable work of Catholic nuns in California.

The result was to make Barron just another high-level corporate manager who lacked the power of a major stockholder. Even with the stock options that he exercised over ten years as chief executive, Barron still owned only a tiny percentage of the company by 1985.

What Barron did was to enter into litigation, seeking control of the foundation's shares. His chances of winning the case, which had dragged on for years, were uncertain. For one thing, he had the sort of adversaries you want to avoid in a litigation: nuns and priests of the Catholic Church.

Conrad's will had specified that if for any reason the foundation was unable to accept his stock bequest, Barron had the right to purchase the stock at its market value as of 1979. Federal law prohibits charitable foundations and their affiliated parties from together owning more than 20 percent of a public company. Therefore, Barron could legitimately argue that he was entitled to purchase for himself the 7 percent of the foundation's shares that were in excess of the foundation's allowable 20 percent.

But Barron tried to take his claim much further. Basically, he tried to argue that for byzantine legal reasons he was entitled to buy out the foundation's entire stake. Moreover, by buying its stock for the 1979 price of 24⅝—at a time when the stock was trading around 72—in effect he'd be paying $170 million for $500 million worth of stock.

It's called a great deal. It may also be called trying to rewrite your father's will. My strong suspicion is that Barron knew his chances of winning the litigation were questionable. More to the point, if he couldn't get control of the stock, he was in a far weaker position to fend off Steve Wynn or any hostile takeover threat. Finally, so long as he held on to his Atlantic

City facility but remained unlicensable, he was also highly vulnerable to shareholder lawsuits.

I have no doubt how I would have reacted if I had been Barron Hilton. I would have fought Steve Wynn and his takeover threat, and I would also have fought for my license at the rehearing. I'm not saying I would also have won, but if I went down, it would have been kicking and screaming. I would have closed the hotel and let it rot. That's just my makeup. I fight when I feel I'm getting screwed, even if it's costly and difficult and highly risky.

But then, I wasn't running a public company, so I didn't have to worry constantly about Wall Street and shareholders and the next quarterly-earnings report. The only person I had to please was myself. In the end, I think, Barron decided that he just wasn't prepared to fight on two fronts at the same time—for licensing as well as for control of his company. And of the two, control of the company obviously came first.

Steve Wynn helped me in two ways. By pursuing a takeover, he put Barron on the defensive and kept him from focusing on his relicensing hearings. At the same time, the more Wynn's aggressive style offended Barron, the more likely it was that Barron would turn to me as a white knight.

It's not a role I'm accustomed to, but Wynn played right into my hand. Wynn grew up in his father's bingo parlor, the son of a compulsive gambler. Later he made the right friends in Las Vegas, managed to buy a small stake in the Golden Nugget Hotel, and eventually took over. His entire world has been Las

Vegas and Atlantic City and gaming. He's got a great act. He's a smooth talker, he's perfectly manicured, and he's invariably dressed to kill in $2,000 suits and $200 silk shirts. The problem with Wynn is that he tries too hard to look perfect and a lot of people are put off by him. Barron Hilton was one.

It's hard to imagine two people with more different styles. Barron is a member of what I call the Lucky Sperm Club. He was born wealthy and bred to be an aristocrat, and he is one of those guys who never had to prove anything to anyone. He doesn't try to impress with his style or his clothing or anything else. If Steve Wynn tries too hard, it might be said that Barron Hilton doesn't try hard enough.

Although Steve would probably never admit it, I'm convinced that he thought he was in a no-lose situation when he launched his takeover bid against Hilton. I believe Steve figured he'd end up buying Hilton's Atlantic City hotel, and quite possibly at a favorable price. Many people thought that the hotel was all Steve really wanted. There was even a certain logic to it. Under siege from all sides, Barron could kill two birds with one stone by dealing with Steve. He could say, "Look, I'll sell you my hotel if you'll agree to give up trying to get control of my company."

But Steve Wynn underestimated how much he'd become anathema to Barron. That's where I came in. One day after Wynn made his takeover bid, Barron Hilton became much more serious about negotiating with me.

My first offer to Hilton was $250 million. As big a

number as that is, I knew Barron wasn't going to sell for that price. He told me when we first met that he had $320 million invested in the facility. Selling out at any price was a horrible prospect for him, but reporting to shareholders that he'd taken a loss on the facility was out of the question. Within a couple of days, I raised my price to $320 million. There was no time to be cute, and no room to be tough in this negotiation. Either I bid the price, or I walked away.

At the time $320 million—even $250 million—represented by far the biggest gamble I'd ever taken in my life. Just a year earlier, I'd completed construction on the Boardwalk facility for less than $220 million. In that case Holiday financed the entire deal and guaranteed me against operating losses.

This time, the risk was entirely mine.

As soon as I decided to bid $320 million, I called John Torell, a good friend who is president of Manufacturers Hanover Trust. We'd already done a great deal of business together and on this occasion we had an amazingly short conversation. "John," I said, "I'm calling because I have an opportunity to buy the incredible Hilton facility in Atlantic City for three hundred and twenty million dollars. I'd like you to lend me the money, and I'm going to need it within a week." John asked me a couple of questions and after two minutes he said, "We have a deal." Just like that. It goes to show you the value of credibility. In return, I did something I'd never done before: I personally guaranteed the loan.

It was a deal based almost entirely on my gut. I made my bid without ever walking through the hotel.

Several of my people had taken a look, and I'd gotten to know a lot about the construction from contractors who'd worked on the facility. However, I felt it wouldn't be appropriate to show up myself in the middle of all the turmoil Hilton was going through. If I'd told my father the story, he would have said I'd lost my mind. I remember very well as a kid, accompanying my father to inspect buildings he was considering buying in Brooklyn. We might have been talking about a $100,000 or $200,000 purchase price, but our inspections were anything but casual. We'd spend hours in the building, checking every refrigerator and sink, looking over the boiler and the roof and the lobby.

Nor would my father have been alone in his horror. In past situations, opinion about deals I was considering had usually been split. In this case, nearly everyone I talked to opposed the deal.

I was having enough trouble on the Boardwalk with Holiday Inns, they pointed out. I had no management for this huge new facility scheduled to open in two months. I'd have to take on huge financial risk personally. I had only a verbal commitment from Manny Hanny, and it wasn't clear what conditions they might ultimately add when documents were drawn—or whether they'd have second thoughts about the whole deal. There was even considerable doubt that the market could support another major facility, particularly one that would have to carry a huge debt service at a time when interest rates were still quite high. Why, everyone said to me, would I even consider this deal?

For one reason only: I believed that, managed well, it had the potential to earn a ton of money.

Once we agreed on a price, we still had a thousand other smaller points to negotiate before we could sign a formal purchase-and-sale agreement. On April 14, 1985, we sat down in Jerry Schrager's offices at 101 Park Avenue, with the lawyers from both sides, to get the deal done.

Often, the easiest part of a deal is price. It's all the other points—in this case, guarantees about construction completion, responsibility for defects, size of deposit, allocation of expenses between contract and closing—that end up creating problems and killing deals. Hilton, from the very start, was taking a fairly hard line. Basically, they wanted to sell the hotel "as is," so that when the contracts were signed, they could walk away from Atlantic City with no further obligations. Barron, by this time, was almost rabid in his hatred of New Jersey and particularly Atlantic City. The sooner he could put this nightmare behind him, the happier he'd be.

The problem for me was that if I didn't win some guarantees about completion of construction, I risked getting killed later on. Say, for example, that it turned out there was a major defect in the plumbing, or the air-conditioning system, and I was forced to rip it out. In a building this size, a major repair could easily run to many millions of dollars.

Early on in the negotiations we seemed to be winning on the deal points that we cared about. But then, about midway through, the person in charge of Hilton's negotiations—Gregory Dillon, the executive vice president of the company—got a call from Barron Hilton, who was back in San Francisco. When Dillon returned to the table, the whole tenor of the negotiation suddenly changed. I can't say for certain, but it's my strong suspicion that Barron had decided he wanted out of the deal, in all likelihood because he'd gotten a last-minute offer for more money. It's even possible that the offer came from Steve Wynn and the Golden Nugget.

In any case, Dillon and the Hilton lawyers suddenly began to raise questions about deal points that we'd agreed on. I've been in a lot of negotiations, and I sensed immediately that they were trying to use these points as deal-breakers. If we couldn't agree on completion guarantees, for example, then they could walk away from the table without appearing to have welshed on the deal merely because they'd been offered a better price.

We reached something of an impasse. Greg Dillon made a suggestion. "We're not getting anywhere," he said, "so let's break this up and we'll come back tomorrow and continue." On the face of it, the suggestion made sense. It was early on Saturday morning. We'd been in the offices around-the-clock for nearly forty-eight hours and everyone was totally exhausted and nearly incoherent. But my fear was that if we put off the negotiations for a full day, the deal would never get done. As a compromise, I suggested we take a break for several hours and get back together about one in the afternoon. The Hilton people agreed, and we broke up.

At that point my lawyers made one more attempt to

convince me to let the deal die, gracefully. In particular, Jerry Schrager was concerned about the financing. Even at that point, we didn't have a formal, signed commitment letter from Manufacturers Hanover. But to me, a verbal commitment from John Torell was as good as a signed commitment. Jerry's point was that even if the commitment was firm, the guarantees I was being asked to make might make it hard for me to borrow money for other large deals.

It was a very strange situation. As I sat in Jerry's office, I wasn't sure who was more eager to break up the deal: my lawyers or theirs.

As it turned out, the Hilton team was more than two hours late in getting back, which only confirmed my suspicions. By the time they finally showed up, around three-thirty, I was convinced that the only way I'd get the deal done was to shame them into doing it. I stood up and began my pitch. How could they shake my hand and then not stand by the commitment? How could they negotiate for three days and then walk away? How could they force me to spend hundreds of thousands of dollars on lawyers and not follow through? It was a disgrace, I said. It was immoral, it was wrong, it was dishonorable.

My tone was more hurt than outraged or angry. I can be a screamer when I want to be, but in this case I felt screaming would only scare them off. Much of the deal had already been negotiated, and under the circumstances, unless I gave Hilton a good excuse, it would be hard psychologically for them to walk away. It's also possible, of course, that Hilton's hard line was all a pose—a way of trying to ensure that they closed the deal with as few contingencies as possible.

In the end, we reached a compromise. They would use their best efforts to ready the hotel for opening, and they'd agree to completion of a specific "punch list" of unfinished items. Also, they would allow me to hold back $5 million of the purchase price, subject to the facility's being delivered complete and in first-class condition, as defined in specific terms in the contract.

I assumed the construction was sound. If it turned out that I was wrong, and the defects I discovered ended up costing an additional $30 million, I believed Hilton would still be legally responsible. At 9:00 P.M. on April 27, 1985, we shook hands and signed a formal contract. I turned over a nonrefundable $20 million deposit, and we set our closing for sixty days later.

On May 1, I made my first visit to the facility I'd just purchased for $320 million. As soon as I walked in, I sensed I'd made a good decision. Much work remained to be done, but it was a spectacular-looking building. Immediately I began pushing all my people—very hard. Over the next six weeks we managed to accomplish what it had taken most other casinos as much as a year or more to do. We got our temporary certificate of occupancy, we finished the vast paperwork for our licensing, we hired 1,500 employees over and above those Hilton had hired, and we got the hotel and casino ready for opening.

We also settled on the name Trump's Castle. My

first choice had actually been Trump Palace, but then Caesars Palace filed for an injunction on the grounds that it had exclusive rights to the name Palace. I decided it just wasn't worth a battle. We needed to get marketing and advertising campaigns under way, and the last thing I wanted was to be forced to make a name change after we'd already spent millions promoting Trump Palace. Ironically, no sooner did I announce my intention to call the facility Trump's Castle than Holiday Inns filed their own suit to prevent me from using the name Trump at all on a competitive casino. Within weeks, however, the suit was thrown out.

Even before we opened Trump's Castle, I began discussions with several investment banking firms about floating a bond issue to replace my bank financing from Manufacturers Hanover. I wanted to take myself off the hook personally, even if it meant paying a higher interest rate to do so. The major problem with floating a bond issue was that Trump's Castle had no performance record by which anyone could calculate how much debt it could reasonably handle. Also, the Trump Organization had no track record running a casino, since we'd yet to manage one ourselves.

In short, anyone who bought Trump's Castle bonds was making a leap of faith. They were betting that we'd make the facility highly successful from the start. That was the only way we could meet a debt service in the range of $40 million a year. To put that in context, there were several existing casinos in town that couldn't come close to supporting that kind of debt service.

Somewhat to my surprise, several investment banking firms bid for the right to handle my offering. In return for a percentage of the total offering, they would guarantee to find buyers for the bonds at a specified price. Among the bidders was Drexel Burnham, which invented the concept of high-yield, junk-bond financing. But Bear Stearns, with whom I'd already done a lot of business, offered to raise $300 million, or nearly 95 percent of the total I needed. Alan Greenberg, the chairman, and Paul Hallingby, managing partner, were willing to bet big on me, and I liked that.

To attract buyers for a speculative offering like this one, you generally have to offer the inducement of a high yield. The bonds Bear Stearns prepared carried about the same yield as other casinos had offered on their own financings, but those casinos had track records and offered far stronger guarantees to buyers.

Bear Stearns did a fabulous job—I got a good deal, but so did the buyers. Anyone who bought the bonds is earning an exceptionally good return and the bonds are now selling at a premium.

The one thing I wanted to avoid above all was a repetition of the sort of problems we had from the beginning at the Boardwalk facility. Rather than hire an outside general manager, I decided to put my wife, Ivana, in charge. I'd studied Atlantic City long enough to be convinced that when it comes to running a casino, good management skills are as important as specific gaming experience. She proved me right.

By closing the deal with Hilton on June 15, we were able to take advantage of the high summer season. The next day, we opened—without a hitch—as Trump's Castle. People packed the casino and we did extraordinary business, way beyond our expectations. On our first day we earned gross gaming revenues of $728,000. For the slightly less than six months we were open during 1985, we grossed just over $131 million. That was better than all but three of our competitors, and far better than the Boardwalk facility had done for the same period under Harrah's.

The one difficulty that arose in the early months had to do with the clause in my contract with Hilton regarding delivery of the hotel in first-class condition. Under the contract, $5 million of my purchase price was held back pending completion of all work. As time went on, however, we discovered that there were numerous outstanding problems—with the cooling tower, the sewage system, the computer system, and the fire alarm, among others.

During the first six months we were open, my representatives and Hilton's quietly negotiated about exactly which defects Hilton was responsible for and which they were not. My people felt strongly that the items not satisfactorily completed ran to considerably more than $5 million. On the other hand, I was eager to resolve the matter amicably.

I liked Barron Hilton, I felt sorry about his experience in Atlantic City, and for months I was the first to defend him in any conversation. As a result, when the argument over who owed money to whom seemed to be getting nowhere, I decided to call Barron myself, in January 1986.

I got him on the phone and I said that since our disputes hadn't been resolved, perhaps we should sit down together and work out some reasonable settlement. Barron seemed delighted that I had called. He said that he would be in New York the following Monday or Tuesday and that he would call me then to set a date.

Instead, when I came into my office on Monday morning I was served with a lawsuit from Hilton, seeking immediate payment of the $5 million the contract authorized us to hold back. I couldn't believe it.

The first thing I did was to call Barron again. "I don't understand this," I said. "I've just been served with a lawsuit, even though you told me we'd sit down and work this out together this week." Barron totally stonewalled me. "I don't know anything about a suit," he said. He suggested that I call Greg Dillon, Hilton's executive vice president. Incredibly, Dillon took the same position: that he knew nothing about the suit. Not for one minute did I believe that both Barron Hilton and his top deputy would be ignorant of a major lawsuit filed by the company.

I recognize that lawsuits are sometimes inevitable, and I accept that as a reality of business. But when a person tells me he's going to sit down with me, I expect him to honor that commitment. If we still can't resolve the situation, that's another story. From that day on I stopped defending Barron Hilton to anyone.

I also immediately ordered my attorneys to file a counterclaim. On April 2, 1986, we did precisely that, listing ninety-four separate deficiencies in the Castle, along with our estimated cost of repair. The figure far exceeded the $5 million we'd been authorized to hold back. Both suits are still pending, and I believe that we'll ultimately be upheld.

But for that one sour note, the story of Trump's Castle has been almost entirely a positive one. Much of the credit has to go to Ivana. No detail escapes her. She has systematically hired the best people in Atlantic City at all levels—from croupiers to hosts to her top executives. She oversaw the decoration of the hotel's public spaces, which are now quite spectacular. The facility is always spotless, because she's meticulous even about that. And great management pays off. In 1986 we grossed $226 million, a record for first-year operations. We are projecting revenues of $310 million and a gross operating profit well in excess of $70 million.

It pays to trust your instincts.

10

LOW RENT, HIGH STAKES

The Showdown on Central Park South

S OMETIMES by losing a battle you find a new way to win the war. What you need, generally, is enough time and a little luck. I had both at 100 Central Park South.

This is a story about a group of tenants who fought very hard to keep me from tearing down the building they lived in and constructing a new one in its place. They succeeded. But by delaying me for several years during which real estate values soared, and by forcing me to totally change my original plans, they inadvertently helped me come up with a less expensive and more profitable project.

Ironically, the easiest part of the whole deal was buying the property. Early in 1981, Louise Sunshine, my executive vice president at the time, came in to say she'd heard there might be an opportunity to buy two adjoining buildings in a great location. The first was 100 Central Park South, a fourteen-story residential building on the corner of Central Park South and Avenue of the Americas. The other was the Barbizon-Plaza, a thirty-nine-story hotel which fronted on Central Park and wrapped around behind 100 Central Park South, so that the east side of the hotel faced Avenue of the Americas.

The buildings were owned by a syndicate that included Marshall Loeb of the Loeb banking family, the Lambert Brussels Corporation, and Henry Greenberg. By virtue of their location, the buildings represented one of the best pieces of real estate anywhere in the world. In addition to being on one of the city's widest and most elegant streets, the buildings looked out over Central Park.

The Barbizon-Plaza was a somewhat run-down middle-price hotel earning a modest profit at best. One hundred Central Park South was a building filled with rent-controlled and rent-stabilized apartments, meaning that the rent roll was barely sufficient to cover the operating costs of the building.

Precisely because of these disadvantages, I was able to negotiate a very favorable purchase price. It helped that the properties hadn't yet been put up for sale on the open market. As long as there were no other bidders, it was much easier for me to make a case that the buildings' problems decreased their value.

It probably also helped that the owners were a group of very wealthy men who had decided to sell not because they needed the money but because one of them was getting older and wanted to put his estate in order. I'm not permitted to say what I paid, but the sum wouldn't be enough today to buy a vacant lot one-third the size in a far less desirable part of Manhattan.

I barely looked at what the two buildings were earning. I was drawn to the real estate value, not the income. I was buying a great location at a modest price, and the way I looked at the deal, there was virtually no downside. Almost immediately I was able to get a mortgage for the buildings, which covered my purchase price. In the worst case, I felt, I could always turn around and sell at a profit. Even in bad times, there are buyers for first-class locations.

Another option was to do a modest renovation of the hotel and raise the rents on the ground-floor stores to market levels as their leases came up. In addition, as tenants in rent-controlled and rent-stabilized apartments passed away or moved out of 100 Central Park South, I could raise the rents on those apartments. Even by doing these relatively minor things, I could earn at least a modest return on my investment.

But then, "modest" isn't my favorite word. The way to derive the most value from the site, I believed, was to knock down both buildings and to construct in their place one huge, beautiful modern luxury condominium tower. That posed two problems. The first, which I recognized from the start, is that it's neither easy nor cheap to demolish a forty-four-story building such as the Barbizon. Still, I was certain that the prices we'd be able to get for new apartments in such a premium location would more than justify any added demolition costs.

The second problem, which I didn't fully understand until much later, is that it's almost impossible to legally vacate a building filled with rent-controlled and rent-stabilized apartments. I knew that some tenants were sure to resist moving, but I figured time was on my side. I could afford delay. I was prepared to be as patient—and as persistent—as I needed to be.

What I underestimated was how much the tenants stood to lose. I soon came to understand a simple axiom: the lower the rent, the bigger the apartment, and the better the location, the harder people will fight to keep what they have. It's no great hardship to consider moving if you're living in a mediocre apartment in a marginal neighborhood. Likewise, if you're paying market rent for a good apartment and you can find a comparable one at the same price, a small financial inducement will often prompt you to move.

But at 100 Central Park South, many tenants were fighting to protect the ultimate in New York real estate: beautiful apartments with high ceilings, fireplaces, and great views—at an unbeatable location. Most important, with rent control and rent stabilization, they were enjoying one of the great windfall subsidies in the free world. On the open market, their apartments would have rented for as much as ten times what they were paying. If I'd been a tenant at 100 Central Park South, I'd have led the fight against anyone who tried to get me to move.

Unfortunately, rent control is a disaster for all but the privileged minority who are protected by it. As much as any other single factor, rent control is responsible for the desperate housing crisis that has plagued New York City for the past twenty years.

Like a lot of failed government programs, rent control grew out of a decent idea that ended up achieving exactly the opposite of its intended effect. Rent control began as a temporary federal policy in 1943. The government froze rent on every apartment in America as a way to provide affordable housing for returning veterans. Having achieved that, the law was rescinded in 1948. But New York City adopted its own rent control law in 1962. Under the city statute, any dwelling built before 1947 was subject to rent control. In effect, the city created an inalienable right for five million New Yorkers—namely, low-price housing.

It sounds wonderful. The only problem was that the city had no intention of underwriting it. Instead, they forced landlords to subsidize tenants. The costs of fuel, labor, and maintenance rose steadily, but the city refused to let landlords raise their rents to keep pace with inflation, much less the market itself.

When landlords simply couldn't make ends meet anymore, they began abandoning their buildings. Between 1960 and 1976, approximately 300,000 housing units in New York were abandoned. The first apartments to go, either by abandonment or arson, were the ones in the worst neighborhoods. Apartments in these buildings had the lowest rents. Landlords therefore earned the smallest profit margins and were least able to absorb rising costs. The other victims were the poor tenants who had been living in these buildings. Whole neighborhoods in the South Bronx and Brooklyn turned into ghost towns. The city, in turn, lost hundreds of millions of dollars in real estate taxes that landlords stopped paying once they'd abandoned their buildings.

Perhaps the worst thing about rent control is that it stopped protecting the people who needed it the most. The best rent-controlled apartments have always been prized and difficult to come by, and people with power and money have always had an inside track on them. During the past year, an independent researcher and writer, William Tucker, has set out to document particularly egregious examples. He cites buildings such as one on Central Park West at 73rd Street. Magnificently designed, it has huge apartments, wonderful detailing, a beautiful double-height marble lobby, and, of course, gorgeous views. It's no surprise that people with money and taste would want to live there. Mia Farrow, for example, has ten rooms overlooking the park. She pays about $2,000 a month for an apartment that might rent for upward of $10,000 a month on the open market. Carly Simon, the singer and songwriter, lives in the same building and pays about $2,200 a month for her ten rooms overlooking the park.

Down the street, Tucker found that Suzanne Farrell of the New York City Ballet has a fourteen-room duplex near Lincoln Center, for which she pays under

$1,000 a month. William Vanden Heuvel, a very prominent attorney who served as ambassador to the United Nations under Jimmy Carter, pays less than $650 a month for a six-room apartment in a terrific building on East 72nd Street near Fifth Avenue. Alistair Cooke, the TV personality, pays about $1,100 for an eight-room apartment on Fifth Avenue. William Shawn, former editor of *The New Yorker*, lives in the same building and pays $1,000 a month for his eight rooms.

The most notorious example of all may be Ed Koch, the mayor of New York. Koch has a very nice three-room rent-controlled apartment with a terrace in a beautiful part of Greenwich Village. He pays $350 a month—perhaps one fifth what it's worth. The worst thing, though, is that Koch doesn't even live in his rent-controlled apartment. He lives in Gracie Mansion, the official residence of the mayor.

Unlike most developers, I don't advocate eliminating rent control. I just think there ought to be a means test for anyone living in a rent-controlled apartment. People below a certain income would be permitted to keep their apartments at their current rent. People with incomes above a certain sum would be given a choice between paying a proportionally higher rent for their apartments or moving somewhere else.

The situation at 100 Central Park South is a perfect illustration. Soon after I purchased the building, I did some research into the financial status of the tenants. What I discovered was fascinating but not surprising. There are three distinct groups. The first, who live in the largest apartments, overlooking the park, on the higher floors, are generally successful, wealthy, and in some cases quite prominent.

Fashion designer Arnold Scaasi, for example, has a six-room duplex facing the park, for which he is paying $985 a month—about what it costs to rent a one-room studio at market rates. Angelo DeSapio, another wealthy tenant and an architect of some eminence, has the entire seventh floor facing the park—nine rooms for a rent of $1,600 a month. Still another tenant owns a beautiful brownstone on 63rd Street worth at least $5 million but also has four combined apartments at 100 Central Park South, with fabulous views of the park from the thirteenth floor and a rent under $2,500 a month. All of these apartments could rent for many times what the current wealthy occupants are paying.

The second group of tenants are what I'd call the yuppies: younger professional people—stockbrokers and journalists and attorneys. While not necessarily millionaires, these people are certainly affluent. A good number of them occupy one- and two-bedroom apartments facing the park.

The third group of tenants live in smaller apartments with tiny kitchens and windows facing the court. Not surprisingly, these people are generally of modest means. A number of them are elderly, living on social security. Their rents are below market, but not nearly to the degree of their wealthier neighbors in the front apartments. A comparable studio in the neighborhood might rent for twice what most of these tenants are now paying.

The leader of the tenants, John Moore, was a man who didn't quite fit into any group. In his early forties, this gentleman came from a family of money and social standing. His grandfather was a major stockholder in Tiffany & Company before it was bought by Walter Hoving, but he himself had not been very successful. I've always been convinced that leading the tenants gave him a way to feel useful and important. Of course, he also had something very valuable to protect: a beautiful two-bedroom parkview apartment for which he paid a very modest rent.

Vacating the Barbizon-Plaza was easy. All I had to do was stop renting hotel rooms. Before I gave up that income, however, I wanted to vacate 100 Central Park South too. Unfortunately, I made a very critical mistake right at the start: I should have gotten involved myself. That's what I'd always done in the past, and that's what always worked for me. But frankly, convincing tenants to move wasn't the kind of work I relished. Instead, I decided to hire a company that specialized in relocating tenants. Citadel Management was recommended to me by several top executives at well-known companies who'd used the firm and vouched for its reputation. I wasn't looking for tough guys. This was a high-visibility location, and a lot of people were gunning for Donald Trump already. The last thing I needed was to create controversy.

My original plan was very straightforward. We'd let the tenants at 100 Central Park South know that we intended to eventually demolish the building, along with the Barbizon next door. Then we'd offer them help in finding suitable new apartments, as well as cash incentives to move.

Very quickly, however, the tenants got organized. They formed a tenants' association and decided to hire a law firm to represent them. Cost was no object. The wealthiest tenants had the most money to lose, and they were more than willing to underwrite any attorney fees. Several agreed to contribute as much as $8,000 a year to the cause. That was cheap, after all, compared with the $10,000 a month they might have to pay for a comparable apartment elsewhere.

The firm that the tenants chose had been somewhat successful representing tenants facing eviction. They made a better living than most landlord attorneys. Their approach was to resist eviction on every front and tie things up in court for as long as possible, perhaps hoping to make as big a settlement as possible with the landlord.

I felt confident that I had every legal right to vacate 100 Central Park South for the purpose of building a new and larger building in its place. To evict the tenants who lived in non–rent-controlled apartments, all I had to show was my plans to demolish the building and put up a new one in its place. To evict the tenants under rent control, I had to meet stricter standards but none that seemed insurmountable.

First, I had to demonstrate that my new building would provide at least 20 percent more housing units than the old one. That was easy enough, since it was obviously in my interest financially to put up a bigger building. Second, I had to prove that the old building was earning a profit, after expenses, of less than 8.5 percent of its assessed value. By virtue of rent control, the assessment was a paltry $1.5 million, meaning the city got almost no taxes from the building. And although I wasn't permitted to include my debt service as part of my expenses, the building still didn't come close to earning an 8.5 percent margin. If my debt service was included, I was actually losing a substantial amount of money. Either way, if the city ruled purely on the merits, I was convinced they'd have to approve our demolition application and order any remaining tenants out.

When Citadel took over management of the building early in 1981, I gave them two instructions: the first was to try to find new apartments for as many tenants as possible; the second was to continue to provide all essential services to the tenants.

It happens to be very easy to vacate a building if, like so many landlords, you don't mind being a bad guy. When these landlords buy buildings they intend to vacate, they use corporate names that are difficult to trace. Then they hire thugs to come in with sledge-hammers and smash up the boiler, rip out the stairways, and create floods by cutting holes in pipes. They import truckloads of junkies, prostitutes, and thieves and move them into vacant apartments to terrorize holdout tenants.

That's what I call harassment. I wouldn't have done that sort of thing for moral reasons, nor would I have done it for practical reasons. I buy buildings in my own name, and I have a reputation to uphold.

The tenants at 100 Central Park South got an abundance of heat and plenty of hot water. I made sure to deal with the building's outstanding violations, however modest, even though you'll find dozens of violations in elegant buildings all over the Upper East Side. The last thing I wanted was to give these tenants legitimate grounds for opposing me.

What I didn't do was run 100 Central Park South as if it were a white-glove Park Avenue building. The rent roll, which barely covered my basic expenses, simply couldn't support luxuries. Nor did tenants paying tiny below-market rents have any right to expect them. For example, when we took over, there was a telephone in the lobby—not a pay telephone but a free telephone. It was supposed to be for emergencies. It turned out that some tenants were using the phone to call their friends in Gstaad and St. Moritz.

The doormen were taken out of their fancy uniforms. That saved a small fortune in dry-cleaning bills. To ensure security, the doormen stopped leaving the door to meet tenants halfway down the street to carry their packages. High-wattage lights in the hallways were replaced with lower-wattage bulbs, because, as any cost-conscious landlord will tell you, that alone saves many thousand dollars a year in electric bills.

What we didn't anticipate was that the tenants would try to use the fact that we were running the building more efficiently as evidence that we were harassing them and making their lives intolerable. In a way it was fitting. We were talking about at least some people, after all, for whom hardship is not being able to get a table on thirty minutes' notice at Le Cirque. If there's one thing I've learned about the rich, it's that they have a very low threshold for even the mildest discomfort.

The tenants even figured out a way to turn our relocation offer into evidence of harassment. We were, they claimed, using "persistent and intense pressure" to get people to move. In reality, each tenant was approached with an offer of help in relocation. If our offer was turned down—which was usually the case, since the tenants had agreed to oppose us on everything—that was the end of it. Some tenants even told us that they had been warned by the tenants' committee not to consider our offer. The irony is that we might well have been able to offer better alternatives to the tenants who lived in the less-desirable apartments.

The one thing I can't deny is that claiming harassment was a clever tactic. Harassment is a virtual buzzword in New York. It prompts instant images of vicious landlords and victimized tenants. If the tenants' attorney could somehow convince a sympathetic jury—probably tenants themselves—that a harassment case had merit, we'd automatically be denied our demolition application. The tenants of 100 Central Park South wouldn't have to move. In the meantime, they could generate plenty of negative press about me merely by alleging that I was harassing them. The fact that I denied the charges would only make it a juicier story.

Unfortunately, we made several moves that played

right into the tenants' hands. For example, we decided
to bring eviction proceedings against any tenant at 100
Central Park South who was in significant arrears on
his rent, or who wasn't using the apartment as a
primary residence, as required by law. Landlords all
over the city bring these proceedings every day. They
are perfectly legitimate, and we won in several instances.

Stupidly, we also brought several cases that were
flawed. In one, for example, we claimed that a tenant
hadn't paid his rent. It turned out he had his canceled
check as evidence, and the payment simply hadn't
been recorded in Citadel's books. When they realized
the error, they told the tenant they'd drop the action if
he produced the check. By then, however, the tenants'
lawyer saw a perfect opportunity to further demonstrate their case. The tenant refused to produce the
check, and obviously we lost this case in court. In
another situation, we failed to give a tenant sufficient
legal notice of an impending eviction proceeding. Our
case was legitimate, but the court ruled that we should
have known the law had been changed recently to
require longer notice.

Another mistake was tinning-up the windows of
vacant apartments. It happens to be exactly what the
city does with its own vacant apartments all over the
city to protect them from vandalism. But then the city
doesn't own buildings on Central Park South. It would
have been smarter—and it would have saved us a lot
of trouble—if we'd come up with a nicer way to deal
with the windows from the start.

Nothing generated as much controversy as my offer

to provide housing for the homeless at 100 Central Park South. By the summer of 1982—about a year after I took over the building—the problem of the homeless in New York was beginning to get a lot of attention. One morning, after passing several homeless people sleeping on benches in Central Park, I got an idea.

I had more than a dozen vacant apartments at 100 Central Park South. Because I still planned to demolish the building, I had no intention of filling the apartments with permanent tenants. Why not, I thought, offer them to the city for use by the homeless, on a temporary basis? I'm not going to pretend that it bothered me to imagine the very wealthy tenants of 100 Central Park South having to live alongside people less fortunate than themselves for a while. At the same time, I genuinely felt it was a shame not to make use of a few vacant apartments when the streets were filled with homeless people.

Almost immediately, the columnists and editorial writers criticized my offer. City officials, sensing a potential controversy, told me "No, thanks." It didn't help make my offer seem sincere when one columnist wrote a story saying that I'd refused a subsequent plea by a group representing Polish refugees seeking to use the apartments. In fact, by then I'd had second thoughts about the whole concept. My attorneys had researched the situation and determined that if I permitted anyone to move into the apartments—even on a temporary basis—I'd have a very hard time ever getting them out legally. That was all I needed.

Saying so publicly, however, might just have made a bad situation worse. Instead, I said nothing, which wasn't much better. It was not one of my best experiences with the media, but it taught me something. You don't act on an impulse—even a charitable one—unless you've considered the downside.

Early in 1984, a group of tenants went to the state and officially filed charges of harassment. Virtually all of the complaints were trivial, but I told my people to take care of every one nonetheless. Even that wasn't enough. In January 1985, the state agreed to consider the tenants' charges of harassment. Obviously, we'd made our share of mistakes early on, but none had caused anyone real hardship. In my view, the tenants' tactics were a clever form of reverse harassment. They knew there had been no real harassment. The case instead was a ploy to hold on to their bargain apartments—or at the very least to exact a rich settlement from me.

The tenants' committee orchestrated the campaign. Nearly fifty tenants were part of the harassment action, and all of them submitted identical boilerplate lists of complaints. They even ended their letters with the same phrase: "Donald Trump is a modern-day Scrooge." When my attorneys did a little further checking, they found out something very interesting. Several of the wealthier tenants had been submitting the same sort of complaints to city agencies for the past ten, twenty, and even thirty years, invariably accompanied by a request for a reduction in rent. The tenants of 100 Central Park South were world experts in the art of living very high for very little.

What the tenants didn't count on is that I'm not one of those landlords who roll over to avoid bad publicity or save a few bucks—particularly when I think the charges are unfair. Fighting back might run up my legal bills and even make me rethink my strategy. But the one thing I wasn't about to do was allow myself to be blackmailed into a ridiculous settlement.

A couple of things did go my way. The most important was the value of New York real estate. It had risen steadily every year since 1974, but in early 1981, about the time I bought the two buildings on Central Park South, it finally took a pause. Over the next two years, during which I'd originally hoped to get my new building finished, the market actually declined. A lot of people thought the big boom was over.

In 1984, however, the market picked up again strongly. The economics were staggering. In the fall of 1981, the average price per room for a cooperative reached as high as $93,000. By early 1983, it dropped as low as $67,000. But by January 1985—when my confrontation with the tenants was reaching a head—the average price per room had jumped up to $124,000. In short, while the tenants were doing all they could to delay me, New York real estate was nearly doubling in value.

Even by building only on the Barbizon site—which I'd decided was the easiest solution—I'd earn more than if I'd developed the entire site two years earlier. In addition, we now had numerous vacant apartments at 100 Central Park South, and with time the number could only rise. The law permitted us to rent some vacant apartments at market rates. In effect, I was sitting on gold.

The other thing that happened during this period is that architectural tastes and trends began to shift. At the time I purchased the buildings on Central Park South, the style in skyscrapers was still very much the sleek, highly modern glass tower. Trump Tower was perhaps the ultimate example. Because that design was so well received and so successful, it seemed to me only logical to design a similarly sleek modern building on the Central Park South site.

By 1984, however, I sensed a new wave in architecture was setting in—and it was the wave of the old. The people who buy top-line apartments in New York tend to be extremely fashion-conscious, in architecture as in everything else. I'm a practical man. If an older look is what people want, that's what I'm going to provide. I'm not interested in buildings that don't sell. Early in 1985, I commissioned an architect to design a new building for the Barbizon-Plaza site—but one that incorporated older, classical elements compatible with 100 Central Park South.

In truth, my heart wasn't totally in it. I'd never been a big fan of postmodernism, the architectural movement that first mixed classical elements with modern design. To me, it often represents the worst of both worlds. The materials and the craftsmanship are rarely first-class because most builders won't pay what that requires, and the classical elements in postmodern designs almost always look imitative. At the same time, these elements interfere with the sleek look of the best modern design.

When my architect showed up with his model for an older-looking building on the Barbizon site, the design was not the first thing that caught my eye. The new building, I noticed, was much smaller than the one it was intended to replace. What, I asked the architect, was this all about?

"It's the zoning," he explained. "When the Barbizon was built, there were no restrictions on size. Now that the zoning is so much stricter, it's no longer permissible to build such a large building on that site."

"Do you mean," I said, "that if I totally gut and rebuild the inside, and leave only the façade and the steel frame intact, that is okay? But if I tear down the old building I have to replace it with a much smaller and less dramatic new one?"

And he said, "Yes, Mr. Trump, that is correct."

"If that's the case," I said, "then why should we knock down an old building to build a new one that will be less than half the size, won't look nearly as good as the old one, and will cost a lot more?"

"It's simple, Mr. Trump," he said. "The reason is that the windows in the Barbizon are much too small for a luxury residential building."

The solution was obvious: leave the building intact, but cut out bigger openings and enlarge the windows.

Coincidentally, my own tastes were changing. I was beginning to appreciate the detailing and elegance of certain great older buildings. Among them were the two buildings I owned on Central Park South. I also began to realize how much a part of the Central Park South skyline these buildings were.

Our preliminary estimate for ripping down the Barbizon and putting up a new structure in its place was $250 million. When we costed out the job of gutting and rebuilding the interior and enlarging all the windows, we came up with an estimate of $100 million for the entire job. The cost of trying to replicate my favorite feature of the Barbizon—the magnificent stone crown at its top—was $10 million alone. Even at that, it would never have matched the original. Renovating wasn't only cost effective, it was also a better design decision.

One last factor helped turn the whole deal around. For several years, I'd been trying to purchase the St. Moritz Hotel, directly across the street from 100 Central Park South. The sellers were Harry Helmsley and Lawrence Wien, two of the greatest real estate men ever. The problem had always been cost. They wanted a huge price for the hotel, which I believed was more than its earnings justified. Several times they made deals with other buyers, presumably for what they were seeking, only to have the agreements unravel before closing. Time and again I've seen that happen with people who offer a top price for a property. Their eyes prove bigger than their pocketbooks, and they end up backing out.

After watching this process repeat itself several times, I called Harry Helmsley and said, "I'd very much like to buy the St. Moritz, and in my case you know the deal will go through, but I don't want to pay the price you have in mind." And he said, "Well, what you're offering is too low." We negotiated back and forth, and finally we settled on a price that I think was fair, based on the hotel's earnings.

But I had an ace in the hole: the 1,400-room Barbizon-Plaza one door up the street. I hadn't told anyone, but my plan was to close down the Barbizon as soon as I purchased the St. Moritz. The logic was simple. When I closed the Barbizon, I could move Charles Frowenfeld, a great hotel manager, and all of his best people over to the St. Moritz. In addition, many of the Barbizon's customers would inevitably follow, since the St. Moritz was the only other moderate-price hotel on Central Park South. While I'd obviously lose some customers when I closed down the Barbizon, I'd pick up a lot of them at the St. Moritz. At the very least, I figured, occupancy and revenues at the St. Moritz would increase by 25 percent virtually overnight.

The banks apparently agreed. When I went seeking financing for the purchase, I was able to get an immediate commitment for $6 million more than my purchase price. In short, I was able to buy the St. Moritz without putting up any money at all—and I ended up with $6 million to put in my pocket. When we got to closing, Harry Helmsley was leafing through the papers and he noticed the size of my mortgage. He didn't look thrilled. But the sale was also a great deal for Harry and Larry. After all, they'd paid practically nothing to purchase the hotel years earlier.

I took over the St. Moritz in September 1985 and closed the Barbizon soon after. During the first year, business at the St. Moritz increased by 31 percent, or slightly more than I'd predicted. But by virtue of more efficient management, the margin of profit nearly quadrupled.

The one remaining issue I faced was the harassment suit at 100 Central Park South. Because I no longer intended to vacate and raze the building, a harassment finding no longer threatened my plans. Still, several of my lawyers urged me to settle the case purely to resolve an unpleasant situation. Specifically, they suggested I work out a deal under which the tenants would drop their harassment suit in return for my selling them the building outright for $10 million.

On its face, the deal wasn't a bad one for me. Based on my original purchase price, I stood to earn a very substantial profit by selling 100 Central Park South for $10 million. But in the end I said no. Temperamentally, I just couldn't accept the idea that the tenants were using harassment charges as a lever against me so that they could buy a building for less than market value. This is where the tenants and their lawyers caused themselves the loss of a tremendous windfall. Today in New York almost everyone wants to buy their apartments.

Meanwhile the harassment case stalled in the courts. A state supreme court judge ruled in August 1985 that there was no clear evidence that harassment had occurred. In December 1986, the appellate division of the state supreme court unanimously upheld the lower court's ruling.

The lawyers kept talking settlement. Finally, late in 1986, nearly all the tenants agreed to drop any further claims against me. Since I no longer planned to demolish the building anyway, I agreed to drop all eviction proceedings and to give them new leases on their apartments. I also agreed to excuse from three months' rent every tenant who was party to the agreement, and in return, all tenants who'd been withholding rent—in some cases for as long as a year—agreed to pay up. The total figure exceeded $150,000.

While the state dropped its case, the city insisted that it intended to continue pursuing the harassment case against me. Even John Moore, the leader of the tenants' group, was surprised. For the city to push the case, he said to a reporter, "is like beating the horse after the horse has come back to the barn." The real victims were the taxpayers. The city was choosing to spend money and manpower on a nonissue that had been resolved—at a time when many important issues had not. It is my opinion that this case continues purely because I beat the hell out of Ed Koch on the Trump Tower tax abatement and embarrassed him with Wollman Rink.

In the meantime, I renamed the Barbizon-Plaza Trump Parc, and began my renovation. One of the first things I did was to hire a company called Holes, Inc. Talk about surreal specialization. These people did nothing but cut holes for a living. Fortunately, they did it very well. In a matter of weeks, they'd turned the Barbizon's tiny windows into huge picture-window openings. Those openings alone were immensely valuable, because a great view is worth a small fortune.

In a market about to be flooded with new buildings,

we had something unique to offer: the best of the old and the new. The detail and ornamentation of the building's exterior remained, including the crown. So did features such as the twelve-foot ceilings in the apartments, which no developer would even consider in a new building, because the cost is simply too great. At the same time, the new construction gave the building several advantages over most older ones: new plumbing, smooth walls, modern wiring, fast elevators—and, of course, huge Thermopane windows.

The building is scheduled to be completed in the fall of 1987, but we put the apartments on the market in November 1986. Within eight months, we'd sold 80 percent—nearly 270 apartments. One individual bought seven apartments, for a total of $20 million. When the building sells out—in all likelihood before a single person has moved in—we'll have grossed in excess of $240 million. And that's before I do anything with 100 Central Park South and the stores along the street.

All's well that ends well. The tenants at 100 Central Park South kept their apartments, Central Park South retained two of its landmark buildings, and the city will soon be earning far greater taxes from the property than ever before. As for me, I'll ultimately earn a profit of more than $100 million on a deal that many people thought would turn out to be a total loser. And it was largely because the tenants managed to delay me.

11

LONG SHOT

The Spring and Fall of the USFL

ALL MY LIFE I've believed in paying for the best. But when it came to the United States Football League, I decided to go a different route entirely.

By the time I bought the New Jersey Generals in the fall of 1983, the league was already failing badly. It had lost nearly $30 million. The Generals alone, under the ownership of an Oklahoma oilman named J. Walter Duncan, had lost more than $2 million, not to mention nearly every game they'd played. In real estate terms, I was buying the South Bronx instead of Fifth Avenue and 57th Street.

But I didn't look at the Generals as a typical deal. I viewed it instead as a long shot, a lark that I could afford to take. I've always been a football fan. I love sports, and having my own team seemed the realization of a great fantasy. I also liked the idea of taking on the NFL, a smug, self-satisfied monopoly that I believed was highly vulnerable to an aggressive competitor.

As long shots go, I liked the odds on the USFL. My initial investment was relatively small, and the potential rewards were quite great. For less than $6 million, contingent on the league's continuing—compared with the $70 million an NFL franchise might cost—I was able to purchase a professional football team in one of the greatest areas in the world. If I could help turn the team and the league around, I stood to earn back many times my initial investment. At the very least, I would have a lot of fun trying.

The main problems with the USFL seemed fairly clear-cut and not all that difficult to remedy. The first was that the league was playing its games in the spring. Sports have their seasons, and fans like their football in the fall. The television networks, which essentially underwrite professional sports, won't pay large sums for the rights to televise spring football. At the time I bought the Generals, ABC was paying $1 million a year for exclusive network rights to the USFL spring schedule. Meanwhile, the three networks together were paying a staggering $359 million a year for rights to the NFL fall games. The first thing the USFL had to do was move to the fall.

The second challenge was to build a first-class product. To me, that meant spending whatever money it took to sign top players, promote our teams, and create the sort of excitement that would make us a legitimate competitor for the NFL's fans and TV dollars.

Two leagues had been launched previously in competition with the NFL, and the outcome in each case was highly instructive. The American Football League was formed in 1962 by eight very wealthy entrepreneurial men. They signed top players and absorbed substantial losses in the service of building the league's credibility during the early years. By 1966, the AFL had signed away dozens of the NFL's best players and was widely seen as the more exciting of the two leagues. With the AFL raids escalating, NFL commissioner Pete Rozelle surrendered. He suggested a merger of the two leagues, and today those original AFL teams are among the NFL's most successful franchises. But even without a merger, the AFL would have prospered.

The other venture that tried to compete with the NFL was the World Football League. It was launched in 1973, but by men of much less wealth and more limited vision. In contrast to their AFL counterparts, the WFL owners signed very few name players, placed their franchises in smaller cities, and failed to attract any kind of television contract. Within two years, the WFL was bankrupt. Its founders didn't lose a fortune—but only because they didn't invest a fortune.

I foresaw two possible outcomes if we moved the USFL to the fall and began to build quality teams, and both of them were potentially good. The first was that at least one of the three networks would offer us a substantial fall television contract, which would help us continue to build an even stronger league fully competitive with the NFL. The second was that the three networks, all fearful of alienating the monopoly NFL, would refuse to give us a fall television contract, no matter how strong a product we had to offer. In that case, I believed, we'd have strong grounds for an antitrust case against the NFL.

If we went the latter route, obviously we could lose, and then our league would be dead. But I believed the more likely outcome was some sort of victory. If the suit went to a jury and we were awarded reasonable damages—particularly given the fact that any damage award is trebled in an antitrust case—we'd have the financial base we needed. Another possibility was that the NFL, anticipating a costly and humiliating court defeat, would offer some sort of settlement, much as they'd done twenty years earlier with the AFL.

I made no secret of my views. Two years later, the NFL would try to claim in court that my plan to move our league's season to the fall was somehow secret and sinister. In fact, within days of taking over the Generals, I told any reporter who called me exactly how I felt. Then, on October 18, 1983, a month after purchasing the Generals, I attended my first owners meeting in Houston, Texas. I wasn't shy there, either.

When my turn came to address my fellow owners, I stood up and explained that I hadn't bought into the USFL to be a minor-league owner playing in the off-season of spring. I pointed out that the greatest number of fans, and by far the biggest pool of network television dollars, were concentrated in the fall. I reminded my fellow owners that because the NFL had just gone through a long, bitter players' strike the past fall, many fans were feeling restless and alienated. And finally, I argued that we had a chance to put the NFL even further on the defensive by moving aggressively to sign top NFL players whose contracts were coming up, as well as the best graduating college players.

If there was a single key miscalculation I made with the USFL, it was evaluating the strength of my fellow owners. In any partnership, you're only as strong as your weakest link. Several of my fellow USFL owners were strong as hell financially and psychologically. Among them were Michigan Panthers owner Al Taubman and Philadelphia Stars owner Myles Tanenbaum, both of whom, coincidentally, had made their personal fortunes building shopping centers, as well as Memphis Showboats owner Billy Dunavaut and Jacksonville Bulls owner Fred Bullard.

Unfortunately, I quickly discovered that a number of USFL owners lacked the financial resources and the competitive vision to build the sort of top-quality league necessary to defeat the NFL. They shuddered at the prospect of any direct confrontation with the NFL, they were quite content to play in obscurity in the spring, and they spent much more time thinking about ways to keep their costs down than about how to build the league up.

My most immediate priority was the team I'd just

purchased. The New Jersey Generals were a disaster. They'd just come off a season in which they'd won only four games and lost fourteen. The team had one great athlete and superstar, Herschel Walker, the Heisman Trophy running back from Georgia, but even Herschel had yet to play near his potential. Meanwhile, although the Generals had just completed a full season of playing professional football across the river from the media capital of the world, they had attracted virtually no press attention and very few fans.

The best way to turn that around was to turn the Generals around. Fans like winners. They come to watch stars—great, exciting players who do great, exciting things. Herschel was obviously one, but in football, the team rises or falls on the quarterback. Nothing helped promote the AFL—and the New York Jets—as much as the signing of a University of Alabama quarterback named Joe Namath, for a then-unprecedented $400,000 a year. Namath eventually led the Jets and the AFL to their first Superbowl victory. But even before that, he earned his salary simply because he became the AFL's most colorful, charismatic drawing card.

The first player I went after was Brian Sipe, the quarterback for the Cleveland Browns. Sipe had been the NFL's most valuable player a couple of seasons earlier, and he was a bona fide superstar. He was also in the option year of his contract, meaning that he'd be available in a matter of months. Getting Sipe was a chance to help the Generals and the USFL and simultaneously to hurt the NFL. The negotiations proved to be long and difficult, but on December 27, 1983, I held a press conference to announce we'd signed Sipe to a long-term $800,000-a-year contract with the Generals.

By the time we got Sipe, we'd already lured away several other top NFL players. The first was Gary Barbaro, an All-Pro free safety from the Kansas City Chiefs, whom we signed on November 5. Signing Barbaro had a side benefit: it showed other NFL players that we were serious about paying top dollar to build a top team. On November 28 we signed Kerry Justin, who'd been a starting cornerback for the Seattle Seahawks. In December we signed a pair of linebackers from the Super Bowl–champion San Francisco Forty-niners, Willie Harper and Bobby Leopold. To protect Sipe, we signed a veteran offensive guard from Cincinnati named Dave Lapham.

Another negotiation that got some attention during that period was the one I conducted with Don Shula, coach of the Miami Dolphins. Shula was one of the most successful coaches in NFL history, but he was also vastly underpaid. I immediately offered Shula far more than he'd been earning. I was willing to meet most of his demands, but when he threw in a request for an apartment in Trump Tower, I drew the line. I can afford to buy football teams in part because I don't give away apartments. Still, the negotiation ended up helping Shula: it forced the Dolphins to renegotiate his contract at a far higher salary, which he certainly deserved.

We got the most attention of all for signing Lawrence

Taylor, the All-Pro linebacker for the New York Giants and perhaps the best all-around player in the NFL. On December 31, 1983, we announced that Taylor had signed a four-year contract with the Generals, for a total of $3.25 million. The catch was that it wouldn't take effect until 1988, when his contract with the Giants expired. In a way, that was even better than getting him immediately. By signing a player of Taylor's stature to a "futures" contract, we were serving notice on the NFL that none of their players—not even those under multiyear contracts—were beyond our reach.

As it turned out, when Taylor's deal was announced the Giants went nuts. Two weeks later, on January 17, 1984, they offered him a six-year $6.55 million extension of his contract. In effect, I forced the Giants to increase Taylor's salary by $3 million just to prevent him from departing three years down the road. Then, in return for my letting Taylor out of his Generals contract, the Giants agreed to pay me a penalty fee of $750,000.

My aggressiveness in signing NFL players also seemed to inspire other USFL owners. The second USFL draft was held on January 4, 1984. The Pittsburgh franchise drafted Heisman Trophy–winner Mike Rozier from Nebraska and signed him five days later. The team's season-ticket sales immediately jumped from 6,000 to 20,000. Brigham Young quarterback Steve Young, a college superstar, signed a multimillion-dollar contract with the USFL's Los Angeles Express. Don Klosterman, the president of the LA Express, also managed to sign fourteen other draft picks, every one of whom was a good NFL prospect. Altogether, USFL teams signed nearly half of the top college players we went after. *Sports Illustrated* posed the obvious question in an article about the success of our draft: "How many more players like Rozier and Young can the NFL afford to lose?"

When our owners met in New Orleans on January 17, I pushed again to move our season to the fall. Given our success in luring NFL players and signing top college prospects, the time couldn't have been better. I suggested a fall vote right then and there, but the reluctant owners managed to vote through a compromise instead: appointing a long-range planning committee to study the spring-fall question. To me, committees are what insecure people create in order to put off making hard decisions. But at least I'd gotten the fall question on the table as a serious issue. I was made a member of the new committee and I was confident I'd ultimately persuade a majority of owners that the fall was our best hope.

Meanwhile, the NFL was beginning to run scared. The best evidence was a meeting the league held in Cambridge, Massachusetts, in February 1984 to discuss its future—and specifically the threat of the USFL. The main seminar—which we didn't learn about until much later—was conducted by a highly respected Harvard Business School professor named Michael Porter, who had prepared a forty-seven-page document entitled "The USFL vs. the NFL." Some sixty-five NFL executives attended his presentation, among them Jack Donlan, executive director of the

NFL management council, as well as numerous team owners.

Porter bluntly outlined a multipart plan for declaring total war on our league, by employing numerous anticompetitive strategies. His two-and-a-half-hour presentation was divided into sections such as "Offensive Strategies," "Guerrilla Warfare" and "The Art of War—China 500 B.C." Porter's suggestions included trying to "dissuade" ABC from continuing even its spring television contract with the USFL; encouraging USFL players to unionize in order to drive up our costs; and attempting to co-opt the most powerful and influential USFL owners by offering them NFL franchises.

As we launched our second season in the spring of 1984, we weren't yet aware of the NFL's secret campaign to destroy us, but we were probably feeling its effects. Several of our more vulnerable owners—most particularly those in Chicago, Washington, San Antonio, and Oklahoma—had begun to experience severe financial problems. The danger to the league was less losing a couple of franchises than having our credibility damaged. As long as we had problems, it was difficult to get the press to focus on our stronger teams. Instead, sportswriters wrote about declining attendance in the weaker cities, and the personal financial problems some owners were having.

Meanwhile, as I feared, the long-range-planning study dragged on. A majority of owners had voted to hire an outside consultant, McKinsey and Company, to conduct the study. McKinsey is probably the best in its business, but I like consultants even less than I like committees. When it comes to making a smart decision, the most distinguished planning committee working with the highest-priced consultants doesn't hold a candle to a group of guys with a reasonable amount of common sense and their own money on the line.

McKinsey's study took three months and cost a princely $600,000. Finally, on the morning of August 22, 1984, McKinsey executive Sharon Patrick presented her conclusions to the USFL owners, who had gathered in Chicago. The league's best hope, she told us, was to continue to play in the spring, to limit expenditures severely, and perhaps to consider a move to the fall somewhere down the line. Among other things, she reported that a majority of fans who'd been surveyed in a poll wanted the USFL to stay in the spring. You can probably guess how much stock I put in polls.

The reality was that we just couldn't afford to adopt the McKinsey conclusions. Even if we cut our losses in the spring, there was no foreseeable chance of making a profit, and a lot of our weaker owners couldn't afford to lose another dime. We needed to take radical action—and that's what I stood up and said. Within two hours of Patrick's presentation, I managed to get the issue of moving to the fall put to a vote. It passed by more than the required two-thirds majority. That same afternoon we announced the decision, to take effect following one last spring season.

The other thing we began to discuss at the meeting was bringing an antitrust suit against the NFL. Specifically, we authorized our commissioner, Chet Simmons, to send NFL commissioner Pete Rozelle a letter putting the NFL on notice. Simmons stated our views gently: "The position of the USFL as a new sports enterprise, and the market position of the NFL, make it essential to the survival of the USFL that the NFL and the NFL owners operate within the bounds of the laws and regulations which govern the conduct of a business having a dominant market position." Put more bluntly, our message was this: If you try to hurt us, we'll sue you.

By October, it was clear that something had changed dramatically in the tenor of our discussions with CBS and NBC. So long as we were just considering a move to the fall, both networks seemed interested in discussing a deal. No sooner did we announce our move, however, than they both backed off totally. It was obvious to me that the NFL was putting enormous pressure on the networks not to do business with us in the fall—particularly on ABC, with whom we already had a contract for the spring.

Pete Rozelle later testified that he'd never even discussed the issue with Roone Arledge, the head of ABC Sports. To me, that was preposterous. Rozelle and Arledge are longtime colleagues and good friends. Would anyone seriously believe that Rozelle, highly concerned about the implications of the USFL's move to the fall, wouldn't make his views known to his friend Arledge? And is it really possible that Arledge, a man who made millions of dollars for ABC by inventing *NFL Monday Night Football*, wouldn't be highly concerned with keeping Rozelle happy?

The irony is that all three networks—not just ABC but NBC and CBS as well—were actually losing money on NFL games. After total rights fees in excess of $350 million a year, the networks, by their own estimates, lost many millions televising games during 1985.

Even so, no network wanted to risk alienating the NFL. Football is the prestige TV sport, and in order to remain competitive with one another, the three networks were resigned to carrying the NFL as a loss leader. As for the USFL, we were left with no option. On October 17, 1984, we filed an antitrust suit in the southern district court of New York. Specifically, we asked that the NFL be limited to contracts with no more than two of the networks, and that we be awarded damages of $1.32 billion.

In the meantime, we had a more immediate problem: staying alive.

On January 3, 1985, the USFL held its third draft of college seniors. While the Generals had improved greatly, to 9–5, and averaged more than 40,000 fans a game, other teams were falling more deeply into the red. We very much needed a shot in the arm.

My own solution was to go after the best and most exciting college senior. There was little doubt who that was. Doug Flutie of Boston College was a lock to win the Heisman Trophy. In his final game, playing against the University of Miami on national television, Flutie capped his career by throwing a last-second fifty-yard bomb for a touchdown, giving Boston College a 47–45 victory. Very quickly, the pass became one of those instant-replay classics, transforming Flutie into an overnight sports legend. I must have seen the pass at least two dozen times on various newscasts and sports shows.

I also liked the fact that Flutie had great media potential. He was good-looking, well-spoken, and gutsy—the sort of guy the press loves to write about. There were two minor problems. One was that the Generals already had a very talented quarterback named Brian Sipe. The other was that Doug Flutie stood just five feet ten and weighed only 170 pounds. A number of scouts were skeptical that he could make it in the pros, where virtually every defensive lineman is six feet six and weighs at least 260 pounds.

In the end, I went with my instincts. Brian Sipe was a proven star, but he was also thirty-five years old, and his best years were probably behind him. Doug Flutie, on the other hand, had the potential to become the USFL's Joe Namath. In the worst case, he'd generate a lot of press, which would help the Generals' season-ticket sales and the image of the league generally. In the best case, he'd be a great player, too.

On February 5, we signed Flutie to a five-year contract at over $1 million a year—which I personally guaranteed. I don't like to do that, but a player of Flutie's stature wasn't about to risk signing with a financially shaky league unless he had some guarantees. If the league ever did go under, I figured, I could sell his contract to an NFL team.

On February 6, I solved the issue of Brian Sipe by trading him to the Jacksonville Bulls. I wasn't about to have a very highly paid quarterback sitting on the bench.

Flutie made his debut on February 24, in an away game against the Birmingham Stallions. He started slow but came on very strong and almost pulled out a victory by leading the Generals to three touchdowns in the fourth quarter. As for his box-office value, it was even greater than I expected. The game was televised by ABC and drew a 9 rating—nearly twice what we'd averaged the previous season.

Two other notable events occurred that first weekend of the season, both having to do with quarterbacks. One was the opening-game performance of a quarterback named Jim Kelly of the Houston Gamblers. Kelly threw for 574 yards and five touchdowns, proving that he was as good as any quarterback in either league. Unfortunately, the other quarterback news was not good. Brian Sipe, playing his first game for Jacksonville, suffered a separated shoulder, which seemed almost certain to end his season—and perhaps his career.

On March 10, we had our home opener against the L.A. Express. If I had to pick a high point for the USFL, it was probably that game. Over 60,000 fans turned up, anticipating a duel between the newcomer Flutie and the USFL's best proven quarterback, Steve Young. Both players put on dazzling shows, and better yet, the Generals came out on top. Flutie threw for two fourth-quarter touchdowns, to give us the victory, 35–24.

The day after Flutie's great game, I wrote a letter to

Harry Usher, our new commissioner, suggesting that the cost of Flutie's contract be shared among all USFL owners—on the grounds that Flutie's promotional value was leaguewide. I knew it was highly unlikely that the other owners would go along—and they didn't—but my attitude is that you can't get hurt asking.

Flutie, Kelly, and Young represented the good news about the USFL. The bad news was that we were still stuck with a lot of weak teams led by mediocre quarterbacks.

My worst fears about the consequences of having weak partners came true midway through our 1985 season. John Bassett was the owner of the USFL franchise in Tampa Bay. Previously he'd been one of the founders of the ill-fated World Football League. From the very start, Bassett and I had been on opposite sides of nearly every issue—and specifically the move to the fall. I'd managed to bring the majority of my fellow owners over to my way of thinking, but Bassett never stopped fighting me, though he finally, reluctantly, did vote with the majority. Despite our disagreements, I liked him personally, and I felt sympathetic to his situation. On this Sunday afternoon in late March, it was widely known within the league that Bassett had cancer, that he was fighting for his life, and that his behavior had become increasingly unpredictable during the previous few months.

What I'll never know is whether Bassett's illness affected his judgment that day. In any case, Bassett agreed to be interviewed by ABC announcer Keith Jackson, who began by asking what he thought was wrong with the USFL. What followed was a tirade. Before a national TV audience, Bassett viciously criticized the concept of moving the USFL to the fall. He called the league its own worst enemy. He said the USFL was guilty of mismanagement and virtually every other horrible sin he could conjure up. I caught the interview on a TV monitor in the press box, and I couldn't believe what I was hearing. My first thought was that Bassett would make a great witness for the *NFL* in our antitrust suit. My second thought was that he was just a terribly frustrated man, thoughtlessly venting anger.

If any one person had the potential to offset the damage wrought by Bassett and our other weaker owners, it was probably Harvey Myerson, the attorney we hired in the middle of 1985 to take over our antitrust case. Myerson was the head of the litigation department at the firm Finley Kumble, and he was an expert in antitrust litigation. He also had the sort of pugnacious, confrontational attitude you need when you're the underdog taking on the establishment. Most of the other USFL owners had long since written off the possibility that we'd win the antitrust suit. The NFL, they believed, was just too entrenched. But from the first time Myerson met us in April 1985, he told us he felt we had a very strong case. He said that we should pull out all the stops to bring it to trial, and that there was a better-than-even chance we'd win.

In the meantime, one bright spot amidst all the USFL's troubles was the fact that the Generals—and specifically Herschel Walker—were playing so well.

For the first two weeks of the season Herschel simply wasn't being utilized. He'd call me up in my office, depressed, and say, "Mr. Trump, I can run over these guys, if they'd just give me the ball." I ranted and raved to our coach, Walt Michaels, but it wasn't until I literally threatened to fire him that he got the point. In the seventh game of the season, Herschel was finally let loose. He ran the ball thirty times for almost 250 yards, setting a league record. In each of the next ten games, he ran for more than 100 yards. By the end of the season he'd racked up 2,411 yards. That broke the all-time professional football rushing record, held previously by Eric Dickerson of the NFL. I got a great kick out of that.

Unfortunately, Doug Flutie was injured late in the 1985 season, and that almost certainly cost us the USFL championship. In the playoffs, we lost by three points to the transplanted Baltimore Stars, while Flutie stood on the sidelines.

In February 1986 we agreed to reduce the number of USFL teams from fourteen to eight. In the process, we weeded out the owners with the biggest financial problems. We also consolidated our strengths. The Houston Gamblers, for example, merged with my Generals. As a result, we created a dream backfield that I'm convinced had no equal in professional football: Herschel Walker at running back and Jim Kelly at quarterback. The other teams that survived the consolidation were also all among our strongest and most popular: Memphis, Baltimore, Jacksonville, Tampa, Orlando, Arizona, and Birmingham.

In April we got more good news when a federal judge named Peter Leisure set a jury trial to begin the next month in our antitrust suit against the NFL. That ensured us a verdict before the start of our first fall season. If we won the suit, we'd be in great shape to launch. If we lost, I considered it highly unlikely that the USFL could survive—but at least we'd finally be able to cut our losses.

The future of the USFL now rested in the hands of the six jurors chosen to hear our case.

The jury system is designed to ensure the fairest possible trial. The problem is that a pool of randomly selected jurors isn't necessarily qualified to make judgments on complicated issues. Sometimes that isn't bad, particularly if you have a case that's weak and a lawyer who is very persuasive. The problem is unpredictability. You can have a great case and come out a loser, and you can have a terrible case but come out a winner.

We got to present our side first, and very quickly, a consensus formed in the courtroom that Harvey Myerson was beating the living daylights out of the NFL. He put Commissioner Pete Rozelle on the stand and almost literally took him apart. For twenty-six years, Rozelle had been running the NFL very successfully and very smoothly. Of course, you don't have to be a genius to run a monopoly. Put that same man up against a tough competitor, and it may be a whole different story.

Myerson pressed, and Rozelle got flustered. He mumbled, stumbled, and spoke badly, he turned red, and he took back statements. At times he appeared to be flat-out lying. Halfway through his week of cross-examination, Rozelle had become physically sick. His performance was so weak that I found myself actually feeling sorry for him. In retrospect, however, I realize that the jury probably felt at least as sorry for Rozelle as I did, and that may well have helped save the NFL's case.

Rozelle was least credible, I thought, when he talked about the Harvard seminar entitled "The USFL vs. the NFL"—the linchpin of our case. Rozelle claimed he hadn't known anything about the seminar, and that he got "physically ill" when he first heard about it, weeks after the fact.

"To your stomach, sir?" asked Harvey Myerson, totally deadpan.

"Yes," said Rozelle.

"I see," said Myerson. "How long did it take you to recover?"

"About half a day," Rozelle replied. I doubt that a single person in the courtroom believed Rozelle during that exchange.

At another point, Myerson introduced some devastatingly incriminating comments that Rozelle had made before a congressional committee, back in 1961. At the time, the NFL's games were being shown on just one network, CBS. "If all the networks were tied up by one football league," a senator asked Rozelle during his testimony, "wouldn't the other league possibly be at a major competitive disadvantage?"

"I should certainly think so," Rozelle said, quickly

adding, "There is no intention on our part of using more than one network." By 1987, of course, the NFL had all three networks tied up. Didn't that put our league at a major competitive disadvantage? Rozelle could only hem and haw.

The one time I myself directly contradicted Rozelle's testimony was over his description of a meeting the two of us had in March 1984. At the time, the USFL owners were still debating whether to move to the fall. The Porter seminar at Harvard had taken place several weeks earlier, and one of Porter's main strategies for destroying the USFL had been to try to co-opt the strongest USFL franchise owners by promising us NFL franchises.

At Rozelle's suggestion, I rented a suite at the Pierre Hotel for a meeting on March 12. I like to keep every option open in life, and I was certainly interested in what the commissioner of the NFL had on his mind. Rozelle testified at the trial that during our meeting I told him I was interested in purchasing an NFL franchise, and that I'd get out of the USFL if I could get into the NFL. It was ridiculous on the face of it. I never had any interest in owning a football franchise outside of the New York area, and I had long since determined that neither of the two New York–based NFL teams—the Giants or the Jets—was up for sale.

What really happened at the meeting is that Rozelle tried to woo me, plain and simple. He said he considered me a good candidate for an NFL franchise, whether it was the Generals, through merger, or an

NFL team, which he said he could help me get. In return, he said, he wanted two things: that the USFL not move to the fall, and that the league not bring an antitrust suit against the NFL.

I had no doubt about what Rozelle was up to. He was testing the waters. If he could get rid of the USFL merely by absorbing a couple of our teams into the NFL, he was prepared to do that, I'm certain. At the same time, by merely dangling an offer he gave himself deniability, in the event that I turned him down. That's exactly what I did. Sure enough, he rewrote the story of our meeting.

We called eighteen witnesses in all during the first month of the trial, and we scored a lot of points. Myerson showed how the NFL had bullied the three networks into refusing to consider giving the USFL a TV contract. He showed why the USFL could not survive without such a contract. He offered endless evidence—led by the Porter study—that the NFL had consciously and illegally set out to destroy the USFL.

By the time we'd finished presenting our witnesses, even the press was beginning to sense the possibility that we might win the case. The headline of a story in *Sports Illustrated* caught the mood best. GIVE THE FIRST ROUND TO THE USFL, it said, followed by an even more devastating subhead: "The embattled younger league has scored tellingly against the NFL in the trial of its $1.32 billion antitrust suit. Now the NFL has the ball."

Looking back, I think our strength may have back-fired, just as the NFL's weakness ended up prompting the jury's sympathy. Myerson's style—the silk hand-kerchief in the pocket of his perfectly tailored suit, his theatrical way of speaking, the methodical relentlessness of his attack—may have come off as too aggressive and too slick. By contrast, I think, the NFL came off as the beleaguered underdogs. Like Rozelle, who became sick and was so unconvincing during his cross-examination, the NFL lawyer, Frank Rothman, was so weak and ashen-faced the last days of the trial that everyone, including me, felt very bad for him. Many didn't even believe he would be able to finish, and in fact he was rushed to a hospital for a major operation shortly after the trial's conclusion. I believe Rothman's troubles elicited further sympathy from the jury.

I was part of the problem. As a witness, I was well spoken and professional, I think—very much a contrast to Pete Rozelle. But that probably played into the NFL's hands. From day one, the NFL painted me as a vicious, greedy, Machiavellian billionaire, intent only on serving my selfish ends at everyone else's expense. "The USFL," attorney Frank Rothman told the jury in his opening remarks, "is controlled and dominated by Donald Trump, who can buy and sell many of the owners in the NFL."

In truth, of course, the wealthy, powerful NFL owners cowered only to the extent that it served their ends. In retrospect, we might have been better off to put on the witness stand several of the smaller USFL owners who'd lost their shirts and had genuinely sad stories to tell.

The other way the NFL beat us was in pure public relations. I've got to give this to Rozelle: he's always been great at promoting his league. His chief spokesman is a guy named Joe Brown, and Rozelle deserves credit for using him well. After each day's testimony, Brown would go to the halls and lobby the press masterfully, telling them what a great day it had just been for the NFL. It drove me crazy. I'd say to Harry Usher, our commissioner, "Why aren't you out lobbying the press?" And he'd say, "It isn't important. It's the jury we've got to convince."

Unfortunately, that's not the way it works. Although the jury is instructed not to read any newspaper coverage or watch any television reports about the trial, it's nearly impossible to resist reading about a case you're part of, particularly one that's getting massive attention. Even if some jurors did resist, they undoubtedly heard about the trial coverage from their friends and family. Why else, after all, would Rozelle assign Joe Brown to lobby reporters every day for six weeks?

For all that, when the jury finally began deliberations on July 25, 1986, I was convinced we'd made the more effective case, and that they'd find in our favor.

What I never anticipated was that we could win—and end up losing anyway. After four days of deliberation, the six-member jury concluded on July 29 that the NFL had violated antitrust laws by conspiring to monopolize professional football, and that they did illegally damage the USFL. But then they voted to award us only a token one dollar in damages. It was a hollow victory. Without damages, the decision had no teeth, since the NFL didn't get punished for breaking the law.

When the jurors were interviewed by reporters immediately after the verdict was announced, it turned out that they'd been deeply divided. At least two of them had wanted to award us substantial damages. One, a schoolteacher named Miriam Sanchez, had favored giving us damages of $300 million but said that she'd misunderstood the mechanism for doing so. "I didn't understand the instructions," she told reporters, "so I had to put my faith in the judge, hoping he would give the USFL more money."

I wasn't happy about the outcome, but in a way I was relieved. My attitude is that you do your best, and if it doesn't work, you move on to the next thing. By the time the trial took place, I had lost quite a lot of money on the Generals—and the USFL had lost many times my number. Without the prospect of a fall network television contract, there wasn't any point in investing more money.

Most of my fellow owners agreed. One week after the decision, the USFL owners met and voted to suspend the season. At the same time we voted to appeal the jury's ruling. Unfortunately, the fans come out the biggest losers. The NFL's monopoly power is secure again, and the owners have less reason than ever to consider adding new teams in cities that have long been seeking franchises.

Meanwhile the best USFL players have been picked up by NFL teams. Herschel Walker was signed by the

Dallas Cowboys. Because I'd personally guaranteed Walker's contract, he could have collected $1.2 million from me for each of the next six years and never played football. But Herschel's a competitor, and the money was secondary.

As it turned out, I made a very good deal with Dallas. They could have refused to pay for his big contract. But figuring that Dallas was under intense fan pressure to sign Herschel, I told them I was interested in letting Herschel go only if they picked up the full cost of his contract. Sure enough, they agreed. It was good for me, it was good for Herschel, and it's even turned out to be good for Dallas. Herschel joined the team in August, and although he had virtually no time to practice, he finished the season as the Cowboy's leading combined rushing and receiving yardage gainer.

Jim Kelly also immediately became a star as quarterback for the Buffalo Bills. Freddie Gilbert, one of our defensive lineman, went to Atlanta and established himself as one of the team's best players. Even Doug Flutie, who everyone said was too small for the NFL, was signed by the Chicago Bears. Dozens of USFL players were signed to NFL contracts and many have become stars on their new teams.

Watching players like Herschel Walker and Jim Kelly play in the NFL does sometimes make me wish our league could have survived. I'm convinced that if the USFL had played last season, the Generals would have fielded one of the best teams in professional football.

Not that I've ever given up entirely. I'm a big believer in comebacks, and the USFL is appealing this ridiculous verdict. In recent months, I've received numerous calls from a very smart, very persistent guy who is trying to put together an entirely new fall league. He wants me to take the New York franchise—and I'm seriously considering it.

12

ICE CAPADES

Rebuilding
Wollman Rink

I NEVER had a master plan. I just got fed up one
day and decided to do something about it.

On the morning of May 22, 1986, there was a
story on the front page of the *New York Times* saying
that New York City officials had decided to start all
over in their effort to rebuild the Wollman Skating
Rink in Central Park. If everything went well, said the
city, the rink would be ready to reopen in approximately two years.

I couldn't believe it.

First of all, there was no reason to believe *anything*
would go well, much less everything. The Wollman

Rink, built in 1950, had first closed for renovations in June 1980. The work was scheduled to take two and a half years. Even that seemed like a long time to rebuild an ice-skating rink.

Coincidentally, in June 1980, I broke ground for Trump Tower, a sixty-eight-story skyscraper with six floors of shopping, thousands of square feet of office space, and 263 residential apartments. Two and a half years later we completed Trump Tower, on time and on budget.

From my new apartment, I had a view of Wollman Rink. It was not a pretty sight. Although millions of dollars had already been spent on its renovation, it was obvious, even from a distance, that the rink was nowhere near finished.

Three more years passed, millions more dollars were spent, and things just got worse. So bad, in fact, that on this May morning in 1986 the city felt compelled to announce it was starting the whole process over from scratch.

I knew absolutely nothing about building ice-skating rinks, but I did know something about construction. If it took me two and a half years to put up a major skyscraper, surely it was possible to build a $2 million ice-skating rink in a matter of months. Two years earlier, when the job was already a disaster, I'd called Henry Stern, commissioner of parks, and offered to take over construction from the city, for no fee. He turned me down. Now, after reading about this latest debacle, I called Henry again and repeated my offer.

He had the same response. "No, thanks," he said. "We can do it ourselves."

"That's great, Henry," I said, "except that you told me the same thing two years ago and look what happened." I decided to write a very strongly worded letter to Ed Koch, the mayor of New York. I was appalled by the city's incompetence. I genuinely felt I could get the job done, and I believed the rink was something hundreds of thousands of New Yorkers— including my own children—had a right to enjoy. Whatever anyone may think, my motive was that simple.

"Dear Ed," my letter began. "For many years I have watched with amazement as New York City repeatedly failed on its promises to complete and open the Wollman Skating Rink. Building the rink, which essentially involves the pouring of a concrete slab over coolant piping, should take no more than four months' time. To hear that, after six years, it will now take another two years, is unacceptable to all the thousands of people who are waiting to skate once again at the Wollman Rink. I and all other New Yorkers are tired of watching the catastrophe of Wollman Rink. The incompetence displayed on this simple construction project must be considered one of the great embarrass-ments of your administration. I fear that in two years there will be no skating at the Wollman Rink, with the general public being the losers."

Then I got to the real point:

"I am offering to construct and pay for a brand-new Wollman Ice-Skating Rink and have it open to the public by November of this winter. I would lease the rink from the city at a fair market rental, and run it properly after its completion.''

I sent the letter to Ed Koch on May 28, 1986. He wrote me a response by return mail. Somewhat to my surprise, he belittled my offer. The city wasn't about to let me operate the rink, he said, but they'd be delighted if I'd donate the $3 million to rebuild it and supervise the construction. He made a few more sarcastic comments and ended by saying, ''With bated breath I await your response.''

The tone of the mayor's letter irritated me. Fortunately, I wasn't the only one who was put off by it, and I have Koch himself to thank for that. I hadn't released my letter to the press because I didn't want to be accused of grandstanding. Koch, however, decided to release his letter. Apparently, he figured that if he made fun of my offer publicly, I'd just quietly slink away.

He totally underestimated the press reaction. First, the press thrives on confrontation. They also love stories about extremes, whether they're great successes or terrible failures. This story had it all. Perhaps most important, many reporters tend to see themselves as consumer advocates. Almost nothing gets them as outraged as a boondoggle that victimizes average citizens. The city's fiasco at the Wollman Rink was an absolute classic.

Even I was surprised at how totally the press took my side. Obviously, that doesn't always happen. But this time, within three days, there were dozens of articles and editorials attacking Koch for his reaction to my offer.

"The Koch administration," said the *Daily News* in an editorial, "is hemming and hawing over Donald Trump's offer to rebuild and operate Wollman Rink in Central Park. Why? The offer is genuine, with no apparent strings attached. Koch should grab it and heave a sigh of relief that a long-running, costly disaster is off his hands. So far the Mayor has raised a lot of phony objections. . . . Maybe the problem [is that] Koch & Co. are embarrassed that they've squandered $12 million on Wollman."

"Trump is offering to take over the Wollman project, to rebuild the rink, and to have it open by November at no cost to the city," wrote the *New York Post*. "After the whole 13-year multimillion-dollar debacle, you would think that they'd be jumping for joy. Not so. City officials seem more interested in thinking up reasons not to go forward than in making a deal. The city should give Donald Trump a speedy hearing—the Wollman farce has been running long enough."

"Let him have a go at it," said *Newsday*. "After all, the city has proved nothing except that it can't get the job done."

If there's one thing I've learned from dealing with politicians over the years, it's that the only thing guaranteed to force them into action is the press—or, more specifically, fear of the press. You can apply all kinds of pressure, make all sorts of pleas and threats, contribute large sums of money to their campaigns, and generally it gets you nothing. But raise the possibility of bad press, even in an obscure publication, and most politicians will jump. Bad press translates into potential lost votes, and if a politician loses enough votes, he won't get reelected. If that happens, he might have to go out and take a 9 to 5 job. That's the last thing most politicians want to do.

What you have to understand about Ed Koch is that he's a bully, pure and simple. Bullies may act tough, but they're really closet cowards. The only people bullies push around are the ones they know they can beat. Confront a strong, competent person, and he'll fight back harder than ever. Confront a bully, and in most cases he'll fold like a deck of cards.

Sure enough, the tide turned, overnight. No sooner did the press jump on Koch's case than he reversed field completely. Suddenly, the city was virtually begging me to take on the Wollman Rink job. On June 6, I sat down in my office with city officials, including Henry Stern, to negotiate the terms under which I'd rebuild the Wollman Rink. Until then, the city had insisted on competitive bidding, as is required on any city-financed construction job. I suggested a simple solution. I'd put up all of the money for the construction of the rink myself. In turn, I'd be reimbursed, over as many years as it took, from any profits the rink earned. In other words, I'd not only supervise construction, I'd also lend the city $3 million for an indeterminate period—and forever if the rink didn't prove profitable.

The city, in its infinite wisdom, balked. "There's no

way we're going to allow that," city officials told me. "There's no way we're going to allow you to make a profit on the rink."

"No, you don't understand," I said. "If the rink does make money, I'll use it to reduce my loan. I'm not looking for personal profit. In fact, if I ever do get my money back, I'll give any subsequent profits to charity." To my astonishment—and to the astonishment of my own lawyers—the city wouldn't budge. Instead, they came up with a counterproposal. I'd still put up the $3 million, as a way of getting around the competitive-bidding issue, but on the day I finished, the city would reimburse me in full.

It's fortunate for those city officials that they chose to go into city government rather than business. The deal they were suggesting was far worse for the city than the one I'd originally offered. I wasn't about to fight them at my own expense.

By the end of the day on Friday, June 6—ten days after my original offer—we came to an agreement, subject to final approval by the city's Board of Estimate. I'd put up the construction money and agree to complete the work by December 15. At that point, the city would reimburse me for my costs, up to a cap of just less than $3 million, but only if the rink worked. If I came in under budget, the city would pay me back only what I'd spent. If I went over budget, I'd cover the overruns myself. That much the city was graciously willing to let me do.

I had just one challenge left: building the skating rink fast and building it right. If I failed—if I was even one day late, or one dollar over budget—my plan was to pack my bags and take the next plane to Argentina. There was no way Ed Koch or anyone else would ever let me live it down.

Since I myself knew absolutely nothing about building rinks, I set out to find the best skating-rink builder I could. Logic suggested that the best place to look was Canada. Ice skating is to Canadians what baseball is to Americans—the national pastime. The top builders, I figured, were probably the companies that built rinks for Canada's professional hockey teams. Sure enough, everyone I talked with agreed that a company called Cimco, based in Toronto, was the best of the best. Among other projects, they'd built a rink for the Montreal Canadiens. I got their top guy on the phone, and I began with a very basic question: "What does it take to build a great outdoor skating rink?"

He gave me a very quick course in rink construction. The key choice, he said, was which ice-making system to use. The city had originally decided to use a relatively new technology in which the freezing agent is Freon. The rationale was that a Freon system requires less electricity, which translates into some minor energy-cost savings. The disadvantage of the Freon system is that it's far more delicate, temperamental, and difficult to maintain—particularly in a public facility where personnel turns over frequently. Among ice-skating facilities that used the Freon system, my friend from Cimco told me, at least one third had experienced problems.

The other option, which had been used in hundreds

of skating rinks for decades, was a brine system, in which salt water is circulated through the pipes. It costs a little more to run than a Freon system, but the advantage is that it's highly reliable and incredibly durable. The Rockefeller Center Skating Rink has used a brine system since it opened in 1936 and has never experienced a major problem.

By the time I finished my first call, I'd made up my mind to use a brine system in rebuilding the Wollman Rink. The city, in fact, had finally come to the same conclusion. The only difference was that they first wasted six years and millions of dollars.

I soon discovered that the city's incompetence on the Wollman Rink project had extended to every imaginable detail, large and small. On June 16, one week after I'd made my deal to take over rebuilding the rink, a city report was released on mistakes made at the Wollman Rink over the past six years. The study had taken fifteen months to complete—four times what I'd given myself to totally rebuild the rink. Worse yet, while the report provided endless examples of incompetence, it came to absolutely no conclusions about who was responsible for the fiasco and what could be done to avoid such failures in the future.

The one thing the report did provide was an astounding chronology of sloppiness, indecision, incompetence and sheer stupidity. If it weren't so pathetic, it would have been almost comical.

The city first closed the rink for renovations in June 1980. By the time plans had been drawn and the bidding process completed, almost a year had passed.

In March 1981, work finally began on installing approximately 22 miles of the very delicate, expensive copper piping used in a Freon cooling system. In the meantime, however, the Parks Department had second thoughts about where to locate the compressor room and what sort of refrigeration equipment to use. Even as the piping was being installed, all work was halted on the equipment that would eventually be needed to operate the rink's cooling system.

Even if the ice-making equipment had been finished and installed, the design of the rink was such that it never had a chance of working. Specifically, the base of the rink was designed on a pitch, so that it was approximately eight inches higher at one end than at the other. The pitch had a purpose. The fact that it ended up being eleven inches was an accident. The point of the pitch was that during the summer the city hoped to use the rink as a reflecting pond, and apparently a pond reflects light better if its base is sloped. In the winter, however, that same sloped base would cause a problem.

It doesn't take a genius to realize that when you try to make ice under those circumstances, there are only two possibilities. The better one is that ice will form, but that because the depth of the water varies, the consistency of the ice won't be uniform. The worse and far more likely result is that the water at the deeper end of the rink simply won't freeze at all, no matter how powerful the ice-making machinery.

Even that issue soon became secondary. In July, two months after the laying of the pipes began, a torrential rain flooded the rink, depositing a thick layer of silt on the newly laid pipes. It wasn't until September that the Parks Department finally got around to hiring a crew to repair the damage.

In the meantime, a new dispute had emerged within the Parks Department about how the concrete sidewalk surrounding the rink should be designed. The result was that the pouring of all concrete—including the concrete meant to form the rink's base—was held up nine months while a debate over the sidewalk raged on. So, unfortunately, did winter. For nine months, the newly laid delicate copper pipes were exposed to horrible weather. There were major snowstorms and flooding. In addition, because copper is quite valuable, vandals climbed over the fences and tried to cut off pieces of the pipe to resell. By the spring, it was as if those twenty-two miles of pipes had been through a war. Nonetheless, not one person thought to check them for possible damage.

In June of 1982, two years after the rink was first closed, the concrete was finally poured over the untested copper pipes. Contractors often use a vibrating machine when they pour over uneven surfaces, since it helps prevent bubbles from forming. However, the vibrating had an unforeseen result: it began shaking loose the joints of the copper pipes. At the same time, the contractor had even bigger problems to contend with: he had underestimated by a great deal how much concrete it would take to cover the rink. The key to pouring concrete is to do it all at once, on a continuous basis, because that's the only way to ensure it will adhere and mesh uniformly. Rather than interrupt his pour, the contractor decided to dilute his concrete mixture with water. It was a recipe for disaster.

Less than a week went by before cracks began appearing on the surface of the newly poured concrete slab. Not coincidentally, the cracks were concentrated at the end of the rink where the cement content had been diluted, and where the vibrating machine had been turned off.

Delays in deciding where to locate the refrigeration equipment prompted another problem. By the time the city made its decision—after sixteen months of deliberations—the contractor originally hired to install the equipment insisted on a "modification" of his original agreement. Specifically, he demanded more money. Those negotiations took another twelve months, and it wasn't until July 1983 that the city approved a new contract—on the contractor's terms. The completion date on installation of the refrigeration equipment was pushed forward yet again, to September 1984.

In the late fall of 1984 the system was finally tested for the first time. It proved unable to sustain pressure for long enough to create ice because it turned out that there were leaks in the pipes beneath the concrete slab. Between October and December of 1984, six leaks were found and repaired. No luck. The system was tested again and still couldn't make ice.

It was at that point that I called Henry Stern and made my first offer to take over construction of the rink. When he turned me down, I said, "Listen, would you like to walk over together and take a look, and perhaps I can at least make some suggestions?'' A few days later, in the dead of winter, we walked over to the rink. I was shocked by what I saw.

There were literally hundreds of tiny cracks in the concrete slab. Worse than that, there were at least a dozen huge gaping holes cut into the slab at various places. When I inquired, I found out that the holes had been cut through the concrete in order to get at the leaks in the pipes underneath. Unfortunately, the jackhammers used to make holes in concrete are very violent, and the pipes underneath are very delicate. In the effort to get at the leaking pipes, these violent men with their violent jackhammers actually made the problem much worse.

Right then and there I turned to Stern and said, ''You have a major problem. You'll never find these leaks. In the meantime, you'll just create bigger leaks. Forget it. Start all over.'' Henry tried to be polite, but it was clear that starting over was the last thing he'd consider.

In the spring of 1985, the city came up with a wonderful new idea. At a cost of $200,000, they hired an outside engineering consultant to study why Freon was leaking from the pipes, and to recommend solutions. The firm promised to have its report within four months. Nine months later—in December 1985—the firm announced that they'd been unable to isolate the cause of the leaks.

Nearly six years had now passed since the Wollman Rink was first closed for renovations. Nearly $13 million had been spent on the effort. The Parks Department finally concluded that the Freon system would have to be scrapped and replaced by a brine system. On May 21, 1986, they announced the new $3 million renovation plan and the eighteen-month timetable. That was when I finally convinced the city to let me take over.

By mid-June, when the Board of Estimate approved the deal I'd negotiated with the city, I had already begun work. One thing I discovered was that the city had agreed to pay a $150,000 fee to yet another consulting company, this time to provide recommendations about how to build the rink with a brine system. The city's contract specified that the company, St. Onge Ruff Associates (SORA), would begin work on July 1, 1986, and deliver its report by the end of December. In other words, I had agreed to finish rebuilding the rink before the city was scheduled to get the report on how it ought to be done.

On the off chance that the consultants might have some intelligent suggestions, I decided to sit down with them. I probably shouldn't have been surprised by what I discovered: the two gentlemen who ran the firm were specialists in refrigeration but had never before been involved in building a skating rink. They hadn't the faintest idea what it entailed. So much for their help.

I hired Cimco to build the refrigeration and piping equipment for the system and to advise me generally. To build the rink itself, I hired HRH, the construction company that had already built the Hyatt and Trump Tower for me and had proved themselves high-quality general contractors. In this case, they generously offered to do the work at cost. Meanwhile, Chase Manhattan, with whom I had a long banking relationship, stepped forward and offered to lend all the money for construction, again at no profit. It was the sort of project everyone could relate to and appreciate.

When I went to see the rink, things were even worse than I'd imagined. For example, there were gaping holes in the roof of the skaters' house, and the result had been massive water damage to the interior of the building. But even the smaller things I noticed reflected the city's approach to the job. For example, as I walked into the rink, I came upon a row of canvas sacks, abandoned and half covered by weeds. When I looked inside, I discovered that the sacks were filled with plants, which were once intended to be part of the new landscaping. Instead, they'd been left on the ground, unopened, and had died.

Just as I was making this discovery, a city worker walked by and stepped right on one of the few living plants on the site. He didn't look back. In a way, it was a perfect metaphor: the rink being trampled by one of the people who was being paid to fix it.

The incident reminded me of a time, several years earlier, when I was walking by the rink on a beautiful summer day. It was about two in the afternoon, and there, right in the middle of the unfinished rink, were perhaps thirty laborers. Not one of them was working. I figured they were on coffee break. Perhaps an hour later, I walked past the rink again. The same men were there, in exactly the same positions, as if they were on a permanent siesta. I didn't fully realize the implications of the scene at the time. Now I saw it as a symptom of the bigger problem at Wollman Rink: there was absolutely no one in charge.

Leadership is perhaps the key to getting any job done. There wasn't a single day when I didn't check on the progress we were making on the rink. Most days, I visited the site personally. I'd given myself six months to finish, and based on the city's record, meeting that deadline would be a minor miracle. By my own calculations, however, six months actually left me a cushion of a month, in case anything significant did go wrong. If absolutely everything went right, I felt it was possible we'd finish the job in four months.

One of the first decisions we made was to build the new rink on top of the old one, rather than rip it out altogether. By the first of August, we were able to lay a level subbase for the new rink, on top of which we would install the piping and pour the concrete for a flat-bottomed rink. Cimco was busy building two huge, 35,000-pound refrigeration units. I hadn't realized, when I offered to take on the job, how big Wollman Rink actually is. At nearly three quarters of an acre, it is one of the largest man-made skating rinks in the country.

Even before we began construction, we were besieged by calls from the press, seeking progress reports. Reporters who normally had no interest whatsoever in construction suddenly wanted to know the smallest details about the laying of pipe, the pouring of concrete, and the building of a compressor room.

After the first dozen or so calls, I decided to hold a press conference to answer everyone's questions in a single forum. On August 7, with only the subfloor in place, we met the press at the rink. To my surprise, perhaps three dozen reporters, photographers, and cameramen showed up, including representatives from every local television station and both wire services. I had no earthshaking news to announce. All I could report was that everything was proceeding right on schedule and that we expected to be open by December. That was enough. The next day there were stories in every newspaper with headlines like TRUMP HAS AN ICE SURPRISE FOR SKATERS and TRUMP PUTS THE ICING ON WOLLMAN CAKE.

There were those who said I went a little overboard holding press conferences about Wollman Rink. Perhaps they're right, but I can only say that the press couldn't get enough of this story. At least a dozen reporters showed up for every press conference we held.

Nor did the story of the rink generate just local attention. Dozens of newspapers as far away as Miami, Detroit, and Los Angeles ran long pieces about the Wollman Rink saga. *Time* magazine devoted a full page in its "Nation" section to the story. It was a simple, accessible drama about the contrast between governmental incompetence and the power of effective private enterprise.

From September 7 through 10, we laid twenty-two miles of pipes. On September 11, a convoy of cement trucks arrived and we began a continuous pour that lasted ten hours. There was no shortage of cement. The next day, when the engineers checked to see how evenly the pour had turned out, it was perfectly level. On September 15, the newly built refrigeration equipment was installed in the renovated compressor room. The only obstacle left was the heat. On the day we poured the concrete, the temperature climbed to 87 degrees. It occurred to me that we were going to be ready for skaters before the weather was ready for us.

By the end of September, all of our ice-making equipment was in place. All we needed to test our system was a succession of four days during which the temperature stayed below 55 degrees. Instead, for two weeks, one beautiful unseasonably warm day followed another. For the first time in my life, I found myself wishing for winter.

Finally, on October 12, the temperature dropped below 55 and it stayed down for several days. On October 15, we conducted our first test of the new system, sending brine through the piping. There were no leaks and the pressure held. That night, following a rainfall, ice formed on the rink—beautiful, clear, long-awaited ice. It was almost four months to the day since I'd gotten approval to renovate the rink. We'd also managed to come in more than $750,000 under our $3 million budget. With the city's blessing, we used the leftover money to renovate the adjacent skatehouse and restaurant.

During most of the construction, the city stayed out of our way—in large part because I instructed my men to keep park officials off the site. When they did try to interfere, it invariably turned into disaster. As an example, after we'd finished the rink, a crew from the Parks Department showed up carting a small tree, which, they announced, the city wanted to plant in my honor. It wasn't enough for one or two guys to handle the job. A crew of perhaps a half dozen men came, among them a park horticulturist to supervise the job. The tree itself was transported in a tractor with a back-hoe loader.

By total coincidence, I walked up to the rink just as the men were beginning to plant the tree. It happened to be one of the ugliest, scrawniest little trees you're ever likely to see. I could have lived with that. What got me absolutely nuts was the way they were planting the tree. Just the previous day, we'd planted beautiful specimen sod all around the perimeter of the rink. It had rained the night before and the ground under the newly planted grass was soft. What do these men do but drive their tractor right over the new grass, completely trampling it. In a matter of minutes, these six men—most of whom weren't needed in the first place—managed to totally destroy a beautiful planting job that had taken two days to complete and now would require three months to grow back in.

Around this time, I got a letter from Gordon Davis, the parks commissioner before Henry Stern. Davis wrote to say that as the person primarily responsible for the early problems at the rink he was "delighted and relieved to see how superbly [his] mistakes had been corrected." I happen to believe that Davis was far from the only person responsible. But what struck me most about his gracious attitude was how radically it contrasted with that of Henry Stern.

Throughout the Wollman project, Stern took numerous opportunities to minimize to reporters what we were accomplishing. The *Daily News*, noting one particularly snide comment Stern made, snapped back in an editorial. "Try saying thanks, Henry," they wrote. "It's more dignified, under the circumstances."

Koch himself was not exactly effusive about what we'd accomplished. Again, I think the media may have been a factor. In October, all the local newspapers ran stories that surely must have made him a little defensive. The *Times*, for example, ran a lead editorial that began, "New York City bungled the job of reopening Wollman Skating Rink for six years, wasting millions," and ended by saying, "The lessons of the Wollman Rink ought not to be forgotten."

Whenever they were asked, both Koch and Stern told reporters that after the job was done, the city intended to meet with me, and my people, to see whether the lessons of Wollman Rink could be applied to other city projects. If I heard them make that statement once, I must have heard it a dozen times, including in several speeches on November 13, the day we officially opened the rink to the public.

I've yet to get a call from any city official seeking a meeting. I can't honestly say I'm surprised. The bad press has died down, and that's all any of them were really concerned about.

Still, I believe there *are* some lessons the city could

take away from what we accomplished at Wollman Rink. At one point, Koch offered his own explanation for why we were able to do what the city could not. "Trump put in a cushion," Koch said, "and then he was able to reduce it by working as hard as he could with an elite crew, who knew that if they screwed up the job, they would never work for Donald Trump again."

That explanation wasn't totally wrong. What Koch didn't understand is that the city could have done some of the very same things I did. I'm not suggesting they would have been able to complete the job in five months, as I did, or even in six months. But there is no conceivable excuse for not completing it in a year, much less for failing for six years. That's incompetence, plain and simple, and incompetence was at the heart of this whole sad saga.

City officials invariably cite two reasons why they can't move as quickly as private developers. The first is that, by law, the city must award any contract to the lowest bidder, regardless of whether that person is best qualified to do the work. There is at least a partial solution. Objective qualifying standards ought to be adopted for any bidder on a city job. Provable past performance, for example, should be required across the board. In addition, any contractor who does good work for the city—coming in on time and on budget— ought to be given priority on future city jobs.

The other disadvantage city officials cite is the so-called Wicks law. It requires that on any public construction job budgeted over $50,000, the work must be divided among at least four separate contractors. The law was designed to increase competition and reduce building costs, but it does just the opposite. No single general contractor is permitted to have overall responsibility, and the result is frequent delays, disputes, and overruns.

I don't deny that these laws put a crimp on the city, but I believe a far bigger problem is leadership.

I know from my own experience that the only way to get even the best contractor to finish a job on time and on budget is to lean on him very, very hard. You can get any job done through sheer force of will—and by knowing what you're talking about. As it is now, a contractor will come in and say to a city official, "I'm sorry, but we've run into this problem, and we're going to need another one million or two million dollars to finish the job." No one argues back, because virtually no one in city government knows anything about construction.

Worst of all, no one in the city government bureaucracy is held accountable for failure. I'll give you what I consider the classic example. Back in 1984—by which time the city had already spent four years trying to rebuild Wollman Rink—a man named Bronson Binger held a press conference. At the time, Binger's title was assistant parks commissioner, and his primary responsibility was the renovation of Wollman Rink. Binger made a bold, confident announcement to the reporters who showed up. If the Wollman isn't ready to reopen in time for next season, he told them, then he'd resign his job.

A year passed, the rink obviously didn't reopen, and Binger was true to his word. He resigned. There was just one catch. A short time later he was named deputy commissioner in charge of prison construction for the State of New York. I don't know much about building prisons, but one thing is certain: renovating ice rinks is a lot easier. You don't reward failure by promoting those responsible for it, because all you'll get is more failure.

The one group that does benefit from the city's incompetence are the contractors who do the work. When a subway project or a new highway or a bridge goes over budget by millions of dollars, contractors clean up. You won't read the names of these people on the Forbes Four Hundred and they may not all speak perfect English, but I'll guarantee you this: many of them have become immensely wealthy working for New York City. They earn vast sums from huge, unwarranted cost overruns that city officials approve—and taxpayers underwrite.

The gala opening celebration for the rink was produced by former skating champions Dick Button and Aja Zanova-Steindler. They managed to bring together for one show most of the world's best skaters: Peggy Fleming, Dorothy Hamill, Scott Hamilton, Debbi Thomas, Robin Cousins, Toller Cranston, the teams of Torvill and Dean and Blumberg and Seibert, and others. It was a great occasion.

Had the city then turned over the finished rink to a second-rate operator, this story might still have a bad ending. But because normal competitive bidding would have led to a new delay in opening the rink, the city asked me to operate the rink on a temporary basis for the first season. Again, I just looked for the best rink managers available. The answer I came up with was Ice Capades. Besides doing great ice shows, Ice Capades operate some of the best rinks in the country.

They've done an impeccable job with Wollman Rink. It's not only beautifully run, it's been highly successful. During the 1970s, when the rink was still open and run by the city, it earned an average gross of approximately $100,000 a year and never took in more than $150,000. Although we charged prices below those of any private city rink—$4.50 a session for adults, $2.50 for children—we earned $1.2 million in revenues during our first season. Profits exceeded $500,000 after expenses, and all of it went to charity and the Parks Department. But equally important, more than a half million skaters enjoyed the Wollman Rink.

Even now, as I write this in the spring of 1987, I get a real kick every time I look out the window of my living room in Trump Tower and see hundreds of skaters on the Wollman Rink. However, I won't be one of them. People have been waiting for years to watch me fall, but I'm not about to help the cause. Skating isn't my strong suit.

13

COMEBACK

A West Side
Story

THE TOUGHEST business decision I ever made
was giving up my option on the West Side
yards—seventy-eight riverfront acres between
59th Street and 72nd Street—in the summer of 1979.
The easiest business decision I ever made was buying
back those same hundred acres in January 1985.

I have a tendency to get very enthusiastic about any
deal I make, but I suspect few people would argue that
those hundred acres represent the single best undeveloped piece of property in America today.

It has been reported that I paid $95 million for the
West Side yards, or about $1 million an acre, which is

not far from the correct figure. Taking the time value of money into account, I paid less to purchase the site in 1985 than I would have if I'd exercised my option to buy them in 1979. During the intervening years, the price of most Manhattan real estate increased as much as five times. Even before I put up a single building, I'm certain I could sell the property at a very substantial profit, and I've turned down numerous offers already. Consider just one comparison. Very shortly after I bought the West Side yards, another group of developers paid approximately $500 million for the Columbus Circle Coliseum site, a tiny property by comparison, and just four blocks away.

I got the yards at a great price because a bank was foreclosing on a desperate seller, because I made the deal before the property was offered for sale on the open market, and because I was one of the few developers both willing and able to pay millions of dollars a year in carrying costs for as long as it took to get the yards developed.

Securing the option to purchase the West Side yards from the Penn Central Railroad back in 1974 was the first major deal I made in Manhattan. At the time, as I've said, the city was on the verge of bankruptcy, and the West Side was hardly considered a great place to live. But I had a simple conviction: I couldn't go very wrong buying spectacular riverfront property in the middle of Manhattan at a bargain-basement price.

Over the next five years, however, government subsidies dried up for the kind of middle-income housing I was proposing, community opposition to any development on the West Side reached a fever pitch, and banks remained reluctant to finance any large-scale developments. Perhaps most important, I was launching other projects—among them the Commodore/Hyatt, Trump Tower, and my first Atlantic City casino. Nor was I eager to load myself down with huge carrying costs while my personal resources were still very limited.

By devoting myself to other deals instead, I generated a cash flow large enough to support the carrying costs on virtually any project. I also built a record of success that made banks happy to lend me money for nearly any deal.

Shortly after I gave up my original option in 1979, the Penn Central sold the West Side yards to my friend Abe Hirschfeld. Very quickly, Abe went out and got himself a partner on the deal. Francisco Macri became wealthy in the 1960s building bridges for the government in his native Argentina. Under the deal with Hirschfeld, Macri agreed to take over the job totally. Hirschfeld retained a substantial percentage of profits but no ongoing role in the project. Macri, in turn, gave the job of overseeing the project day-to-day to a man named Carlos Varsavsky, a former physics professor who'd been running Macri's Argentinian company, BA Capital.

The Macri team had plenty of brainpower. What they lacked was practical experience, especially in New York City, where it is so difficult to do any sort of real estate development.

The first key to developing any huge Manhattan site

is getting the necessary approvals to build a job that is economically viable. Rezoning is a complex, highly political, and very time-consuming process that ultimately involves a dozen city and state agencies, as well as local community groups and politicians.

Macri did finally manage to get his zoning for the project he named Lincoln West. But in the process he made far too many concessions to the city. Being forced to sell out may have been the best thing that ever happened to him. If Macri had ever tried to build the project under the terms to which he'd agreed, he would have lost hundreds of millions of dollars.

It was sad, in a way, because Franco Macri is a wonderful and well-meaning man. But he made a critical misjudgment from the start: he assumed that in a project as big as the West Side yards, he could afford to absorb nearly any costs and still end up with a huge profit. The truth is that unless you design a project to be self-supporting as you build it, you risk getting eaten alive before you've turned the corner into profit.

One of Macri's problems was that he tried to apply the principles of bridge-building to a residential development. When you build a bridge, under contract to the government, you calculate the costs and sign a contract for a set amount. All you need to do to earn a profit is bring the project in on budget. In developing real estate, it's a whole different ball game. You can budget building costs, but you can't truly project revenues, because you're always at the mercy of the market. The variables include how much you get per unit, how long it takes to sell out, and what your

carrying costs are along the way. The less you commit
to spend up front, the less you're at risk later.

Instead, Macri spent three years mostly in the business of giveaways. The city, eager to get all it could in
return for approving the project, asked Macri for
concession after concession. Macri began by agreeing
to provide $30 million to refurbish the 72nd Street
subway station nearest to the project—even though the
projected renovation amounted to little more than
widening a single platform by four feet. For $30
million, you ought to be able to totally rebuild a
station.

Next, Macri threw in a $5 million pledge for a
railroad flat-car operation in the South Bronx to replace the one he'd be eliminating in the West Side
yards. Then he promised to chip in $30 million for a
public park within his development. Later, he agreed
to build a new public through street connecting with
the existing city grid—a job that would have surely
cost tens of millions of dollars.

When Con Edison asked Macri to underwrite the
cost of rebuilding a smokestack the company owned
on the site, he even agreed to that. This I found
particularly preposterous. Con Edison already gets one
of the highest utility rates in the country. When I met
Macri, I asked him why he'd agreed to do anything for
Con Ed. Wasn't it enough, I asked, that over the years
he was going to be buying billions of dollars worth of
electricity from them?

"They told me they were going to oppose my

project," Macri explained. "And anyway, what's the big deal? How much can a smokestack cost?"

Suddenly I understood: Franco Macri hadn't bothered to check. But I did. To put a needle 500 feet into the air, it turns out, costs nearly as much as putting up a building. "It could run to thirty or even forty million dollars," I told Macri. He still didn't seem fazed. By the time he'd finished being generous to anyone who asked, Marci had committed more than $100 million in giveaways. Worse yet, he'd agreed to pay in full for much of it before he'd erected any buildings—much less sold a single apartment.

Equally bad was the zoning to which Macri finally agreed. By the time the process was finished, he'd been negotiated down to less than 4,300 residential units on his hundred-acre site—a density lower than you find in some six-story apartment complexes in the suburbs. More specifically, Macri agreed to build just 850 units in the most valuable part of his site—68th Street to 72nd Street—which was adjacent to an existing residential neighborhood. The great majority of his apartments he agreed to put in the undeveloped industrial southern end of the site, where the residential market remained totally untested.

Antidevelopment forces on the Upper West Side barely had to fight with Macri. He became his own worst enemy.

The last major mistake Macri made was that he never set out to create any excitement about his Lincoln West project. During the four years when he owned this terrific piece of property, virtually not a word was written about it. Even the name Lincoln West implied that, despite the fact that this represented one of the largest and potentially most important developments in the United States, it was merely a job located west of Lincoln Center.

An average 150-unit luxury high-rise building in New York takes two years to sell out—and that assumes a strong market and good promotion. To sell literally thousands of units in a new development requires that you have both something unique to sell and a very aggressive approach to selling it. Macri had neither. The Lincoln West development he had proposed—two dozen relatively short brick buildings —was as bland and uninspiring as any of a dozen public housing projects that were thrown up around Manhattan during the 1960s. It was scarcely surprising that not one of at least a dozen banks Macri called on over three years was willing to lend him money for his construction, even though banks were practically throwing money at dozens of other New York City developments.

By late 1983, Macri also had personal cash problems. The war in the Falklands apparently had hurt his business interests in Argentina. By this point, counting outlays for architectural staff, environmental-impact studies, and carrying costs, Macri was probably in to Lincoln West for more than $100 million. Caught in a crunch, he began defaulting on the original loan he'd taken from Chase Manhattan to purchase the land.

In the spring of 1984 I got a call from Abe Hirschfeld. He told me that Macri was in trouble and was interested in selling. I went to see Macri, and we began a long negotiation. He was eager to get out with a profit. At the same time, the bank was breathing down his neck. Sure enough, in November, we finally agreed to an all-cash price of approximately $100 million, and Chase agreed to finance a good part of the transaction.

One of the reasons Franco Macri agreed to sell to me, I'm convinced, is that I'd done him a favor long before we finally made a deal. Shortly after our first meeting in early 1984, we agreed on the terms of a tentative deal under which Macri would sell me the project. He wasn't yet certain that he wanted to sell, but he was willing to consider signing at least a letter of intent. One of the first things that anyone should learn about real estate—and New York real estate in particular—is never to sign a letter of intent. Years can be spent in court trying to get out of a seemingly simple and "nonbinding" agreement.

Macri did not fully realize this, and in addition, my lawyer, Jerry Schrager, drafted a letter of intent that was significantly more binding than most.

It was with an eye to getting this letter signed that Jerry and I sat down in mid-1984, in an extraordinary apartment at the Sherry Netherland Hotel, along with Macri, his young son, and a beautiful interpreter named Christina. She was a true Latin beauty, and all of us were somewhat distracted. I'll never forget Christina's stopping in the middle of translating a complex legal point and saying to Macri, "You really should get a lawyer to help you understand the meaning of this document. It's very complicated."

"No, no, Christina," he said. "As long as I can get out of it, it's not so important." And he went ahead and signed.

As it turned out, Macri retained his dream of proceeding with the project, and several months later he called and asked me to let him rescind his letter of intent. I declined, but he asked if we could meet, and I agreed.

Macri explained that the project was killing him, but that he desperately wanted to make one last effort to get his financing and move forward. I couldn't help feeling sympathetic, having spent years myself working to launch difficult projects. I also appreciated his openness.

I took the letter of intent out of a folder and tore it in two, in front of Macri. And then I said to him, "If you should ever again decide to sell, I hope you'll think of me first. In the meantime, good luck."

When I told Schrager what I'd done, he wasn't happy, but to this day I'm convinced that my ripping up that letter—which may or may not have been binding—is the reason that Macri did come back to me, instead of going to any of a dozen other potential bidders, when it finally became clear that he couldn't get his financing after all.

Even before I signed the purchase papers in January 1985, I had the basic elements of my plan in mind. I intended to build many fewer buildings than Macri, and all along a single block. Views were the site's single strongest selling point, and I wanted every apartment to have unobstructed views either of the Hudson River to the west, the extraordinary cityscape to the east, or both. I also intended to build much taller buildings than Macri had planned, to take full advantage of the views and also because I believed tall buildings would make the project more majestic and alluring.

I also envisioned a huge retail shopping promenade on the ground level, along the riverfront in front of the buildings. What the Upper West Side of Manhattan needs more than anything else, I believe, is basic shopping services—large supermarkets, shoe stores, pharmacies, and hardware stores. Rents along Broadway, Amsterdam Avenue, and Columbus Avenue have gotten so high that small shopkeepers have been driven out. It's easier today to find a $100 pair of leather gloves on Columbus Avenue than a loaf of bread. One advantage of my low land cost is that I will be able to charge more reasonable rents to retail tenants.

My plans were contingent, of course, on what sort of zoning I could get. I didn't have to undertake complex cost analyses to know that the only way to make the project feasible was to get approval for many more units and total square feet of buildable space than Macri got. Unlike Macri, I was prepared to hold out for as long as it took—even into another city administration if necessary—to win approval for a plan I believe can be economically workable.

My first goal was to put as much distance as possible between Macri's approved project and my own vision for the site. Any link to his project could only hurt me.

At the time he sold to me, Macri had yet to sign any formal contract with the city, and the city had yet to issue him a final building permit. I was under no obligation, therefore, to deliver on his many promises. Starting the process over from scratch meant I'd have to spend much more time and money, but I felt there was no other choice.

My first critical challenge was to make the project exciting and attractive to the city so that they'd be inclined to give me the zoning approvals I needed. The key was to find a mutual interest. Deals work best when each side gets something it wants from the other. By luck, I picked up the newspaper one morning soon after purchasing the site, and the answer came to me. It turned out that NBC, which had long had headquarters in Rockefeller Center, was looking to relocate. Edward S. Gordon, a top New York real estate broker, then confirmed this to me. Among the possibilities NBC had in mind was a move across the river to New Jersey, where they stood to save considerable money by virtue of that state's lower taxes and land costs.

For the city to lose any large company is obviously bad, but there could hardly be a worse blow than losing NBC. Pure economics are part of the issue. The city's economic development agency has estimated that if NBC moves, it will cost New York some 4,000 jobs, and perhaps $500 million a year in revenues.

The psychological loss would be at least as great. It's one thing to lose a manufacturing company no one has ever heard of. It's another to lose a company that is a crucial part of what makes New York the media capital of the world. The two other networks, ABC and CBS, now produce nearly all their programs in Los Angeles. NBC still does the *Today* show, the *NBC Nightly News*, *Late Night with David Letterman*, *The Cosby Show*, *Saturday Night Live*, and other shows from New York. You can't put a specific dollar value on the excitement and glamour of being home to the number-one network and its top-rated shows. It's like trying to assess what New York would be like without the Empire State Building or the Statue of Liberty.

With the West Side yards, I had something to offer NBC that no other New York developer could possibly match: enough space to build huge single-story studios in the style of Hollywood backlots. NBC was making do at Rockefeller Center with a cramped 1.2 million square feet of space. On my site, I could offer them 2 million square feet, as well as room for future expansion, and I'd still have plenty of room left over to build the rest of the project I had in mind.

In addition, because my land costs had been so low, I was in a position to offer NBC a price per square foot far below what they might otherwise get in New York. Even at that, to be truly competitive with a New Jersey offer, I knew I'd need a tax abatement from the city. But I also knew that it was in the city's economic interest to provide incentives for NBC to stay.

The more I thought about it, the better I liked the idea. Even if NBC ultimately decided not to move to my site, it was still a perfect place to build television and motion picture studios. With or without NBC, I felt studios would be a good, high-profile business. Before I got a commitment from the network, I decided to design my project around the studio concept. The first step was the name: Television City.

My second challenge was to find a way to immediately capture the public imagination with my project. The more awareness and excitement I could create early on, the easier it was going to be to attract buyers down the line. A lot of developers build first and promote later, if at all.

The world's tallest building was a project I'd considered undertaking even before I purchased the West Side yards. I've always loved very tall buildings. I remember coming in from Brooklyn as a kid with my father and pleading with him to take us to see the Empire State Building, which at the time was the world's tallest building. But then Chicago built the Sears Tower and took away the title. I loved the challenge of bringing the world's tallest building back to New York, where I felt it really belonged.

In a way, I saw the building as a loss leader. When you build any structure higher than about 50 stories, the construction costs escalate geometrically. If maximum profit is your sole motive, you're far better off putting up three 50-story towers than one 150-story skyscraper. On the other hand, I felt the building would ultimately pay for itself as a tourist attraction and an overall lure. After all, how many millions of tourists have come, as I once did, to see the Empire State Building?

The next challenge was to find an architect who was as enthusiastic as I was about making such a building the centerpiece of this project. In the end, I interviewed only two architects. The first was Richard Meier, who represents the epitome of the New York architectural establishment. Critics adore Meier, and he has a big following. But what I discovered very quickly is that Meier is not the sort of guy who jumps in with great energy and enthusiasm. He prefers to spend time pondering and analyzing and theorizing. For weeks, I waited for him to bring me a scale model of a plan, or at least some preliminary drawings. Nothing came.

In the meantime, I also met with Helmut Jahn. I liked him for very different reasons than I liked Meier. Jahn was an outsider: German-born, Chicago-based, in no way part of the New York architectural establishment. He was a bit of a dandy personally, a very good promoter, and he'd gotten very good notices for some very daring work. Among other things, Jahn designed the Xerox Center in downtown Chicago and the high-tech State of Illinois building. At the time I talked with him, he had four major buildings under way in midtown Manhattan.

What I liked most about Helmut was that he believed, as I did, that big can be beautiful. He liked spectacle. Less than three weeks after we first talked, he arrived in my office with a scale model of a project that incorporated the basic elements I'd told him I wanted, as well as several of his own. In the summer of 1985, I hired Jahn to be the project's chief architect.

By the fall, we'd batted back and forth a dozen

possible designs for the site. Both of us felt that the site was so big and so distinctive that it made no sense to try to create something that blended into the surrounding community. Instead, we saw this as a chance to build a self-contained city, with a look and a character wholly distinct from the disparate surrounding neighborhoods.

On November 18, we held a press conference to announce our plan for the site. For years, while Macri pursued his Lincoln West plan, the media had ignored him. This time, no fewer than fifty reporters—local and national—showed up for our announcement. I ran down the basic elements. We were calling it Television City, and we hoped to lure NBC as our prime tenant. We intended to build a mixed-use development totaling 18.5 million square feet of commercial, residential, and retail space. The project would include approximately 8,000 residential units, 3.5 million square feet of TV and motion-picture studios and offices, 1.7 million square feet of retail space, 8,500 parking spaces, and almost forty acres of parks and open space, including a thirteen-block waterfront promenade. At the center of the site, we'd erect the world's tallest building—1,670 feet high—or about 200 feet higher than the Sears Tower in Chicago.

To me, the beauty of the plan was its simplicity and its grandeur. In addition to the world's tallest building, we'd put up just seven other buildings—three at the north end, four at the south. A decked-over three-level platform in front of the buildings—including parking and enclosed shopping—would permit us to put a pedestrian promenade on top, at a level slightly higher than the adjacent West Side Highway. The result would be to provide an unimpeded view of the river from virtually any spot on the site. We'd also have enormous space for parks. In all, our proposal was about 50 percent bigger than Macri's—but even at that, the overall density was lower than that of many smaller developments squeezed onto tiny midtown sites.

Most reporters, I find, have very little interest in exploring the substance of a detailed proposal for a development. They look instead for the sensational angle. In this case, that may have worked to my advantage. I was prepared for questions about density and traffic and the mix of housing on the site, but instead, all the reporters wanted to talk about was the world's tallest building. It gave the project an instant mystique. When I got home that night, I switched on the *CBS Evening News*, expecting to hear news from the opening of the summit between Ronald Reagan and Mikhail Gorbachev. Dan Rather was in Geneva anchoring the program, but after summarizing the day's developments, suddenly he was saying: "In New York City today, developer Donald Trump announced plans to build the world's tallest building." It demonstrated how powerful and intoxicating a symbol I'd found for my project.

The reaction to the world's tallest building was hardly uniformly positive, but I fully expected that. The controversy actually helped keep the project in the news. Critics insisted that such a building was unnecessary, that people wouldn't want to live up so high, and that I'd never be able to build it anyway. *Newsweek* did a full-page story about the building, headlined DONALD TRUMP'S LOFTY AMBITION. The *New York Times* ran an editorial about my plan, which probably added to its credibility. "Time alone," the editorial said, "can distinguish between great dreams and vain illusions. It's too early to know which describes Donald Trump's desire to loom over New York and all other cityscapes with a 150-story tower."

My favorite reaction to the world's tallest building came from columnist George Will. I've always liked Will, in part because he's not afraid to challenge fashion. "Donald Trump is not being reasonable," Will wrote. "But, then, man does not live by reason alone, fortunately. Trump, who believes that excess can be a virtue, is as American as Manhattan's skyline, which expresses the Republic's erupting energies. He says the superskyscraper is necessary because it is unnecessary. He believes architectural exuberance is good for us [and] he may have a point. Brashness, zest and élan are part of this country's character."

My only regret was that George Will didn't have a seat on the City Planning Commission.

To my surprise, as time passed, opposition to the world's tallest building seemed to diminish. Critics focused instead on other aspects of the development, which I'd expected to be less controversial. In particular, the *Times* architecture critic, Paul Goldberger, launched something of a crusade against Television City. A week after I announced my plans, Goldberger wrote a long piece entitled "Is Trump's Latest Proposal Just a Castle in the Air?" His major criticism, aside from the fact that he simply doesn't like tall buildings, was that the project hadn't been sufficiently integrated into the rest of the neighborhood.

That, of course, was precisely what I liked best about it. The worst thing I could do, I was convinced, was to build something that blended into the surroundings. Ten years earlier, I'd taken the same position on the rebuilding of the Commodore/Hyatt Hotel. The Grand Central neighborhood was dying, and I felt the only chance at success was to build a spectacular new hotel sheathed in reflective glass, so that it stood apart from the dull, older buildings in the neighborhood. The hotel became an enormous success, and eventually even the critics came around. Reading Goldberger, I felt I was reliving the Commodore experience.

I felt certain I'd get far better reviews from Paul Goldberger and certain other critics simply by cutting my buildings in half and making them look more like the better-known prewar buildings on the West Side. The problem was that my project would no longer be majestic or distinctive, and it wouldn't sell. It irritates me that critics, who've neither designed nor built anything themselves, are given carte blanche to express their views in the pages of major publications, whereas the targets of their criticism are almost never offered space to respond. Of course, I can be irritated all I want and it won't do any good. So long as a critic writes for a newspaper like the *New York Times*, his opinion will continue to carry great weight—whether I like it or not.

By the spring of 1986, the project we'd proposed was at something of a standstill with city planning. Much of the explanation was that city government itself had become almost completely paralyzed, under the mayoral administration of Ed Koch.

Koch has achieved something quite miraculous. He's presided over an administration that is both pervasively corrupt *and* totally incompetent. Richard Daley, the former mayor of Chicago, managed to survive corruption scandals because at least he seemed able to operate his city efficiently. Under Koch, the problem of the homeless has grown far worse, the vast majority of the city remains unwired for cable, highways have gone unrepaired, subway tunnels have been left unfinished, companies have continued to flee to other cities and city services have deteriorated inexorably.

Meanwhile, no fewer than a dozen Koch appointees and cohorts have been indicted on charges of bribery, perjury, and accepting kickbacks, or have been forced to resign in disgrace after admitting various ethical transgressions. The criminally indicted include Jay Turoff, the former head of the Taxi and Limousine Commission, John McLaughlin, the hospitals chief, and Anthony Ameruso, the former transportation commissioner. Victor Botnick, one of Koch's closest personal advisers, quit after it was revealed that he'd lied about his educational background and had taken numerous unnecessary trips under the pretext of doing city business. Bess Myerson, the cultural affairs commissioner and one of Koch's best friends, resigned in disgrace and was eventually indicted after it came out that she'd given a job to the daughter of a judge she was seeking to influence and had then lied repeatedly about her involvement. Later it came out that Koch ignored evidence that Myerson had acted improperly.

The irony is that Koch made his reputation by boasting about his integrity and incorruptibility. It doesn't seem to occur to him that if the people he appoints prove to be corrupt, then in the end he must take the responsibility. To the contrary, at the first hint that any of his friends might be in trouble, Koch can't run fast enough the other way. For example, when his close friend Donald Manes, the late Queens borough president, came under investigation and tried to commit suicide, Koch immediately called him "a crook," even though Manes had yet to be indicted for anything. At the time, Manes was recovering in a hospital. Weeks later, he did succeed in killing himself.

As for the Koch appointees who managed to avoid criminal indictment, the scandal is their sheer incompetence. Many just lack talent. Others seem to have concluded that the safest approach to protecting their jobs is to stop making decisions of any kind; at least then they can't be accused of breaking the law. The problem is that when officials in a huge city government stop making decisions, you get the bureaucratic equivalent of gridlock. Dishonesty is intolerable, but inaction and incompetence can be every bit as bad.

In any case, the city was also stonewalling my

project as a means of trying to force me to make changes. In my view it was a form of economic blackmail. So long as I resisted their ideas, they held up my approvals, and my costs mounted.

Specifically, city planning wanted me to provide more direct access to the waterfront, add more east-west streets connecting the project to the existing city street grid, and move the world's tallest building south, away from the existing residential neighborhoods. I disagreed with their suggestions, but I also recognize that zoning is always a matter of negotiation. As hard as I push, in the end I'm practical. If it took making some compromises to get the project moving forward, and the result didn't undermine the project's economic viability, I was prepared to make the changes.

In March, I decided to move the location of the world's tallest building south to 63rd Street. The people at city planning were immediately more enthusiastic. Around the same time, the *New York Times* had made public an environmental-impact study of the site. Some of its conclusions, I felt, would ultimately help my cause. I'd always believed that any concerns about density were unwarranted. In truth, the West Side of Manhattan is relatively underpopulated. According to the census, the area declined in population from 245,000 in 1960 to 204,000 in 1980. Only 3,100 new apartments went up in the neighborhood between 1980 and 1984. Adding several thousand more hardly represents development run amok.

The study also pointed out several benefits that

would come from the project. For example, the study predicted that the West Side would gain business worth at least $500 million a year from new residents, as well as tens of thousands of jobs, both during construction and permanently on the site. Providing jobs, in my view, is a far more constructive solution to unemployment than creating welfare programs. Finally, the study found that any added vehicular congestion in the area—a major concern among some critics—could be eased by improvements in local subways and the addition of a jitney service, which I'd already proposed.

Even after moving the location of the world's tallest building, I began to believe that I might also have to make a change in architects. I liked the fact that Helmut Jahn was an outsider, but I think it hurt us with the people at city planning. No one at the commission ever seemed quite comfortable with Helmut. It was never anything more specific than that, but in the end I felt that was enough. If the project was going to move forward, there had to be some spirit of cooperation. Reluctantly, I decided to make a change.

A lot of people were surprised that I chose Alex Cooper. Even more than Richard Meier, Cooper was Jahn's antithesis. Legendarily civic-minded, he'd built his reputation as an urban planner, served five years on the City Planning Commission, and helped write the rules of the planning process I was now going through. Along with his partner at the time, Stanton Eckstut, Cooper had just finished work on the master plan for a development at the southern tip of Manhattan called Battery Park. The critics loved it, calling it a classic example of enlightened urban architecture.

I wasn't a total fan of the Battery Park project myself. For example, while the project was situated on the waterfront, many of its apartments faced other buildings and therefore had no water views at all. In addition, I felt that a number of the buildings were totally undistinguished architecturally. However, Cooper's contributions to the master plan—the placement of streets, parks, and other amenities—I did like, and I felt he could bring some of those ideas to our site.

I had first interviewed Cooper in October 1985, shortly before going public with the Helmut Jahn plan for the site. There were already indications that the city might have problems with the way we'd designed our open space, and I was interested in hiring Cooper to work with Jahn just on that. Working together didn't appeal to either of them, however, so I put the idea on the back burner.

I called Cooper again in May 1986 and offered him the chance to take over sole responsibility for the Television City job. In my opinion, he was the guy best positioned to get my project moving forward. As for him, although we might have been on different sides of the fence in the past, what smart, ambitious architect could pass up such an opportunity? Television City was probably the best and most challenging design job available anywhere. It was about time, I challenged Alex, that he got associated with something big and bold, instead of small and precious. To his credit, Alex jumped at the opportunity. "My God," he told a reporter later, "it's three quarters of a mile of Hudson frontage, so you don't lightly just walk away."

We had our differences, but I quickly discovered that Alex had far grander instincts than many people realized, and we got along better professionally than most people assumed we would. Alex added more streets and pedestrian walkways providing direct access through the project to the waterfront. He designed parks that were easily reached by anyone coming from outside. We agreed to increase the number of buildings and to make each one a little smaller. In front of the taller buildings, Alex added townhouses as a way of varying the scale.

What Alex didn't do was substantially reduce the amount of overall square footage below what I believed was necessary to ensure the project's economic viability. Still, his changes plainly had an impact. Suddenly we started getting more positive feedback from city planning. When we unveiled the plan publicly on October 23, 1986, even our toughest critics were more enthusiastic than they'd been about the original plan. The head of the local community board, John Kowal, still objected to the superskyscraper, but he described Alex's new approach as a "brilliant answer to Trump's desires" and "a far better plan."

Cooper himself, who'd been skeptical of the size of the project at first, grew more enthusiastic as he got more involved in the design. In April 1987, he told the *New York Times*, "I hope that the project can be dealt with on its merits. The problem is that the antidevelopment spirit in this city is very, very strong right now. What we are trying to do at Television City is different. There is room by the river, and we are providing a level of public amenity that makes this immense size justifiable—parks, waterfront promenades and so forth. The world's tallest building demands an extraordinary situation. But if there is any place that such a skyscraper makes sense, it is here."

I couldn't have said it better myself.

As for attracting NBC to the site, I felt our cause got a boost when General Electric purchased RCA—owner of NBC—in mid-1986. I knew Jack Welch, Jr., the chairman of GE, and he struck me as a brilliant big thinker who would immediately see the advantage of locating NBC on a site like Television City. Welch went on to name Bob Wright, one of his top GE executives, to head NBC, and I got the same feeling about Wright. They are exceptional men—even if they don't choose my site.

At the time GE took over, NBC had been actively considering no less than four New York City sites, in addition to the one in New Jersey. In January 1987, NBC announced that aside from the possibility of remaining at Rockefeller Center, they'd narrowed their choice to just two sites: ours and the marshland owned by Hartz Mountain Industries in Secaucus, New Jersey. Eliminated from the competition were three other New York City sites.

The result was to make the issue very simple: either NBC came to my site, or they moved to New Jersey. The city had already announced a willingness to offer

NBC tax concessions, mostly in the form of property tax abatements, as an inducement for the network to remain in New York. The question now was whether they'd offer a package competitive with New Jersey's proposal.

Incredibly, the city seemed content to sit back and do nothing. I say incredible because in early 1987, Mobil Oil, one of the largest corporations in the world, announced that it was abandoning New York and moving to Virginia. A short time later, J. C. Penney, another huge employer, revealed that it too was leaving, and taking along many thousands of jobs. You'd think the city, faced with yet a third big company threatening to leave, would spring to action. Not under Ed Koch, however.

In late February 1987, the *Daily News* ran an editorial that I thought captured the dilemma perfectly. After suggesting that the loss of NBC would be "a major blow to the city—an enormous loss of jobs, revenues and prestige," the editorial addressed the significance of my site. "Television City is far from a certainty," it said. "The project must work its way through the city approval process, where anything from bureaucratic inertia to political cowardice can kill it. That's not a case for City Hall's blindly accepting Trump's plan in toto. But it is an argument for swiftness and efficiency in making crucial yes-or-no decisions. The goal of city policy must be to keep NBC home. The worst possible result would be to lose it to cowardice."

In my view, that's precisely what was happening.

Early in May 1987, I went to the city with a proposal for a tax-abatement program that would make it possible for me to offer NBC a deal competitive with New Jersey's. Alair Townsend, the city's head of economic development, had said herself that without abatement, NBC stood to save up to $2 billion over a twenty-year period by moving to New Jersey.

I suggested a deal under which I'd build NBC's headquarters myself, at a cost of between $300 million and $400 million. I'd also subsidize NBC's rent for thirty years by charging only $15 a square foot, which is less than half the break-even rent. Finally, I'd agree to give to the city 25 percent of any profits Television City earned for a period of forty years. In return, I'd get a twenty-year tax abatement on my entire site. Even then, my savings would begin only when I got the project up, which was years away, at best. In the meantime, I'd be subsidizing NBC out of my own pocket, to the tune of at least $30 million a year.

Ironically, there was almost total opposition to my offer within my own organization. Robert, Harvey Freeman, and Norman Levine felt that for me to agree to give NBC $30 million a year in subsidies before we knew what revenues we'd be earning was too great a risk. My feeling was that the risk was worth taking. A tax abatement for our residential apartments would make them more marketable. In addition, NBC would be a prestigious addition to the site, and a lure. For the city, it was no-lose: they put up no money at all to keep NBC, and in lieu of taxes they'd share a substantial percentage of any profits we ultimately earned.

My proposal sparked the first serious negotiations we'd had with the city. Ed Koch didn't participate, but the city officials under him seemed receptive to the general structure of the plan. On May 25, however, after more than three weeks of intense negotiations, Ed Koch turned the deal down cold. I'm convinced that he made the determination not on the merits, but rather because he didn't want to make any deal with me—no matter how good it was for the city.

The next day I wrote Koch a letter that I'd held off writing for more than a year. "Dear Ed," it said, "Your attitude on keeping NBC in New York City is unbelievable and, I predict, will lead to NBC leaving the city, as so many other major companies have, for New Jersey." I again ran down the benefits of keeping the network, and ended by saying, "I am tired of sitting back quietly and watching New Jersey and other states drain the lifeblood out of New York."

Koch replied exactly the way I expected him to. He refused to respond to my specific points, and he tried to turn the issue into a personal contest of wills—Koch, the great protector, against Trump, the greedy developer. For months, he'd been looking for a way to get back at me for embarrassing him by building Wollman Rink so quickly and efficiently. The West Side yards, he apparently decided, was the perfect vehicle. When I came back with yet another suggestion for saving NBC—selling nine acres of my site at below my cost directly to the city—Koch rejected it without so much as a discussion.

I can't say I was surprised when the *New York Times*

came out against my plan. The writer of the editorial was longtime Koch ally Herb Sturz. Until joining the *Times* editorial board only a few weeks earlier, Sturz had been head of the City Planning Commission, with specific responsibility for Television City. In my view, letting Herb Sturz write editorials about New York City is analogous to permitting Caspar Weinberger to write editorials about Reagan's military policy.

I did get strong editorial support, however, from the *Daily News*. "The mayor is correct in saying there are limits to how much the city can give NBC," the *News* wrote. "But that's no excuse for inaction. Koch should personally bring together the decision-makers from NBC, Rockefeller Center and Trump's outfit. He should lay out a strong plan—and knock heads if that's what it takes."

Instead, Koch offered NBC a half-assed, watered-down tax-abatement proposal, which he said they could apply at any Manhattan site they chose. He even offered a little free advice about some new sites they might consider. Free advice, of course, tends to be worth what you pay for it. No sooner did Koch make his suggestion than an NBC spokesman said the network wasn't interested in considering more sites. In the meantime, the executives at Hartz Mountain Industries weren't sitting idly by. Recognizing an opportunity to force NBC's hand, they announced on June 1 that the network had thirty days to accept the terms that they were offering and which New York was no longer willing to match.

There were some who told me that I was hurting my

chances for zoning approval by taking on Koch in the media. They may well have been right. But I felt there was a bigger issue at stake. I've come to believe Ed Koch is so incompetent and destructive to New York that someone has to stand up and say so, publicly. When the *Daily News* polled its readers as to whether they agreed with Koch's position on NBC or with mine, the results were very satisfying. Nearly 10,000 readers sided with me. Only 1,800 went with Koch.

I've waited a long time to build on the West Side, and I can wait longer to get the zoning I feel is necessary. In the end, I will build Television City with or without NBC and with or without the current administration.

I continue to keep all my other options open too, because, as I've said, it's the only way you truly protect yourself. If the residential real estate market remains strong, I'll undoubtedly do very well selling large, riverview apartments in that location. If the market generally falls—and that can only be temporary in a city like New York—I may choose to build only the shopping complex. I'll do very, very well just with that.

My time—and Television City's—will come. I'm lucky that I can afford to wait, because that way I'll be able to do it right. The one thing I know is that I'll be doing business in New York City long after Ed Koch has moved out of Gracie Mansion.

14

THE WEEK
THAT WAS

How the Deals
Came Out

I SAID AT THE START that I do it to do it. But in the
end, you're measured not by how much you
undertake but by what you finally accomplish.
What follows is an accounting of how the deals that
crossed my desk in the week I chose to describe have
since turned out.

Holiday Inns

Several weeks after selling my Holiday stake for a
profit, which was substantial but not the reported $35

million, I began purchasing stock in another casino company, Bally Manufacturing Corporation. In a short time, I accumulated 9.9 percent of the stock. Bally responded by adopting poison pill provisions aimed at thwarting any attempt at a hostile takeover. When they also sued to try to keep me from buying any more stock, I countersued.

Two days after I initiated my suit, Bally announced an agreement to purchase the Golden Nugget casino at the highest price ever for an Atlantic City casino, almost $500 million, including the cost of the bonds. Once again, the real goal seemed to be to thwart me. No company is legally permitted to own more than three casinos in Atlantic City, and if I took over Bally after they'd purchased the Golden Nugget, I'd own four.

In effect, however, they put me in a win-win position. By paying such a huge price for the Nugget, Bally could only serve to increase the value of all casinos in town, including the two I already owned.

In the end, Bally offered me a settlement I couldn't refuse. I agreed not to stand in the way of their purchase of the Nugget. In return, they agreed to buy back my 9.9 percent stake in their company at an average price much higher than I paid, giving me a profit on my brief investment of more than $20 million.

In March 1987 I made my third attempt to purchase a casino company, Resorts International, but this time on a friendly basis. In the wake of the death of Resorts founder James Crosby, several other parties had launched bids for the company, but none had been successful. In the meantime, I'd developed a close relationship with several members of Resorts who controlled the company. In April 1987 I came to an agreement with the family to buy or tender for 93 percent of the voting stock in the company at $135 per share.

Several other bidders subsequently offered a higher price, but the family stuck by our agreement. Among other things, they believed I was the bidder with the best credentials to complete construction on Jim Crosby's pet project, the Taj Mahal on the Boardwalk. Designed as the largest and most lavish hotel-casino in the world, the Taj Mahal had already gone many millions of dollars over budget and was still nowhere near completion at the time Crosby died.

I hope to have the Taj open by October 1988. In order to create a more efficient operation, I may close the casino in the existing Resorts facility adjacent to the Taj Mahal and use it to service the Taj. Of course, I could always sell it to another casino operator for the right price. Who knows? Maybe Bally or Holiday Inns might be interested.

Annabel Hill

We ended up raising more than $100,000 for the Annabel Hill fund, which we used to pay off her mortgage and save her farm. To celebrate, we flew Mrs. Hill and her daughter to New York, where we held Trump Tower atrium's first—and, I suspect, its last—mortgage-burning ceremony.

United States Football League

The owners voted unanimously to appeal the ruling under which the USFL was awarded just one dollar in damages, despite the jury's antitrust finding against the National Football League. I think the grounds for an appeal are as strong as our original case.

Wollman Rink

The rink came in at $750,000 under budget and opened a full month ahead of schedule in November 1986. More than a half million skaters enjoyed the rink during the first year. Before the opening the city predicted a major operating loss. For the first full season of operation, we earned almost $500,000 in profits—all of which went to charity.

Palm Beach Towers

Lee Iacocca became my partner in the purchase of two condominium towers in the Palm Beach area, which we bought for approximately $40 million. When we took over the project, only a few units had been sold. In a short period of time, operating in a glutted market for condominiums in southern Florida, we sold or sale/leased nearly fifty units and managed to turn a bankrupt operation into a big success story. During the next year we intend to open a major restaurant on the ground level of one of the towers. Among those who've bid for the space are the owners of the 21 Club in New York, and Harry Cipriani, owner of Harry's Bar. Sir Charles Goldstein was dismissed as counsel to Lee before the deal was concluded.

The Australian Casino

Although we were among the finalists being considered to operate the second-largest casino in the world (after the Taj Mahal in Atlantic City), I thought better of it at the last moment. The idea of running a business which is a twenty-four-hour plane trip from New York City just didn't make sense—particularly when I have so much to occupy my attention in my own backyard. Shortly before the decision was to be announced by officials in New South Wales, I let them know that I was withdrawing my bid.

The Beverly Hills Hotel

The hotel was finally sold to the highest bidder, oilman Marvin Davis, for a price far in excess of what I was willing to pay. After having the property inspected, I kept my own bid low. Of course, should Davis ever choose to sell, I'm sure he'll earn a profit.

Marvin Davis subsequently became one of the bidders

for Resorts International as well. After I'd already made my deal, he not only offered a higher price but also tried to get the Murphy and Crosby families to renege on their agreement with me. They refused, and the court approved my deal, after which the New Jersey Casino Control Commission also approved it by a 5–0 vote.

Right around the same time, I happened to be at a fabulous party in California thrown by Merv Adelson and Barbara Walters, and a reporter asked me about Marvin Davis's bid for Resorts. Kiddingly, I said that Davis, who happens to be terribly overweight, should focus on losing 200 pounds instead of wasting time trying to break my deal with Resorts. I heard later that Davis was incensed by my remark, but I can't say I felt bad. I don't go out of my way to be cordial to enemies.

The Parking Garage

In October 1986, several months after construction on our new parking garage had begun, I got an emergency call one morning, just before I was scheduled to make a speech to a group of businessmen in New York. My construction manager, Tom Pippett, was calling. It seemed that the operator of a huge megaton crane had reached his boom out too far for a pickup, and the result was the crane and a twenty-two-ton beam toppled over onto the garage. Pippett told me that a huge section of the garage had literally collapsed. "What about the workers?" I asked. "Was anyone hurt?"

He told me that at least a hundred men had been working on the site and that a head count was under way. I told him to keep me posted, and went off to make my speech, trying to put the issue out of my mind while I spoke. As I was walking out after the speech, I was handed a message from Tom. I called back immediately. "You're not going to believe this, Mr. Trump," he said, "but we've accounted for everyone, and no one was hurt."

Losing even one life would have been horrible and devastating. In this case, only the sheer luck that the men at the site happened to be working on another part of the garage at that moment saved their lives.

It goes to show you how fragile it all really is. Those men were very lucky, and so was I.

The job was finished without further incident. In May 1987 we opened 1,200 new spaces in the parking facility connected by a walkway to Trump Plaza on the Boardwalk. During the week that followed, our slot-machine revenues more than doubled—mostly from the increased pedestrian traffic through our facility. By July, we had all 2,700 parking spaces opened, along with the bus terminal and the limousine dropoff—all on time and on budget.

Las Vegas

I withdrew my application for a gaming license in Las Vegas. Between Resorts and my two other casinos in

Atlantic City, I had enough to occupy me in the casino business closer to home. My focus now is on Atlantic City, but I don't rule out building or buying in Nevada at some point in the future.

The Trump Car

A decision has been made to go into production on two Cadillac-body limousines using my name. The Trump Golden Series will be the most opulent stretch limousine made. The Trump Executive Series will be a slightly less lavish version of the same car. Neither one has yet come off the line, but the folks at Cadillac Motors Division recently sent over a beautiful gold Cadillac Allante as a gift. Perhaps they felt I needed more toys to keep me busy.

The Drexel Deal

I decided not to go forward with the hotel company deal that Drexel Burnham Lambert brought me, and I have continued to keep all my investment banking business with Alan Greenberg and Bear Stearns. It's been a rough time for Drexel.

Trump's Castle

I said you can't bet against Ivana, and she proved me right even sooner than I expected. When the figures were announced for the first three months of 1987, Trump's Castle had the biggest increase in revenues among all of the twelve casinos in Atlantic City and was the most profitable hotel in town. The Castle took in $76.8 million in those three months—a 19 percent gain over the comparable period during the previous year. Good as that performance is, there is no way Ivana will be happy until she's far outdistanced the field.

Gulf & Western

I've been continuing to talk to Martin Davis, the chairman of Gulf & Western, about the theaters. In addition, I've since purchased a great deal of stock in the department store chain Alexander's. The chain's flagship location between 58th and 59th streets and Third and Lexington avenues, next to Bloomingdale's, is another perfect site for theaters— as well as for a mixed-use commercial and residential skyscraper.

Mar-a-Lago

The pool and the tennis court are finished, and both are as beautiful as I'd hoped they would be. As little as I'm interested in relaxing, I enjoy Mar-a-Lago almost in spite of myself. It may be as close to paradise as I'm going to get.

Moscow Hotel

In January 1987, I got a letter from Yuri Dubinin, the Soviet ambassador to the United States, that began: "It is a pleasure for me to relay some good news from Moscow." It went on to say that the leading Soviet state agency for international tourism, Goscomintourist, had expressed interest in pursuing a joint venture to construct and manage a hotel in Moscow. On July 4, I flew with Ivana, her assistant Lisa Calandra, and Norma to Moscow. It was an extraordinary experience. We toured a half dozen potential sites for a hotel, including several near Red Square. We stayed in Lenin's suite at the National Hotel, and I was impressed with the ambition of the Soviet officials to make a deal.

Trump Fund

I decided against setting up a separate fund to buy distressed real estate, using money raised from outside investors. I don't mind taking risks myself, but the idea of being responsible for the money of a lot of other people—particularly when they're bound to include some friends—just wasn't appealing in the end. For the same reason, I've never been tempted to take any of my companies public. Making choices is a lot easier when you have to answer only to yourself.

My Apartment

The renovation on my apartment was finally finished in the fall of 1987. I could afford to take my time, and I'm happy that I did. There may be no other apartment in the world like it.

Airplane

I finally found a plane. I happened to be reading an article in *Business Week* in the spring of 1987 about a troubled, Texas-based company named Diamond Shamrock. The article described how top Shamrock executives were enjoying incredible perks, actually living like kings. Among the examples cited was a lavishly equipped company-owned 727, which executives flew around in at will.

I sensed an opportunity. On Monday morning, I called the office of the Diamond Shamrock executive who had been pictured on the cover of the *Business Week* article. It turned out that he was no longer there and a new chairman, Charles Blackburn, had just been named. I was immediately put through to him, we talked for a few minutes, and I wished him well. Then I said that I'd read about the company's 727, and that if he had any interest in selling, I was interested in buying. Sure enough, Blackburn said that as much as they all loved that plane, selling it was one of the first things on his agenda. He even offered to send it up to New York, so that I could take a look at it.

The next day I went out to La Guardia airport for a look. I had to smile. This plane could seat up to two hundred passengers, but it had been reconfigured for fifteen, and it included such luxuries as a bedroom, a full bath, and a separate working area. It was a little more plane than I needed, but I find it hard to resist a good deal when the opportunity presents itself.

A new 727 sells for approximately $30 million. A G-4, which is one fourth the size, goes for about $18 million. However, I knew that Diamond Shamrock was hungry to sell, and that not very many people are in the market for 727s.

I offered $5 million, which was obviously ridiculously low. They countered at $10 million, and at that point I knew I had a great deal, regardless of how the negotiation ended. Still, I haggled some more, and we finally agreed on a price of $8 million. I don't believe there is any other private plane in the sky comparable to this one.

What's Next

Fortunately, I don't know the answer, because if I did, that would take half the fun out of it.

This much I do know: it won't be the same.

I've spent the first twenty years of my working life building, accumulating, and accomplishing things that many said could not be done. The biggest challenge I see over the next twenty years is to figure out some creative ways to give back some of what I've gotten.

I don't just mean money, although that's part of it. It's easy to be generous when you've got a lot, and anyone who does, should be. But what I admire most are people who put themselves directly on the line. I've never been terribly interested in why people give, because their motivation is rarely what it seems to be, and it's almost never pure altruism. To me, what matters is the doing, and giving time is far more valuable than just giving money.

In my life, there are two things I've found I'm very good at: overcoming obstacles and motivating good people to do their best work. One of the challenges ahead is how to use those skills as successfully in the service of others as I've done, up to now, on my own behalf.

Don't get me wrong. I also plan to keep making deals, big deals, and right around the clock.

Index

369